Benjamin Church

The History of the Eastern Expeditions

1689, 1690, 1692, 1696, and 1704

Benjamin Church

The History of the Eastern Expeditions
1689, 1690, 1692, 1696, and 1704

ISBN/EAN: 9783744704267

Printed in Europe, USA, Canada, Australia, Japan

Cover: Foto ©ninafisch / pixelio.de

More available books at **www.hansebooks.com**

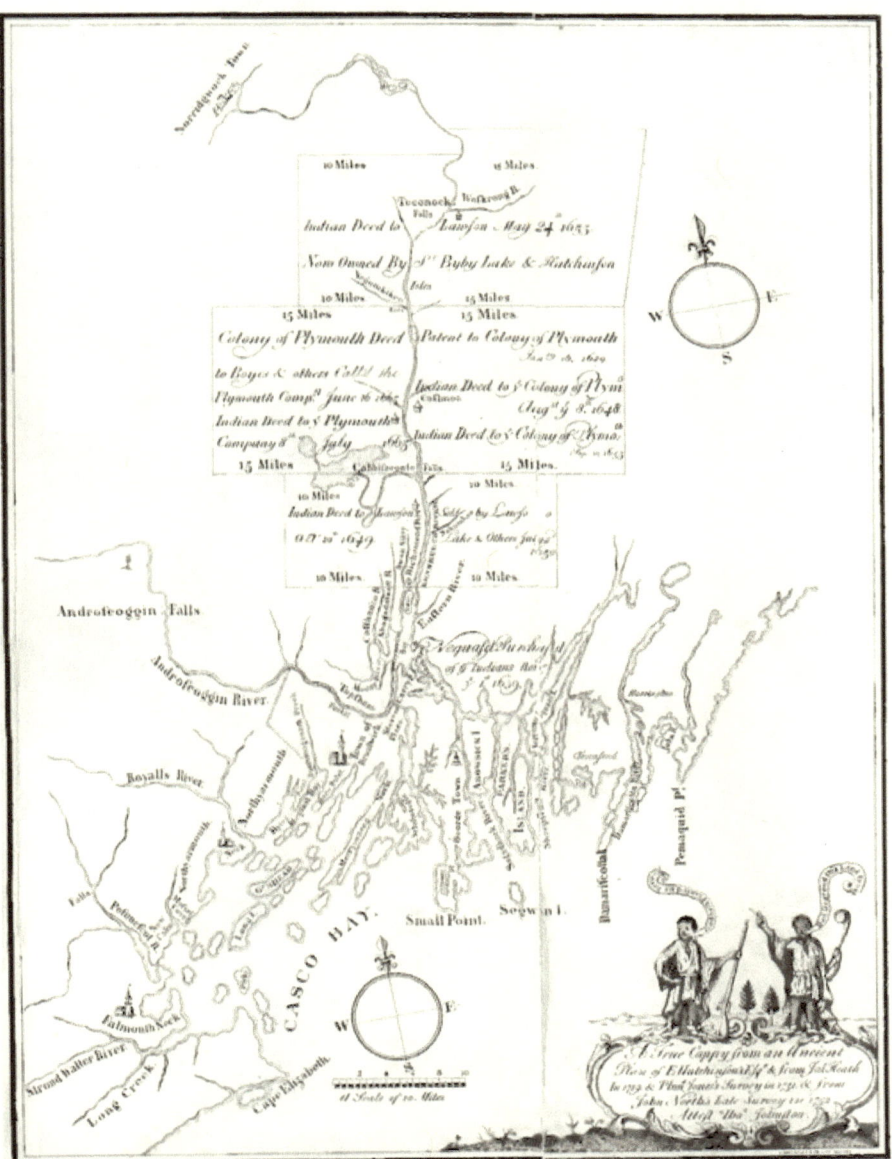

The History

OF THE

Eastern Expeditions

Of 1689, 1690, 1692, 1696, and 1704

AGAINST THE INDIANS AND FRENCH

By BENJAMIN CHURCH

WITH AN INTRODUCTION AND NOTES

By HENRY MARTYN DEXTER

Boston

J. K. WIGGIN AND WM. PARSONS LUNT

MDCCCLXVII

Entered according to Act of Congress in the year 1867, by
WIGGIN AND LUNT
In the Clerk's Office of the District Court of the District of Massachusetts

EDITION

Two Hundred and Fifty Copies, Small Quarto
Thirty-five, Royal Quarto

CAMBRIDGE: PRESS OF JOHN WILSON AND SON

PREFATORY NOTE.

T was not anticipated, when the First Part of these "ENTERTAINING PASSAGES" was issued, in the summer of 1865, that so long a period would elapse before the publication of the Second Part, relating to the later Eastern Expeditions. But various labors and engagements have necessarily delayed the progress and completion of the work, both of editing and printing, until the present time. It is hoped that the kind welcome accorded to the portion relating to Philip's War may not be withheld from this completing glance at the later Indian warfare, which engaged the prowess, if it did not materially augment the fame, of the brave man from whose later reminiscences the story was set down.

The endeavor has been constantly in mind to make this a fit companion volume for the First Part, — in carefulness and abundance of illustration, in exact accuracy of reprint, and in all general features.

PREFATORY NOTE.

The map is a "True Coppy from an Ancient Plan of E. Hutchinson Esq. &c. &c.," which was reproduced from an engraving of 1753, to accompany Mr. S. G. Drake's late edition of Baylies's "Historical Memoir of the Colony of New Plymouth"; and has been kindly granted for use by that gentleman, — for whose varied courtesies in the preparation of these reprints their editor desires here to express his gratitude.

In addition to acknowledgments already tendered, it is due also that thankful mention should here be made of the kindness of Dr. A. G. WILBOR, of Boston, and Mr. A. E. CUTTER, of Charlestown, for the loan of copies of the rare first edition, to aid the accuracy of the work of revision.

H. M. D.

HILLSIDE, ROXBURY,
12th April, 1867.

HISTORICAL INTRODUCTION.

HEN the murder of *Sassamon*, in the winter of 167¼, led to the breaking-out of "Philip's War," Plymouth had been settled fifty-four years; Dover, fifty-one; Boston, forty-four; Wethersfield, forty; Providence, thirty-eight; and Kittery, twenty-seven. There appear to have been then, within the boundaries of what is now Maine, thirteen towns and plantations; * within what is now New Hampshire, † four; within what is now Massachusetts, sixty-four; ‡

---

* Kittery; York; Wells; Cape Porpoise; Saco; Scarborough; Falmouth; Pejepscot; the plantations on the Sagadahoc and Kennebec; Sheepscot and Capenewagen; Damariscotta; Pemaquid; Monhegan, with Gorges Islands and the opposite settlements upon the mainland.

† Dover, Portsmouth, Exeter, Hampton.

‡ Plymouth, Salem, Charlestown, Boston, Dorchester, Roxbury, Watertown. Medford, Cambridge, Ipswich, Newbury, Springfield, Concord, Weymouth, Dedham, Braintree, Lynn, Hingham, Scituate, Duxbury, Barnstable, Sandwich, Yarmouth, Gloucester, Rowley, Salisbury, Sudbury, Woburn, Reading, Eastham, Taunton, Marshfield, Haverhill, Wenham, Andover, Hull, Bridgewater, Manchester, Rehoboth, Marblehead, Middleborough, Medfield, Topsfield, Malden, Northampton, Chelmsford, Billerica, Groton,

within what is now Rhode Island, six;* within what is now Connecticut, twenty-three.† Vermont, as yet, was not. It is probable that the entire population of New England at this time, excluding Indians, was not far from eighty thousand.‡

The best computation suggests, on the same territory, at the same time, not far from 10,500 Indians, distributed among the tribes as follows: —

Pequots	1,200
Narragansetts	4,000
Pokanokets, Nausets, &c.	700
Massachusetts	1,200
Pautuckets	1,000
Nipmuks	2,400
	10,500

When the war broke out, Josias Winslow was Governor of Plymouth Colony — where William Bradford had been dead seventeen years; Miles Standish, eighteen; Edward Winslow, nineteen; and William Brewster, thirty; and where John Howland had been dead scarcely one year.

Marlborough, Hadley, Hatfield, Dartmouth, Swansea, Amesbury, Beverly, Milton, Wrentham, Lancaster, Mendon, Deerfield, Brookfield, Sherborn, Edgartown, and Tisbury.

* Providence, Newport, Portsmouth, Warwick, Westerly, and New Shoreham (Block Island).

† Wethersfield, Hartford, Windsor, New Haven, Guilford, Saybrook, Milford, Fairfield, Stratford, Greenwich, Stamford, Branford, Farmington, New London, Simsbury, Middleton, Norwalk, Stonington, Norwich, Killingworth, Lyme, Haddam, and Wallingford.

‡ See estimate of 78,416 in *Coll. Am. Statis. Assoc.* i : 141.

HISTORICAL INTRODUCTION.

Indeed, of that one-half of the Mayflower's company (fifty) who survived the first year of the settlement, at least thirteen were still in the land of the living, though not all still within the limits of the Old Colony. George Soule and John Alden, in a hale old age, resided at Duxbury; and Susannah White — who had enjoyed the singular honor of being first the first mother in the new Colony, and then the first bride — was keeping still the house at Careswell, which her second husband, the honored Gov. Edward Winslow, had left to her possession. These three were already adults when they first saw the New World. And, of the children who romped along the Mayflower's decks, there were still living Resolved White, who seems now to have been a resident of Salem; Giles and Constantia Hopkins, both at Eastham, — the latter the widow of Nicholas Snow; Henry Sampson, of Duxbury; Joseph Rogers, of Eastham; Samuel Fuller, of Barnstable; Samuel Eaton, of Middleborough; (Rev.) John Cooke, of Dartmouth; Mary Allerton, — who was destined to be the last survivor of the Mayflower company, dying in 1699, æt. 89, — who still lived at Plymouth with her venerable and excellent husband, Elder Thomas Cushman, who came in the "Fortune," 1621; and Mary Chilton, now the recent widow of John Winslow, of Boston. Nathaniel Morton, who, five years before, had published his *New-England's Memoriall*, was still Secretary of the Colony.

HISTORICAL INTRODUCTION.

In Massachusetts, John Leverett was Governor, and Edward Rawson, Secretary. Here Winthrop and Shepard had been dead twenty-five years; John Cotton, twenty-two; Dudley, twenty-one; Saltonstall, sixteen; John Norton, eleven; Richard Mather, five; John Allin, three; and John Davenport and Charles Chauncy, two; and here Thomas Cobbett still lived at the age of sixty-six, John Eliot at seventy, and Simon Bradstreet at seventy-seven.

William Coddington was Governor, and John Sanford Recorder, of the "Providence Plantations," where Roger Williams was still hale and hearty (and ready to earn a new title as "Captain" in this war) at the age of seventy-five; and William Blaxton was very soon to be carried from his dreams among his folios to his rest on the banks of that beautiful river, which bears his name as it ripples by his grave.

John Winthrop (son of Gov. John of Massachusetts) was Governor of the now united Colonies of Connecticut and New Haven; where Samuel Eaton had been dead thirty-two years; Thomas Hooker, twenty-seven; Theophilus Eaton, seventeen; Samuel Stone, eleven; and John Warham, four.

The settlements in what is now Maine had at this time but a single Congregational Church. In what is now New Hampshire, there were three.* In what is now Vermont,

---

* One had been gathered at Exeter in 1638, but it became extinct in 1641; and no record exists of the formation of another until 1698.

HISTORICAL INTRODUCTION.

there was none. In Massachusetts, there were fifty-seven. In Rhode Island, there was none. In Connecticut, there were twenty-one.

These, with their pastors, — so far as known, — at the breaking-out of the war, were the following; arranged in the order of their formation: —

Plymouth (1620)	John Cotton, Jr.
Salem (1629)	John Higginson.
Boston, First Church (1630)	James Allen.
Windsor (1630)	Nathaniel Chauncey.
Watertown (1630)	John Sherman.
Roxbury (1632)	{ John Eliot. { Samuel Danforth.
Lynn (1632)	Samuel Whiting.
Duxbury (1632)	John Holmes.
Marshfield (1632)	Samuel Arnold.
Charlestown (1632)	Thomas Shepard.
Hartford (1633)	Joseph Haynes.
Ipswich (1634)	Thomas Cobbet.
Newbury (1635)	Thomas Parker.
Hingham (1635)	Peter Hobart.
Weymouth (1635)	Samuel Torrey.
Cambridge (1636)	Urian Oakes.
Concord (1636)	{ Edward Bulkley. { Joseph Estabrook.
Dorchester (1636)	Josiah Flint.
Springfield (1637)	Pelatiah Glover.
Taunton (1637)	George Shove.
Sandwich (1638)	John Smith.
Hampton (1638)	Seaborn Cotton.
Dover (1638)	John Reyner, Jr.

HISTORICAL INTRODUCTION.

Salisbury (1638)	John Wheelwright.
Dedham (1638)	William Adams.
Quincy (1639)	Moses Fiske.
New Haven (1639)	Nicholas Street.
Milford (1639)	Roger Newton.
Barnstable (1639)	Thomas Walley.
Scituate (1639)	Nicholas Baker.
Rowley (1639)	Samuel Phillips.
Sudbury (1640)	Edmund Browne.
Stratford (1640)	No pastor.
Edgartown (1641)	No pastor.
Stamford (1641)	Eliphalet [?] Jones.
Wethersfield (1641)	Gershom Bulkley.
Woburn (1642)	Thomas Carter.
Gloucester (1642)	John Emerson.
Scituate, Second Church (1642)	William Witherell.
Guilford (1643)	Joseph Eliot.
Hull (1644)	Zechariah Whitman.
Rehoboth (1644)	Noah Newman.
Haverhill (1645)	John Ward.
Andover, North (1645)	Francis Dane.
Reading, South (1645)	John Brock.
Topsfield (1645)	William Perkins. / Jeremiah Hobart.
Manchester (1645)	No pastor.
Eastham (1646)	Samuel Treat.
Branford (1647)	John Bowers.
Saybrook (1646)	Thomas Buckingham.
Malden (1649)	Michael Wigglesworth.
Fairfield (1650)	Samuel Wakeman.
New London (1650)	Simon Bradstreet.
Boston, Old North (1650)	Increase Mather.
Medfield (1651)	John Wilson.

HISTORICAL INTRODUCTION.

Norwalk (1652)	Thomas Hanford.
Farmington (1652)	Samuel Hooker.
Chelmsford (1655)	John Fiske.
Beverly (1657)	John Hale.
Hadley (1659)	John Russell.
Lancaster (1660)	Joseph Rowlandson.
Norwich (1660)	James Fitch.
Northampton (1661)	Solomon Stoddard.
Billerica (1663)	Samuel Whiting.
Wenham (1663)	No pastor.
Bridgewater, West (1664)	James Keith.
Groton (1664)	Samuel Willard.
Newton, Center (1664)	Nehemiah Hobart.
Marlborough (1666)	William Brimsmead.
Killingworth (1667)	John Woodbridge.
Mendon (1667)	Joseph Emerson.
Amesbury (1668)	Thomas Wells.
Middletown (1668)	Nathaniel Collins.
Boston, Old South (1669)	Thomas Thatcher.
Hartford, Second (1669)	Joseph Haynes.
Windsor, Second (1669)	Benjamin Woodbridge.
Woodbury (1670)	Zechariah Walker.
Greenwich (1670)	No pastor.
Hatfield (1670)	Hope Atherton.
Portsmouth (1671)	Joshua Moody.
Tisbury (1673)	John Mayhew.
York (1673)	Shubael Dummer.

Besides these eighty-two regular Congregational churches, there were six or seven Indian missionary churches; five Baptist churches — one founded at Rehoboth (Swansey) in 1663, one at Boston in 1665, and three in Rhode Island:—the First Providence (1639), the First

Newport (1644), and the Second Newport (1656); — a society of Friends, which had been formed at Newport in 1656-7; and a church of Seventh-day Baptists, formed at Newport in December, 1671.

We have seen that the estimated number of Indians on the territory of New England at this time, was between ten and eleven thousand. Of these, about four thousand were then reckoned as "Praying Indians," and seem to have been won to some comprehension and practice of Christianity. According to Gookin, whose "Historical Collections of the Indians in New-England" bears date 7th Dec., 1674,* just before the breaking-out of Philip's War, these were, in large part, distributed as follows, viz: —

Nonantum (Natick)	145	*Manamoyik* (Chatham)		71
Punkapoag (Stoughton)	60	*Sawkattukett* (Harwich), *Nobsquassitt*, *Mattakees*, and *Weequakut* (Yarmouth and Barnstable)		
Hassanamesitt (Grafton)	60			
Okommakamesit (Marlborough)	50			122
Wamesit (Tewksbury)	75	*Satuit, Pawpoesit, Coatuit, Maskpee*, and *Wakoquet* (Mashpee)		95
Nashobah (Littleton)	50			
Magunkaquog (Hopkinton)	55	*Codtanmut, Ashimuit, Weesquobs* (Mashpee and Sandwich)		22
Manchage (Oxford)	60			
Chabanakongkomun (Dudley)	45			
Maanexit (N.E. Woodstock)	100	*Pispogutt, Wawayantik*, and *Sokones* (Wareham and Falmouth)		36
Quantisset (S.E. Woodstock)	100			
Wabquisset (S.W. Woodstock)	150	*Cotuhtikut, Assoowamsoo* (Middleborough)		35
Packachoog (Worcester)	100			
Wacuntug (Uxbridge)	50	*Kittaumut* (Sandwich)		40
Meeshawn and *Punonakanit* (Truro and Wellfleet)	72	*Nope* (Martha's Vineyard) and *Chuppaquiddick*		1500
Potanamaquut and *Nawsett* (Eastham)	44	Nantucket		300

* Mass. Hist. Coll. i: 141-226.

HISTORICAL INTRODUCTION.

Rev. Richard Bourne, missionary among the Indians in the Plymouth Colony, reported, in 1674, that one hundred and forty-two could read their own language, seventy-two could write it, and nine could read English.*

It will be seen from this enumeration, that the seat of the successes of the benevolent labor of John Eliot and his compeers was upon the Elizabeth Islands, upon Cape Cod, and in the country neighboring Boston; the great inland and remoter tribes remaining wholly unreached or unaffected by them.

The general aspect of New England at this time, Dr. Palfrey has admirably sketched in a few words. He says: —

"Along a line of rugged coast, from the Penobscot to the Hudson, are scattered settlements of Englishmen, at unequal distances from each other, — closely grouped together about midway of that line, farther apart at the extremities. Almost all of them are reached by tide-water: a very few have been planted in detached spots in the interior; the most distant of these being about a hundred miles from the sea, whether measured from the east or from the south. The surrounding country is not occupied, but roamed over by savages." †

Maine was yet rough and primitive, in the extreme, in the quality of its settlers. Rhode Island was the paradise of schemers and dreamers, and come-outers of all sorts; from the high-souled advocate of pure and entire toleration down to those fussy and unendurable champions of

---

* 1 *Mass. Hist. Coll.* i: 197.   † *Hist. New England*, iii: 132.

queer and petty principles, who were such crooked sticks by nature that they could not lie still even there. Plymouth, badly situated both for commerce and culture, with no good harbor on her coast, and with her thin and sandy soil, had been able, even with the best efforts of her noble men, to move but very slowly forward in the path of empire. While, from the fact that her teachers were taken from her repeatedly by the superior attractions offered by wealthier neighbors, she had been compelled to occupy a lower place in the relative scale, than that to which she would have been entitled from the purity and worth of her founders, and her general patient industry. Massachusetts had advanced more rapidly. Every thing helped her, until she was strong, not merely relatively as compared with her neighbors, but as looked at from the mother-country across the sea. Connecticut, too, was thriving. She had plenty of good land, wise and thrifty oversight, and general prosperity.

Dr. Palfrey draws the picture of daily life with a skilful pencil; thus: —

"In the three associated Colonies, there is great similarity in the ordinary occupations and pursuits. Most adults of both sexes work hard, and nearly all the children go to school. The greater part of the men get a living by farm labor: they provide bread and meat, milk, butter and cheese, for their own tables, and raise stock to sell in the West Indies for money with which to buy foreign commodities. But they are not all farmers. A portion are lumberers, plying the axe through the winter in the thick pine forests, and, at the return of spring, floating down their rafts to a sure and profitable market. Another portion are fishermen, familiar with the haunts of the cod, the mackerel, and the whale, and with all perils of the sea. In the principal towns, various classes of artisans pursue a lucrative trade. The country furnishes some staples for an advantageous foreign commerce; and, especially in Boston, not a few merchants have grown rich." *

Peace had reigned in these Colonies since the close of the Pequot war in the spring of 1636, — nearly forty years. The last colonist who had gained experience in savage warfare in that short but fierce struggle was now dead, or too old for service; while the youngest immigrants who had been trained to arms abroad were now in the same category. Slight and temporary misunderstandings and quarrels had taken place now and then; but the wise and scrupulously just policy which the Pilgrims at Plymouth had first initiated with the good Massasoit, had prevailed, and borne its natural and pleasant fruit. On the whole, the state of the Indians had been improved by the settling of the English at their side. Though they had parted with a good deal of the land over which they had been accustomed to roam, they had still enough reserved for their present wants. They had bettered their position, in their fight with nature for food and shelter, by many implements and suggestions from the superior culture of their white neighbors. And although their exposure to

* *Hist. New England*, iii: 134.

the seductive "fire-water" had wrought them harm, and they were sometimes imposed upon by the cunning greed of crafty and unscrupulous settlers, the Colonial governments were always administered in the endeavor to do them justice and afford them protection; and the proceeds of their hunting, or of their slight farming, now found ready and remunerative sale. In the single matter of the — to the English undesired, yet gradually accomplished — exchange of his bow and flint dagger and stone tomahawk, for the musket, hatchet, and hunting-knife of the white man, the Indian gained, for the legitimate uses of his own savage life, more than all which he had lost from the advent of civilization to these shores.

Massasoit died in 1661-2, and was succeeded in the sachemship of the *Wampanoags* by his eldest son, Alexander [*Mooanam, Wamsutta*]. His life was short after his accession. In a few months' time, it was rumored that he was plotting with the *Narragansetts*, — the bugbear of the Colonies on the west, as the *Maquas* were on the northwest, — and the Plymouth government thought the matter of sufficient consequence to be looked into. It is not improbable that an impression had been for some time gaining ground, that when the venerable sachem, who had welcomed Bradford and Winslow and their company at *Patuxet*, and had become their abiding friend, had passed away, certain tendencies toward disturbance, on which he had kept a tight rein, and which others had repressed through respect for him, might find development. So a message was sent to Alexander to come to Plymouth, and talk over affairs. He ignored the invitation. As the Court had broached the subject, they felt that the general safety required that their summons should not be disregarded in that way; so they sent an armed party, under Majors Winslow and Bradford, to find and bring him. They found him not far off, at *Monponset* (in Halifax), and then, "freely and readily, without the least hesitancy,"* he went with them. He told them that he had intended to come when first invited, but wanted to delay long enough to consult Mr. Willett, in whom he had confidence. Hubbard's story† is, that when he had been dismissed on the promise to send his son as a hostage, he was so enraged at the indignities put upon him, that he fell into a fever, of which he died before he got half-way home. And out of this statement has grown the general representation, that his ill-treatment at the hands of the English was the means of his death, and was laid up as one prominent cause of the war, twelve years later. But the letter of Rev. John Cotton to Increase Mather, — which Judge Davis prints in the appendix of the *Memorial*, and which has every element of trustworthiness, — from the dictation of Major Bradford,

* Davis's *Morton's Memorial*, 426. † *Narrative*, 9.

one of the chief actors, and a most competent witness, desiring expressly to correct Hubbard, puts an entirely different construction upon the event, and one intrinsically much more in harmony with the probabilities of the case. Mr. Cotton says, —

> "Reports being here, that Alexander was plotting or privy to plots against the English, authority sent to him to come down. He came not. Whereupon Maj. Winslow was sent to fetch him. Maj. Bradford with some others went with him. At *Munponset* river (a place not many miles hence) they found Alexander with about eight men and sundry squaws. He was there about getting canoes. He and his men were at breakfast under their shelter, their guns being without. They saw the English coming, but continued eating: and Mr. Winslow telling their business, Alexander, freely and readily, without the least hesitancy, consented to go, giving his reason why he came not to the Court before; viz., because he waited for Captain Willet's return from the Dutch, being desirous to speak with him first. They brought him to Mr. Collier's, that day, and Governour Prince living remote, at Eastham, those few magistrates, who were at hand, issued the matter peaceably, and immediately dismissed Alexander to return home, which he did, part of the way; but in two or three days after, he returned and went to Maj. Winslow's house, intending thence to travel into the Bay and so home; but at the Major's house he was taken very sick, and was, by water, conveyed to Mr. Bradford's, and thence carried upon the shoulders of his men to Tetchquet river,* and thence, in canoes, home, and about two or three days after died."

Upon his decease, his brother Philip [*Pometacom*] reigned in his stead. One of Philip's first acts was to renew the ancient covenant between his father and the

---

* *Titicut*, or Taunton Great River.

colonists; and five years passed quietly away, when a vague charge was made against him of being willing to plot with the French or Dutch against the English. This he denounced as a calumny of *Ninigret* of *Niantic*, and the matter subsided. After nearly four years more, another rumor of his treachery gained so much ground as to demand investigation, and awaken solicitude at both Plymouth and Boston. An investigation revealed proofs of bad faith on his part; and a bad spirit was clearly manifested by him, when questioned concerning them. But this matter was finally issued in his renewed engagements of fealty. Three years passed again, when the Governor of Plymouth was informed by *Sassamon* — a " praying" Indian, who had been schoolmaster at Natick, and who, being able to write as well as read, had sometimes served Philip with his pen, — that there were suspicious circumstances in Philip's camp, which gave color to the rumor that he was endeavoring to excite other sachems to war. This information was given under a demanded pledge of secrecy, as *Sassamon* said that Philip's Indians would kill him if they suspected him as its source. It somehow leaked out to Philip's ear, that the Governor of Plymouth had heard something to his disadvantage, and would send for him to come to the next Court to explain it. He therefore resolved to anticipate the matter by going without summons. He went to Plymouth, accordingly, and saw the Assistants, — the Court not yet being in session, — and protested his innocence. They were not satisfied; but hoped that he would be led to desist by his knowledge of their discovery of his plans, and so dismissed him in a friendly manner, with a warning, that, should further evidence come up, they should be obliged to demand his arms for safe keeping.

Philip went back to Mount Hope; and, a few days after, *Sassamon* was missing. On search, his hat and gun were found on the ice of *Assawompset* Pond, in Middleborough, and his body under the ice. It was dragged out, and buried; and afterwards exhumed and examined, when marks of violence indicating murder, and not accidental drowning, became manifest. Three Indians were soon arrested on suspicion, and tried by a jury, to which six grave friend Indians were added, to insure fairness in the verdict. An Indian came forward and testified, that, by accident, from the top of a hill, he had witnessed the scene, and that *Sassamon* had been murdered by these prisoners. One of the prisoners subsequently confessed that he had stood by while the others did the deed. The jury convicted and sentenced the murderers, the Indians concurring; whereupon two were hanged, and the third, after a respite of two or three weeks, was shot.

This seems immediately to have promoted the outbreak, which took place with very little delay; the first

HISTORICAL INTRODUCTION.

English blood being shed on or about the 24th June, 1675.*

It has been usual to picture Philip as a great king, a sagacious warrior, and a far-sighted patriot; and to represent him as having been for years engaged in planning and perfecting a comprehensive conspiracy among all the Indian tribes on the New-England territory — and even upon that of New York — for the purpose of sweeping away, by one concerted blow, the hated white usurper, and of recovering to their own savage uses the whole of their ancient hunting-grounds. It has been usual to apologize for the ill success of the actual strife, by asserting that it was so hurried up by the death of *Sassamon*, that the first blow was struck before due preparations to follow it up could be completed.

Dr. Palfrey has shown, one would think to the general conviction, that there is a very small foundation of truth indeed on which to build this majestic, one might almost say magnificent, superstructure. He has shown that the English had used Philip habitually well; that he had no real grounds of complaint against them; that his frequent sales of land to them implies no unwillingness that they should have his hunting-grounds if they would pay for them, as they did; that he gave no indications of greatness, whether in council or conflict; that there is no proof

* See Part I. p. 18.

that he directed or approved those hostilities about Mount Hope with which the war began; that his movements immediately after indicated a much keener anxiety for his own personal safety than for the extinction of the colonists; that there is nothing to show that he directed the outbreaks which followed, and no evidence that he was personally present and active in any particular fight; that there was no manifestation of savage wisdom on the part of anybody in the management of the war; that attacks upon particular, much-exposed localities were delayed for weeks and months, which, if any such general conspiracy existed as has been claimed, it is incredible should not have been simultaneous, or nearly so, when they would have been overwhelming; that, instead of hastening to join his waning fortunes with the Eastern Indians, when misfortune pressed him in his ancient haunts, — as he could have done in two days' easy march, — Philip retreated to the den whence he had originally gone forth, and there was shot ingloriously, while, unattended, he was attempting to run away; and that the war was waged at the Eastward, after his death, with more vigor than during his life, for nearly two whole years. In short, Dr. Palfrey makes it out, — and, as it would seem, on the best evidence, — that, instead of being a far-reaching, well-organized campaign, what we commonly call "Philip's War" was merely a succession of unconsidered and indiscriminate murders and pillages, taken up by one body of savages after another, as the intelligence of the attractive example of others reached them; and rightfully connected with his name mainly as having been led off by those bands who centred around *Sowams*, and over whom he had partial control.*

The cotemporaneous records do certainly bear out this general judgment. There is a tradition mentioned by Callender, † as derived both from the white settlers in the vicinity of Mount Hope and from those Indians who survived the struggle, that Philip and his elder chiefs were utterly averse to the war. Increase Mather never seems to have heard of the all-embracing conspiracy, or of Philip's great statesmanship. Even Cotton Mather — much as one would think he would have enjoyed it — never mentions either. Hubbard is the only early writer who says any thing on which the popular judgment could be based. He does say that Philip had been "plotting with all the Indians round about," &c.; but he gives only vague rumor from some prisoners, as his authority, and does not seem himself to have attributed to his own words the importance even which they might naturally convey.

Easton — it is difficult to decide how much of accuracy and weight is to be attributed to the testimony lately published in his name — gives the following account of an

* *Hist. New England*, iii: 223-229.   † *R.-I. Hist. Coll.* iv: 126.

HISTORICAL INTRODUCTION.

interview which he asserts to have been held between Philip and some Rhode-Islanders just before the outbreak. He says:* —

"[Philip] came himself unarmed, and about 40 of his Men armed. Then 5 of us went over [Trip's Ferry], 3 wear Magiftrates. We fate veri friendly together. We told him our bifnes was to indever that they might not refeue or do Rong. They faid that was well; they had dun no Rong, the Englifh ronged them. We faid we knew the Englifh faid the Indians ronged them, and the Indians faid the Englifh ronged them, but our Defier was the Quarrell might rightly be defided, in the beft Way, and not as Dogs defided their Quarrells. The Indians owned yᵉ fighting was the worft Way; then they propounded how Right might take Place. We faid by Arbitration. They faid that all Englifh agreed againft them, and fo by Arbitration they had had much Rong; mani Miles fquare of Land fo taken from them, for Englifh would have Englifh Arbitrators: and once they were perfuaded to give in their Arms yᵗ thereby Jealoufy might be removed, and the Englifh having their Arms wold not deliver them as they had promifed, untill they confented to pay a 100ᴸ, and now they had not fo much fum or muny; yᵗ thay wear as good be kiled as leave all ther Liueflyhode.

"We faid they might chufe a Indian King, and the Englifh might chufe the Governor of New Yorke, yᵗ nether had cafe to fay either wear Parties in the Diferance. They faid they had not heard of yᵉ Way, and faid we oneftly fpoke, fo we wear perfwaided if yᵗ Way had bine tendered they would have acsepted. We did endeavor not to hear their Complaints, faid it was not convenient for us now to confider of, but to indever to prevent War; faid to them when in War againft Englifh, Blood was fpilt, yᵗ ingaged all Englishmen, for we wear to be all under one King; we knew what their Complaints wold be, and in our Colony had removed some of them in fending for Indian Rulers in what the Crime concerned Indians Lives, which they veri lovingly

---

* A Relation of the Indyan Warr, by Mr. Easton, &c., pp. 7–16.

HISTORICAL INTRODUCTION.

acsepted, and agreed with us to their Execution, and faid fo they were abell to fatiffie their Subjects when they knew an Indian fufered duly, but faid in what was only between their Indians and not in Townefhipes, y! we had purchafed, they wold not have us profecute, and y! they had a great Fear to have ani of ther Indians fhuld be caled or forced to be Chriftian Indians. Thay faid y! fuch wer in everi thing more mifchievous, only Diffemblers, and then the Englifh made them not fubject to ther Kings, and by their lying to rong ther Kings. We knew it to be true, and we promifing them y! however in Government to Indians all fhould be alike, and y! we knew it was our King's will it fhould be so, y! altho we wear weaker than other Colonies, they having fubmitted to our King to protect them, others dared not otherwife to moleft them; expreffed thay took that to be well, that we had littell Cafe to doute, but that to us under the King thay would have yielded to our Determinations in what ani fhould have complained to us againft them.

"But Philip charged it to be difoneftly in us to put of the Hering to iuft Complaints, therefore we confented to hear them. They faid thay had bine the firft in doing Good to the Englifh, and the Englifh the firft in doing Rong; faid when the Englifh firft came, the King's Father was as a great Man, and the Englifh as a littell Child; he conftrained other Indians from ronging the Englifh, and gave them Corn and shewed them how to plant, and was free to do them ani Good, and had let them have a 100 Times more Land than now the King had for his own Peopell. But ther Kings Brother, when he was King, came miferably to dy by being forced to Court, as they iudge poyfoned. And another Greavance was if 20 of there oneft Indians teftified that a Englifhman had dun them Rong, it was as nothing; and if but one of their worft Indians teftified againft any Indian or ther King, when it pleefed the Englifh it was fufitiant. Another Grievance was, when their King fold Land, the Englifh wold fay, it was more than they agreed to, and a Writing muft be prove againft all them, and fum of their Kings had dun Rong to fell fo much. He left his Peopell uone, and fum being given to Drunknes the Englifh made them drunk and

HISTORICAL INTRODUCTION.

then cheated them in Bargains, but now ther kings wear forwarned not for to part with Land, for nothing in Cumparifon to the Value thereof. Now home the Englifh had owned for King or Queen, they wold difinheret and make another King that wold give or fell them thefe Lands; that now, they had no Hopes left to kepe ani Land. Another Grievance, the English Catell and Horfes ftill incrafed; that when thay removed 30 Mile from where Englifh had ani thing to do, thay could not kepe ther Corn from being fpoyled, thay never being iufed to fence, and thoft when the Englifh boft Land of them thay wold have kept their Catell upon ther owne Land. Another Grievance, the Englifh were fo eager to fell the Indians Lickers, y! moft of the Indians fpent all in Drynknes, and then raueved upon the fober Indians, and thay did believe often did hurt the Englifh Catell, and ther King could not prevent it.

"We knew before, thefe were their grand Complaints, but then we only indevered to perfuaid y! all Complaints might be righted without War, but could have no other Anfwer but that thay had not heard of that Way for the Governor of Yorke and an Indian King to have the Hearing of it. We had Cafe to think in y! had bine tendered it wold have bine accepted. We indevered y! however thay fhould lay downe the War, for the Englifh wear to Strong for them; thay faid, then the Englifh fhould do to them as they did when thay wear to ftrong for the Englifh.

"So we departed without ani Difcurtioufnefs, and fudingly had Letter from Plimoth Governor thay intended in Arms to conforem Philip, but no Information what y! was thay required, or w! Termes he refufed to have their Quarrell defided; and in a Weke's Time after we had bine with the Indians the War thus begun."

If this is authentic, it is interesting, and indicates the utmost that — from his side of the question — a wily savage could then suggest in extenuation of the proposed outbreak. The insinuated poisoning of Alexander may

HISTORICAL INTRODUCTION.

have been the utterance of an honest suspicion on the part of Philip and his friends: it sounds more like an advantage taken of the impossibility of contrary proof, to urge a conscious and mischievous slander. Nor is there any thing in what Easton says to give color to the notion of a general conspiracy among all the tribes to crush out the whites.

The results of the war were heavy to the Colonies. Ten or twelve towns were utterly destroyed, and two-score of others more or less damaged and depopulated. From five to six hundred men fell in the various fights, were murdered in stealthy assaults, or were carried away captive, never to return. More than £100,000 were expended in the struggle; and, at its close, it is estimated that the Old Colony was left under a debt which exceeded the value of the entire personal property of its people! As a natural consequence, the Plymouth Colonists were nearly discouraged. But, from her thin soil and her various industries, she gradually pushed on to square herself with the world, until she had paid the last dollar of principal and interest!

The causes which aroused those later hostilities, which called out the several Eastern Expeditions recounted in this Second Part, were not different essentially from those which lay at the root of "Philip's War," except as the intermeddling of the French may have had to do with exciting, exasperating, and sustaining them. The Indians grew more and more dissatisfied as they saw the Colonists advancing in wealth and power, and every year fixing themselves with a firmer hold upon the soil. It was this inherent hostility between a savage race and that civilized one which it sees to be too strong for it, and to be menacing its future, added to the Indian's natural love for blood and pillage, which stimulated attacks which were sought to be excused by pretences that this treaty had not been faithfully kept, or that promise had not been honestly performed.

It may be doubted, however, whether even the fierce savage of the eastern wilds would not have chosen to retreat from the coasts toward the Five Nations without risking the chances of conflict, if he had not been urged on and aided and abetted even in his brutalest work, by the deadly hatred then borne by the French settler to his English competitor; in which the old hostility of race was supplemented and intensified by the ferocity of Jesuit-fanned fanaticism.

When the echoes of the last hearty war-whoop died away among the New-England hills, a new leaf was turned in her history. Even her strong men breathed freer as they wrought along her frontiers; and her women slept sweeter, with their little ones around them, everywhere under the deep shadows of her ancestral woods.

HISTORY

OF THE

EASTERN EXPEDITIONS.

[55]

A further Account of the Actions
in the more later Wars againſt the Common Enemy and *Indian* Rebels in the Eaſtern Parts, under the Command of the aforeſaid Capt. *Benj. Church.*[1]

IN the time of Sir *Edmund Androſs's*[2] Government, began that bloudy War in the Eaſtern Parts of *New-England*; ſo that immediately Sir *Edmund* ſent an Expreſs for Capt. *Church*; who then being at *Little Compton*,[3] received it on a Lords Day[4] in

---

[1] See Introduction, for ſome account of the cauſes which led to theſe "more later wars."

[2] *Sir Edmund Andros* was born in Guernſey in 1632; went into the army, where, through favor of the Duke of York, he received promotion; in 1664 was appointed Governor of the Duke's territories in America; arrived at New York 31 Oct., 1674; ſoon began to ſupervife the moral and religious, as well as the civil affairs of the people; in 1675, attempted in vain to extend his authority over Connecticut. In Feb., 1685, the Duke of York, ſucceeding to the throne as James II., appointed Andros Governor of all the New-England Colonies except Connecticut. He arrived at Boſton 20 Dec., 1686, and began to remove old officers, overturn exiſting inſtitutions, and enter upon a practical deſpotiſm. 12 Jan., 1687, he aſſumed the Government of Rhode Iſland; and, 13 June, that of Connecticut, which he claimed by ſupplementary inſtructions. After the news of the landing of the Prince of Orange reached Boſton, an inſurrection took place there 18 April, 1689, and Andros was impriſoned. In Feb., 1690, he was ſent home to England, by command of William III., who, in 1692, appointed him Governor of Virginia, where he for the firſt time had a popular adminiſtration, but returned to England in 1699; was Governor of Guernſey from 1704 to 1706; and died in London, Feb., 1714, at the age of 82. [*Governors of Maſs. Bay*, 403-422.]

[3] Capt. Church muſt have been at *Saconet* on a tranſient viſit, as he was at this time a reſident of Briſtol. [See *Introductory Memoir*, Part I., of this work, p. xxviii.]

[4] The date of this occurrence would ſeem to be approximately fixed by the

[55]

the afternoon Meeting; going home after Meeting, took his Horſe and ſet out for *Boſton*, as ordered; and by Sun riſe next Morning got to *Brantry*,[5] where he met with Col. *Page*[6] on Horſe-back, going to *Weymouth* and *Hingham* to raiſe Forces to go Eaſt; who ſaid he was glad to ſee him, and that his Excellency would be as glad to ſee him in *Boſton* ſo early: ſo parting, he ſoon got to *Boſton*,

probability that it muſt have been between the 20 Oct., 1688, when Andros iſſued his proclamation ſeeking to ſecure peace among the Eaſtern Indians, and that time in the following November (Hutchinſon [*Hiſt. Maſs.* i: 331] ſays "in the beginning of November"; Willis [*Hiſt. Portland* (ed. 1865), 274] ſays "early in November"; Williamſon [*Hiſt. Maine*, i: 589] ſays "late in November"), when he ſtarted, with his force of 700 or 800 men, for the Eaſtern country.

[5] What was then known as Braintree is now known as Quincy; the preſent Braintree being at that time called *Monatiquot*. [*Addreſs at the opening of the new Town Hall in Braintree*, July 29, 1858, by Hon. C. F. Adams, 67; *Vinton Memorial*, 463].

[6] *Nicholas Paige* was in Boſton in 1665; married Ann, daughter of Edward Keayne, and widow of Edward Lane (which Ann was tried for adultery 23 May, 1666, and made confeſſion of "much wickedneſs"); ſerved in Philip's War, and was witneſs to articles of peace with the Narraganſetts 15 July, 1675; was Captain of one of the companies raiſed in Boſton on the overthrow of Andros; was Captain of the Ancient and Honorable Artillery Company in 1695. He is called "Lt. Coll." in 1688. He died, probably, late in 1717. In the repairs made, in 1863, upon the Univerſity Library building in Leyden, Holland, there were found under the floor of that room which for many years was uſed as a chapel by the Scotch Preſbyterian Church, ſix memorial ſtones, and parts of twelve bodies. One of the ſtones bore the following inſcription: —

Here lieth buried *Edward Paige*, onely ſon of *Nicolas* and *Anna Paige*, born at Boſton in New England, Feb. 20, 1622, died in Leyden, Nov. 1, 1680, N.S.

The firſt date ſhould, of courſe, be 1662, and this is clearly the Edward *Lane* of whom Savage ſpeaks [*Gen. Dict.* iii: 50] as the ſon, of that birth-date, of his mother while ſtill the wife of Edward Lane; whoſe name, for ſome wiſe reaſon, was changed to that of his mother's ſecond huſband, after her ſecond marriage. [Savage's *Gen. Dict.* iii: 332. *Maſs. Col. Rec.* iv (pt. 2): 309; Drake's *Hiſt. Boſt.* i: 482. Leyden *MSS.*]

and waited upon his Excellency; who informed him of an unhappy War broke out in the Eaſtern Parts; and ſaid he was going himſelf in Perſon, and that he wanted his Company with him: But Capt. *Church* not finding in himſelf the ſame Spirit he us'd to have,[7] ſaid, he hop'd his Excellency would give him time to conſider of it. He told him he might; and alſo ſaid that he muſt come and Dine with him. Capt. *Church* having many acquaintance in *Boſton*, who made it their buſineſs ſome to incourage, and others to diſcourage him from going with his Excellency.[8] So after Dinner his Excellency took him into his room and diſcours'd freely; ſaying that he having knowledge of his former Actions and Succeſſes; and that he muſt go with him, and be his Second, with other incouragements. But in ſhort, the ſaid Capt. *Church* did not accept, ſo was diſmiſt, and went home.

Soon after this was the Revolution, and the other Government Re-aſſumed;[9] and then Governour *Broadſtreet*[10]

---

[7] This can ſcarcely refer to any feeling incident to advancing age, for Capt. Church was not yet 50.

[8] Andros was at this time ſo unpopular, that very few perſons in Boſton would then be apt to adviſe a friend to aid him, or undertake any thing under him.

[9] The ſmothered flame broke out into the arreſt of the Governor, a portion of his Council, and other obnoxious perſons — about 50 in all — on Thurſday, 18 April, 1689. On the 22 May, the repreſentatives of 54 towns met in Boſton; and, two days after, Gov. Bradſtreet and the Magiſtrates who had been choſen in 1686, reſumed the direction of affairs. [Hutchinſon's *Hiſt. Maſs.* i: 333-344.]

[10] *Simon Bradſtreet* was born — the ſon of a Non-Conformiſt miniſter — at Horbling, in Lincolnſhire, in March, 1603; took A.B. 1620 and A.M. 1624, at Emanuel College, Cambridge; was ſteward of the Earl of Lincoln, and then of the Counteſs of Warwick; came with Winthrop in the "Arbella," 1630; ſettled in Newtown (Cambridge),

fent for Capt. *Church* to come to *Boston*, as foon as his bufinefs would permit: Where-upon he went to *Boston*, and waited upon his Honour;[11] who told him he was requefted by the Council to fend for him, to fee if he could be prevail'd with to Raife Volunteers both *English* and *Indians* to go Eaft; for the Eaftward *Indians* had done great fpoil upon the *English* in thofe Parts;[12] giving him an account of the Miferies and Sufferings of the People there: Capt. *Churches* Spirits being affected, faid, If he could do any Service for his Honour, the Country, and their relief, he was ready and willing: His advice was asked, How he would act, he faid, He would take with him as many of his old Souldiers as he could get, both *English* and *In-*

lived afterward at Ipfwich, Andover, Bofton, and Salem. He was the firft Secretary of the Mafs. Colony; Commiffioner of the United Colonies; Deputy Governor 1672-9; afterward Governor until 1686; was the head of the moderate party, but oppofed Andros's arbitrary acts, and refumed his place at the head of affairs when Andros was depofed, where he continued until Sir William Phipps came, in 1692, with the new Charter. He died 27 March, 1697, aged 94. He married (1) Ann, daughter of Gov. Thomas Dudley, by whom he had Samuel, Dorothy, Sarah, Simon, Hannah, Mercy, Dudley, and John; (2) Ann, widow of Capt. Jofeph Gardner, and daughter of Emanuel Downing. [Savage's *Gen. Dict.* i: 236; *N. E. Hift. & Gen. Reg.* i: 75.]

[11] The date of this is approximately fixed by cotemporary documents. Gov. Bradftreet wrote to Gov. Hinckley, 17 July, 1689, " We have written to Capt. Church"; and 2 Aug., 1689, "Capt. Church having alfo been written to from hence thereabouts, who is now here with the Council treating about that affair," &c. [Hinckley Papers, 4 *Mafs. Hift. Coll.* v: 204-5.]

[12] In April, 1689, the Indians renewed hoftilities at Saco; and 27 June, Cocheco (now Dover, N.H.) was furprifed, and Maj. Waldron and 23 others were killed, and 29 were taken captive, and fold to the French in Canada. 2 Aug., Pemaquid was deftroyed, and the inhabitants Eaft of Falmouth (Portland, Me.) withdrew in terror to that town, or removed to other places of fuppofed fecurity. [Mather's *Magnalia* (orig. ed.), Book vii: 64-5; Williamfon's *Hift. Maine*, i: 610; Willis's *Hift. Portland*, 275.]

dians, &c. The Gentlemen of *Boston* requested him to go [56] to *Rhode-Island* Government to ask their assistance: So giving him their Letter, and about 40 *s*. in Money, he took leave and went home to *Bristol* on a Saturday; and the next Monday Morning he went over to *Rhode-Island*, and waited upon their Governour,[13] delivering the Letter, as ordered; pray'd his Honour for a speedy answer:[14] who said, they could not give an answer presently; so he waited upon them till he had their answer; and when he had obtain it, he carryed it to the *Boston* Gentlemen; who desired him to Raise what Volunteers he could in *Plymouth* Colony,[15] and *Rhode-Island* Government, & what was wanting they would make up out of their's that was already out in the Eastern Parts. The Summer being far spent Capt.

---

[13] *Walter Clark*, eldest son of Jeremiah of Newport, was born about 1639; was a Quaker; was freeman in 1665; 6 Nov., 1672, was member of a committee to audit the accounts between the Colony and its creditors; in 1673 and 1674 was on the committee to see that the election was conducted in an orderly manner; 2 May, 1676, was chosen Governor; for many years afterward was Deputy Governor, and then Governor again in 1686, and once more in 1696; died 22 May, 1714, aged 74. He married (1) Content ———, who died March, 1666; (2) Hannah, daughter of Richard Scott, who died 24 July, 1681; (3) Freeborn, daughter of Roger Williams, and widow of Thomas Hart, who died 10 Dec., 1709; (4) Sarah, daughter of Matthew Prior, and widow of John Gould. [Savage's *Gen. Dict.* i: 403; *R.-I. Col. Rec.* ii: 147, 481, 483, 517, 541; iii: 30, 186, 312.]

[14] When the Revolution ousted Andros, the old Charter Government was resumed in Rhode Island, but the "wary Clark"—who had been Governor when Andros arrived and seized the State—"hesitated to accept his former post; and for ten months Rhode Island was without an acknowledged Governor." [Arnold's *Hist. R.-I.* i: 512.] It was during these ten months that Church "waited upon him"; whence the difficulty of giving "an answer presently" finds ready explanation.

[15] Plymouth Court met 14 Aug., 1689, and voted their "concurrence" accord-

[56]

Church made what dispatch he could, and raised about 250 Men Volunteers, and receiving his Commission from Governour *Hinkley*,[16] which is as followeth, *viz.*

' *The Council of War of their Majesties Colony of*
' *New-Plymouth in* New-England. *To Major*
' *Benjamin Church,* Commander in Chief.

' WHereas the *Kennebeck* & *Eastern Indians* with their
' Confederates, have openly made War upon their
' Majesties Subjects of the Provinces of *Maine, New-Hamp-*

ing to their "weak capacity," in the measures proposed by Massachusetts to subdue the Eastern savages. They instructed their Commissioners (1) to be satisfied as to the grounds of the War; (2) to take care not to be overcharged for its carrying on; (3) to endeavor not to be involved in charges formerly contracted; (4) to secure due allowance to volunteers, and due bounty to the wounded; (5) to arrange for disbursements to be repaid in time convenient; (6) to stipulate that what shall be due to Plymouth soldiers shall be paid here, to prevent charge of transportation and other loss; (7) that it be endeavored to engage the Mohawks as allies. It was also ordered "that the millitary officers of each town forthwith use their endeavour to encourage English & Indians to a volluntary going out in this present expedition under com'and of Capt. Church," &c.: and that if a competent number should not volunteer "then such a number shall be pressed as shall be by the Councill of war agreed upon

in the severall towns where vollunteers enough do not appear."

It was further ordered, and I insert the order as curiously intimating the proportionate strength of the towns of Plymouth Colony at this date, that " the proportion for men and armes for each towne for this present expedition shall be as followeth : each man to be provided with a well fixt gun, sword, or hatchet, a horne or cartouch box, suitable am'unition and a snapsack." viz :—

	Men.	Armes.		Men.	Armes.
Plymouth,	4	3	Rochester,	1	1
Scituate,	6	5	Monamoy,	1	1
Marshfield,	3	3	Succoneffett,	1	1
Duxborough,	2	2	Bristoll,	3	2
Bridgewater,	3	2	Taunton,	4	4
Middleborough,	1	1	Rehoboth,	4	3
Barnstable,	4	3	Dartmouth,	3	2
Eastham,	4	3	Swansey,	3	2
Sandwich,	3	3	Freetown,	1	1
Yarmouth,	3	3	Little Compton,	2	2

[*Plym. Col. Rec.* vi : 212–216.]

[16] *Thomas Hinckley* was born in 1618, in Tenterden, Kent, being son of Samuel, who came to this country in the Hercules,

'*shire*, and of the *Massachusetts* Colony, having committed
' many barbarous Murders, Spoils & Rapines upon their
' Persons & Estates. And whereas there are some
' Forces of Souldiers *English* and *Indians*[17] now raised
' & detached out of the several Regiments & Places within
' this Colony of *New-Plymouth*, to go forth to the assistance
' of our Neighbours & Friends of the aforesaid Provinces
' and Colony of the *Massachusetts*, Subjects of one and the
' same Crown; and to joyn with their Forces for the re-
' pelling and destruction of the common Enemy. And
' whereas you *Benjamin Church* are appointed to be Ma-
' jor & Commander in Chief of all the Forces *English* and
' *Indians* detached within this Colony, for the Service of
' their Majesties as aforesaid. 𝕿𝖍𝖊𝖘𝖊 are in their Majesties
' Name to Authorize & Require you to take into your care
' & conduct all the said Forces *English* and *Indians*, and
' diligently to intend that Service, by leading and exercis-
' ing of your Inferiour Officers and Souldiers, commanding
' them to obey you as their Chief Commander; and to
' pursue, fight, take, kill or destroy the said Enemies, their

---

in 1635. He was Deputy from Barnstable as early as 1645, and Assistant in 1658; Deputy Governor in 1680; and Governor in 1681, holding the office, except when it was usurped by Andros, until the absorption of the Colony, when he was made Councillor of Mass. He died at Barnstable, 25 April, 1705, æt. 87. He married (1) Mary Richards; (2) Mary Glover, daughter of Lawrence Smith, and widow of Nathaniel Glover. One of his daughters married Experience Mayhew, and another Samuel Prince. [Otis's *Hist. Barnstable*, i: 308-313.]

[17] Mr. Drake [*Book of the Indians*, 270] states, on the authority of a MS. letter of Capt. Bassett of this Expedition, that there was an Indian Company commanded by Capt. *Amos*, and another by Capt. *Daniel*; while Church seems to imply that the *Sacouet* Indians who were with him were under Capt. *Numpas*.

'Aiders and Abetters, by all the wayes and means you
' can, as you fhall have opportunity. And you to obferve
' & obey all fuch Orders and Inftructions as from time to
' time you fhall receive from the Commiffioners of the
' Colonies, the Council of War of this Colony, or the Go-
' vernour and Council of the *Maffachufetts* Colony. In
' Teftimony whereof the Publick Seal of the faid Colony
' of *New-Plymouth* is here-unto affixed. Dated in *Ply-*
' *mouth* the Sixth day of *September, Anno Dom.* 1689.
' *Annoque Regni Regis* et *Reginæ* Willielmi *et* Mariæ
' *Angliæ,* &c. *Primo.*

Thomas Hinkley, *Prefident.* [57]

And now Marching them all down to *Bofton,* then received his further Orders and Inftructions: which are as
followeth,

Bofton, Septem. 16*th.* 1689.

*To all Sheriffs, Marfhalls, Conftables, and other Officers
Military and Civil, in their Majefties Province
of Maine.*

'WHereas purfuant to an agreement of the Commif-
' fioners of the United Colonies, Major *Benjamin*
' *Church* is Commiffionated Commander in Chief over
' that part of their Majefties Forces (levyed for the pref-
' ent Expedition againft the Common Enemy) whofe
' head quarters are appointed to be at *Falmouth* in *Cafco*
' *Bay.* In their Majefties Names, You, and every of you

' are required to be aiding and affifting to the faid Maj.
' *Church*, in his purfute of the Enemy, as any Emergency
' fhall require; and to Imprefs Boats, or other Veffels, Carts,
' Carriages, Horfes, Oxen, Provifion and Ammunition, and
' Men for guides *&c*. as you fhall receive Warrants from the
' faid Chief Commander, or his Lieutenant fo to do: You
' may not fail to do the fame fpeedily and effectually, as
' you will anfwer your neglect and contempt of their
' Majefties Authority and Service at your uttermoft Peril.
' Given under my Hand and Seal the Day and Year above
' Written. *Annoque Regi Regis* et *Reginæ* Willielmi *&*
' *Mariæ Primo.*

By Thomas Danforth,[18] *Prefident of the
Province of Maine.*

*By the Governour and Council of the Maffachufetts Colony.
To Major* Benjamin Church.

' WHereas you are appointed and commiffioned by the
' Council of War of the Colony of *New-Plymouth*,
' Commander in Chief of the Forces raifed within the faid
' Colony, againft the Common *Indian* Enemy, now ordered
' into the Eaftern Parts, to joyn with fome of the Forces
' of this Colony; for the profecution, repelling and fubdu-

---

[18] *Thomas Danforth*, of Cambridge, was eldeft fon of Nicolas; was born in England; was freeman 10 May, 1643; Deputy 1657-8; Affiftant 1659-78; Deputy Governor 1679-86, and again after Andros; in 1680 was appointed Prefident for Maine, and, in 1692, Judge of the Supreme Court; died 5 Nov., 1699. He married Mary Withington, of Dorchefter. [Savage's *Gen. Dict.* ii: 8.]

[57]

'ing of the said Enemy. It is therefore Ordered that
'Captain *Simon Willard*,[19] and Capt. *Nathanael Hall*,[20]
'with the two Companies of Souldiers under their several
'Command belonging to this Colony, now in or about
'*Casco Bay*, be and are hereby put under you, as their
'Commander in Chief for this present Expedition. And
'in pursuance of the Commissions severally given to either
'of them, they are Ordered to Observe and Obey your
'orders and directions, as their Commander in Chief until
'further Order from the Governour & Council; Or the
'Commissioners of the Colonies. Dated in *Boston* the
'17th day of *September, Anno Dom.* 1689. *Annoque*

[19] *Simon Willard* was third son of Maj. Simon; born 23 Nov., 1649; freeman 1680; Captain in this war; was Deacon; died 21 June, 1731. He married (1) about 1679, Martha, daughter of Richard Jacob, of Ipswich; (2) 30 April, 1702, Elizabeth, widow of John Walley, and daughter of the second John Alden; (3) July, 1722, Priscilla Buttolph. [Savage's *Gen. Dict.* iv: 555.]

[20] I cannot identify this Captain, except by the supposition that he was the same "Capt. Nathaniel Hall" who joined the Ancient and Honorable Artillery Company in 1692, and who is barely mentioned by name, by Whitman. [*Hist. Anct. & Hon. Art.* 228.] It seems to me that Mr. Savage is mistaken in saying that he was that son of the first John of Yarmouth, who married Anne Thornton, practised as a physician, kept tavern, &c., &c. It is hardly probable that there were two cotemporary Nathaniel Halls of Yarmouth, both of whom fought the Indians. But that Nathaniel Hall who received grants from the Plymouth Colony in July, 1681, and July, 1683, and who was licensed to keep an ordinary, in addition to a grant of £5 per annum, 5 June, 1684, to which £30 more, with the promise of £6 per annum, were added in June, 1685,—all on account of his "contenewed lamenefs" as "a decriped souldier, whoe became soe by a wound received in the late Indian warr," was of Yarmouth. And as he was thus an untitled pensioner up to 1685, it seems unlikely that he could have been the Capt. Nathaniel who marched under Church in 1689. Mr. Otis, however, thinks he was the same. [Savage's *Gen. Dict.* ii: 336; *Plym. Col. Rec.* vi: 65, 112, 130, 132, 169; Freeman's *Hist. Cape Cod*, ii: 203. Otis's *Hist. Barnstable*, i: 241.]

' *Regni Regis et Reginæ* Guilielmi *et* Mariæ *Angliæ*, &c.
' *Primo.*

 Paſt in Council,   S. Bradſtreet, GOV.
Atteſt Iſaac Addington, *Secr.*[21] [58]

> *By the Commiſſioners of the Colonies of the* Maſſachuſetts, Plymouth *and* Connecticut, *for managing the preſent War againſt the Common Enemy.*

' 𝕴𝖓𝖘𝖙𝖗𝖚𝖈𝖙𝖎𝖔𝖓𝖘 for Major *Benjamin Church* Commander
' in Chief of the *Plymouth* Forces, with others of the
' *Maſſachuſetts* put under his Command.

' IN Purſuance of the Commiſſion given you for their
' Majeſty's Service in the preſent Expedition againſt the
' Common *Indian* Enemy, their Aidors and Abettors; re-
' poſing confidence in your Wiſdom, Prudence and Fi-
' delity in the truſt committed to you, for the honour of
' God, good of His People, and the ſecurity of the Intereſt
' of Chriſt in His Churches, expecting and praying that in
' your dependance upon Him, you may be helped &
' aſſiſted with all that Grace and Wiſdom which is requi-
' ſite for carrying you on with Succeſs in this difficult Ser-
' vice; and tho' much is and muſt be left to your diſcretion
' as Providence and opportunity may preſent from time to
' time in places of attendence: Yet the following Inſtruc-
' tions are commended unto your obſervation, and to be

---

[21] *Iſaac Addington*, only ſon of Iſaac, of Boſton, born 22 Jan., 1645; was bred for a ſurgeon, but was choſen Deputy 1685, and next year Aſſiſtant. Under the new Charter, he was one of the Council, and Secretary, in which office he continued many years. He was afterward Judge. He died 19 Mar., 1715, *æt.* 70. [Allen's *Biog. Dict.* 14.]

' attended fo far as the State of matters with you in fuch a
' tranfaction will admit. You are with all poffible fpeed
' to take care that the *Plymouth* Forces both *Englifh* and
' *Indians* under your Command be fixed and ready, and
' the firft opportunity of Wind & Weather, to go on
' board fuch Veffels as are provided to tranfport you and
' them to *Cafco*, where if it fhall pleafe God you arrive,
' you are to take under your care & command the Com-
' panies of Capt. *Nathanael Hall*, and Capt. *Simon Wil-*
' *lard*, who are ordered to attend your Command, whom
' together with the *Plymouth* Forces, and fuch as from time
' to time may be added unto you; you are to improve in
' fuch way as you fhall fee meet, for the difcovering,
' purfuing, fubduing and deftroying the faid Common En-
' emy, by all opportunities you are capable of; alwayes
' intending the preferving any of the near Towns from
' incurfions, and deftruction of the Enemy, yet chiefly
' improving your men for the finding and following the
' faid Enemy abroad, and if poffible to find out & attach
' their head quarters and principal Randezvouz, if you find
' you are in a rational capacity of fo doing; the better to
' inable you thereto, We have ordered two men of War
' Sloops, and other fmall Veffels for tranfportation, to attend
' you, for fome confiderable time. You are to fee that
' your Souldiers Arms be always fixt, and that they be
' furnifhed with Ammunition, Provifions and other necef-
' faries, that fo they may be in a readinefs to repel and
' attach the Enemy. In your purfute you are to take

'special care to avoid danger by Ambushments, or being
'drawn under any disadvantage by the Enemy in your
'Marches, Keeping out Scouts and a forlorn before your
'main Body, and by all possible means endeavouring to
'Surprize some of the Enemy, that so you may gain intelli-
'gence. You are to Suppress all Mutinies and Disorders
'among your Souldiers, as much as in you lies, and to
'punish such as disobey your Officers, according to the
'rules of War herewith given you. [59]

'You are according to your opportunity, or any occa-
'sion more than ordinary occurring to hold correspondence
'with Major *Swaine*,[22] and to yield Mutual assistance when
'and as you are capable of it, and you may have reason to
'judge it will be of most Publick Service; and it will be
'meet you and he should agree of some Signal whereby
'your *Indians* may be known from the Enemy. You are
'to incourage your Souldiers to be industrious, vigorous,
'and venturous in their Service, to search out and destroy
'the Enemy, acquainting them, It is agreed by the several
'Colonies, That they shall have the benefit of the Captives,
'and all lawful Plunder, and the Reward of *Eight Pounds*
'*per* head, for every fighting *Indian* man slain by them,
'over and above their Stated wages; the same being made
'appear to the Commander in Chief, or such as shall be
'appointed to take care therein. If your Commission Offi-

[22] This appears to have been Jeremiah Swain, of Reading, who was Deputy 1686 and 1689, and Assistant the latter year. He was Captain for many years previous to this war, and was at the head of a regiment in 1691. [Savage's *Gen. Dict.* iv: 235; *Mass. Col. Rec.* v: 476, 514.]

'cers or any of them should be slain, or otherwise uncapa-
'ble of Service, and for such reason dismist, you are to
'appoint others in their room, who shall have the like
'wages, and a Commission sent upon notice given, you to
'give them Commissions in the mean time. You are
'to take effectual care that the Worship of God be kept up
'in the Army, Morning and Evening Prayer attended as
'far as may be, and as the Emergencies of your affairs
'will admit, to see that the holy Sabbath be duely Sancti-
'fied. You are to take care as much as may be to prevent
'or punish Drunkenness, Swearing, Cursing, or such other
'Sins, as do provoke the anger of God. You are to ad-
'vise with your Chief Officers in any matters of Moment,
'as you shall have opportunity. You are from time to
'time to give intelligence and advice to the Governour &
'Council of the *Massachusetts*, or Commissioners of the
'Colonies of your proceedings and occurrence that may
'happen, and how it shall please the Lord to deal with you
'in this present Expedition.

'If you find the Vessels are not likely to be Serviceable
'to you, dismiss them as soon as you may.

'Capt. *Silvanus Davis*[23] is a prudent Man, and well

---

[23] *Sylvanus Davis* was at Sheepscot 1659; swore allegiance to the King 1665; was wounded by the Indians at Arrowsick when Captain Lake was killed; removed to Falmouth (Portland) 1680; became a large land-owner there, and had the most extensive warehouse in the Eastern country at that time, being licensed, in 1687, "to retail liquors out of doors in the town of Falmouth"; became unpopular in the days of Andros; commanded the fort; was captured by the French and Indians in May, 1690; was exchanged for a Frenchman 15 Oct., 1690; was put into the Council by the Charter of William and

' acquainted with the affairs of thofe parts, and is writt
' unto to advife and inform you all he can.

' Such further Inftructions as we fhall fee reafon to fend
' unto you, you are carefully to attend and obferve, and in
' the abfence of the Commiffioners, you fhall obferve the
' orders and inftructions directed unto you from the Gov-
' ernour and Council of the *Maffachufetts*.

 Given under our hands in Bofton, *Sept.* 18. 1689.
  Tho. Hinkley   Thomas Danforth, Prefident.
  John Walley [24]   Elifha Cooke [25]
          Samuel Mafon [26]
          William Pitkin.[27]

Mary 1691; lived in his latter days at Hull, Mafs.; died 1704, leaving a wife, but no children. He wrote an account of his capture, &c., &c., which is on file in the Mafs. State Paper Office, and was printed in 3 *Mafs. Hift. Coll.* i: 101–112. [Willis's *Hift. Port.* 21, 131, 208, 226, 231, 234, 258, 263, 284, 293; Savage's *Gen. Dict.* ii: 21.]

[24] *John Walley* was fon of Rev. Thomas, of Barnftable; was born in 1643; was admitted to the Ancient and Honorable Artillery 1671; freeman 1673; Captain 1679; was interefted in the fettlement of Briftol; was one of Andros's Council 1686; was chief military officer of the expedition to Quebec 1690; was Judge of the Superior Court 1700–11; died in Bofton 11 Jan., 1712, *æt*. 68. He publifhed a Journal of the Quebec Expedition, which is contained in the appendix to the firft volume of Hutchinfon's Hiftory of Maffachufetts. He had a fingular controverfy with John Saffin, & in which Judge Byfield became alfo involved. [Savage's *Gen. Dict.* iv: 400; *Hift. Anct. & Hon. Art.* 185; Freeman's *Hift. Cape Cod*, i: 323; Wathburn's *Judic. Hift. Mafs.* 270.]

[25] *Elifha Cooke*, fon of Richard, of Bofton, was a phyfician; freeman 1673; Deputy 1681–3; Affiftant 1684–6; of the Council of Safety 1689; was agent

[26] *Samuel Mafon* was eldeft fon of Maj. John; born at Windfor, Conn., July, 1664; Lieut. 1670; freeman 1673; on the court-marfhal for New London

[27] *William Pitkin* was of Hartford, Conn., fon of Roger; freeman 1662; Deputy 1675; Treafurer 1676; was Affiftant many years; Commiffioner for

[60] The First Expedition, *East.*

BEing ready,[28] Major *Church* imbark'd with his Forces on board the Vessels provided to transport them for *Casco*,[29] having a brave Gale at S. W and on Fryday about 3 a clock they got in sight of *Casco* Harbour; and discoursing two or three small Ships there, not knowing before whether they were friends or enemies; whereupon the said Commander Maj *Church* gave orders that every man that was able should make ready, and all ly close, giving orders how they should act in case they were Enemies: He going in the *Mary* Sloop, together with the *Resolution* went in first, being both well fitted with Guns & Men; coming to the first, hail'd them, who said they were friends;

for Mass. in England, with Oakes and Mather, 1690-1; Judge of Probate 1701; died 31 Oct., 1715. He married Elizabeth, daughter of Gov. Leverett. [Savage's *Gen. Dict.* i: 445; Bradford's *New Eng. Biog.* 111.]

Co., 1676; Deputy from Stonington, 1678-82; Assistant 1683-89; Captain 1685; afterward Major and Commissioner for Conn.; died 30 Mar., 1705. He married (1) —— ? ; (2) Eliz. Peck. [*Col. Rec. Conn.* ii: 132, 201, 484; iii: 3, 17, 36, 66, 75, 106, 114, 170, &c.; *N. E. Hist. & Gen. Reg.* xv: 117, 118.]

the United Colonies 1678; and to treat with Gov. Dungan 1683; Commissioner again later; died 15 Dec. 1694, æt. 58. He married Hannah, only daughter of Ozias Goodwin. [Savage's *Gen. Dict.* iii: 441; *Col. Rec. Conn.* iii: 2, 17, &c.]

[28] "Major Church arrived at Falmouth in the latter part of September." [Williamson's *Hist. Maine*, i: 616.]

[29] "The old Indian name *Casco* continued to be used all the first century after the settlement (for what is now Portland, Me.,) notwithstanding the town had received from Massachusetts the corporate name Falmouth, as early as 1658." The familiar aboriginal titles had then much vitality. [Willis's *Hist. Portland*, 49.]

prefently Man'd their Boat, brought too, and fo came along the fide of them; who gave the faid *Church* an account, That yefterday there was a very great Army of *Indians*, & *French* with them upon the Ifland,[30] at the going out of the Harbour, and that they were come on purpofe to take *Cafco* Fort[31] and Town, likewife inform'd him that they had got a Captive Woman aboard (Maj. *Waldens* daughter of *Pifcataqua*[32]) that could give him a full account of

[30] Jofeph Prout wrote from Falmouth 17 Sept., 1689, that 200 Indians were then on "Palmer's Ifland." [Willis's *Hift. Port.* 277.] Palmer's was what is now Peak's Ifland, perhaps 500 rods E. of the mouth of Cafco River.

[31] *Fort Loyall* had been erected on Cleeves's Neck, on the point, at the foot of what was afterward King Street (now India Street), in 1680, and garrifoned by 13 men, part of whom were fupported by Maffachufetts. 24 May, 1682, an agreement was made with Lieut. Anthony Brackett to keep the fort for one year, by 6 men in the fummer and 4 men in the winter, "by continual watch and ward to keep it as a fort ought to be kept." The next year, Walter Gendall was authorized to take charge of the fort if Brackett declined. [Willis's *Hift. Port.* 226, 249, 254.]

[32] *Richard Waldron* (more properly *Walderne*) was born in Alcefter, Warwickfhire, Eng., where he was baptized 6 Jan., 1615; came to America in 1635, with Mr. Hilton or Mr. Wiggin, to fee the country; ftaid about two years, and returned to England and married a gentlewoman of good family; came back, and fettled at Cocheco Lower Falls. He was, at different periods, Selectman, Deputy, Affiftant, Major, Chief-Juftice of New Hampfhire, and acting Prefident. He was killed by the Indians (fee note 12) 28 June, 1689. He married (1) the Englifh lady above referred to; (2) Anne Scammon, fifter of Richard, fhe died 7 Feb., 1685. By thefe wives he had (1) Paul, d. 1669; (2) Timothy; (3) Richard, b. 1650; (4) Anna; (5) Elnathan, b. 6 July, 1659, d. 10 Dec., 1659; (6) Efther, b. 1 Dec., 1660; (7) Mary, b. 14 Sept. 1663, d. young; (8) Eleazer, b. 1 May, 1665; (9) Elizabeth, b. 18 Oct., 1666; (10) Marah, b. 17 July, 1668. Efther married (1) Henry, fon of Henry Elkins, of Hampton; (2) Abram Lee, "Chymift," who was killed with Major W. by the Indians; (3) Richard, fon of Richard Jofe, of Portfmouth; (4) —— ——; and died in the Ifland of Jerfey. She, of courfe, was the perfon here referred to by Church, having been captured by the Indians at the time of the murder of her father and hufband, three months before, and refcued by a Dutch privateer. [*N. E. Hift. & Gen. Reg.* ix: 55;

their number & intentions: He bid 'em give his Service to
their Captain, and tell him, He would wait upon him after
he had been on fhore and gave fome orders and directions:
being come pretty near he ordered all the Men ftill to keep
clofe, giving an account of the News he had received, and
then went a-fhore, where were feveral of the chief Men of
the Town who met him, being glad that he came fo hap-
pily to their relief; told him the News Mrs. *Lee* had given
them, being the Woman aforefaid. He going to Capt.
Davis's [39] to get fome refrefhment, having not eat a Morfel
fince he came by *Bofton* Caftle; and now having inquired
into the State of the Town, found them in a poor condition
for to defend themfelves againft fuch a number of Enemies:
He gave them an account of his Orders and Inftructions,
and told them what Forces he had brought, and that when
it was dark they fhould all Land, and not before, left the
Enemy fhould difcover them. And then he went on board
the Privateer, who were *Dutch* Men; but as he went call'd
aboard every Veffel and ordered the Officers to take care
that their Men might be all fitted and provided to fight, for
the People of the Town expected the Enemy to fall upon
them every Minute, but withal charging them to keep undifcovered: and coming on board the faid Privateer, was
kindly treated; difcours'd Mrs. *Lee*, who inform'd him

Belknap's *Hift. New Hamp.* i: 199; Williamfon's *Hift. Me.* i: 616.]

[39] Capt. Davis's [fee note 23, *ante*] houfe, to which Church now repaired for refrefhment, ftood on the "great bay" a little E. of the foot of the prefent India Street; his lot there hav-ing a front on the tidewater of 147 ft., and a depth of 630 ft., to the burying-ground.

that the company she came with had fourscore Canoo's: & that there was more of them, whom she had not seen, which came from other Places, and that they told her when they came all together, should make up 700 Men. He ask'd her, Whether *Casteen*[31] was with them? She answered, That there was several *French* Men with them, but she did not know whether [61] *Casteen* was there or not. He then having got what intelligence she could give him, went ashore and viewed the Fort and Town, discoursing with the Gentlemen there according to his Instructions; and when it began to grow dark, he ordered the Vessels to come as near the Fort as might be, and Land the Souldiers, with as little noise as possible; ordering them as they Landed to go into the Fort and Houses that stood near, that so they might be ready upon occasion; having ordered Provisions for them, went to every Company and ordering

[31] Baron *Vincent de St. Castin* was born near the Pyrenees, and became a man of wealth and eminence, and an officer in the body-guard of the King of France. He arrived at Quebec about 1665; and, the regiment which he commanded having been disbanded, he selected the pine-clad peninsula of Biguatus, in Acadie, as his residence, where he erected a fortified habitation, and for over a quarter of a century carried on an extensive and profitable trade, shipping merchandise from France, and exchanging it with the Indians for furs. La Hontan estimated his profits at 200,000 to 300,000 crowns. He himself testified that 80,000 livres could be annually realized at Penobscot from the beaver trade. He married the daughter of *Madockawando*, chief of the Tarratines; and, being a zealous Catholic, gave the English great trouble from his instigation of, and aid to, the enemy in Indian wars. The English, on the other hand, at different times, used him very hardly. He went to France in 1701, and probably never returned. His son, by his Indian wife, continued to reside at Penobscot, and to be influential among the savages. The present town of Castine marks the spot. [*La Hontan*, i: 471; Tibierge's *Mem. Acadie*, 1 Oct., 1695; *Me. Hist. Coll.* vi: 110-113.]

them to get every thing ready; they that had no Powder-
horns nor Shot-bags, fhould immediately make them; ordering the Officers to take fpecial care that they were
ready to March into the Woods an hour before day: and
alfo directing the Watch to call him two hours before
day; fo he haftned to bed to get fome Reft. At the time
prefix'd he was call'd,[35] and prefently ordering the Company's to make ready, and about half an hour before day
they mov'd; feveral of the Town People went with them
into a thick place of brufh, about half a Mile from the
Town;[36] now ordering them to fend out their Scouts, as
they us'd to do, and feeing them all fettled at their work, he
went into Town by Sun rife again, and defired the Inhabitants to take care of themfelves, till his men had fitted
themfelves with fome neceffaries: for his *Indians* moft of
them wanted both bags and horns; fo he ordered them to
make bags like Wallets to put Powder in one end and
fhot in the other: So moft of them were ready for action
(*viz.*) the *Seconet Indians*,[37] but the *Cape Indians*[38] were

[35] This was the morning of Saturday, 21 Sept., 1689.

[36] "A portion of the central part [of the "neck" whereon the city of Portland now ftands] was fwampy and covered with buthes and trees, and furrowed with gullies." [Willis's *Journals of Smith & Deane*, 430.]

[37] See Part I. xxii. Probably all the *Saconet* Indians who ferved in this expedition were under the command of Capt. *Numpas*.

[38] The Indians on Cape Cod had been friendly — with individual exceptions — through Philip's war, and they now furnifhed foldiers freely to aid the Englifh. As late as the Revolutionary war a fingle Continental regiment had 26 *Mafhpee* Indians; and it was stated, in 1783, by Rev. Mr. Hawley, that moft of the *Mafhpee* women loft their hufbands in the fervice, at one time there being 70 widows there. [Freeman's *Hift. Cape Cod*, i : 692.]

very bare, lying fo long at *Boston* before they imbark'd, that they had Sold every thing they could make a Peny of; fome tying Shot & Powder in the corners of their Blankets. He being in Town, juft going to Breakfaft, there was an Alarm, fo he ordered all the Souldiers in the Town to Move away as faft as they could, where the firing was; and he with what Men more were with him of his Souldiers, Mov'd immediately, and meeting with Capt. *Brackits*[39] Sons, who told him their Father was taken, and that they faw a great Army of *Indians* in their Fathers Orchard,[40] &c. By this time our *Indians* that wanted bags and horns were fitted, but wanted more Ammunition: prefently came a Meffenger to him from the Town & inform'd him, That they had knock'd out the heads of fev-

---

[39] *Anthony Brackett*, perhaps fon of Anthony, who was at Portfmouth, 1640, was at Falmouth as witnefs to a delivery of poffeffion 1662; married (1) Ann, eldeft daughter of Michael Mitton, and fettled on the 100 acres granted her at Back Cove by George Cleeves. He fubfequently enlarged his farm to 400 acres. He was conftable 1664; juror 1666; commiffioner 1668; was taken captive, with his wife, five children, and a negro fervant, by the Indians 11 Aug., 1676, but efcaped by the bold ufe of an old, dilapidated birch canoe: his wife Ann died foon after, and, 30 Sept., 1679, he married (2) Sufanna, eldeft daughter of Abraham Drake, sen., of Hampton; was Lieut. 1682; Capt. 1689; was fhot by the Indians in this engagement at his houfe on Back Cove. He had by the firft wife (1) Anthony, (2) Seth, (3) Mary, (4) Kezia, (5) Elinor; by the fecond, (6) Jane, (7) Zipporah, (8) Zachariah, (9) Ann, (10) Sufanna. [Willis's *Hift. Port.* 101, 106, 111, 138, 141, 156, 159, 169, 172, 176, 181, 187, 202, 208, 214, 219, 225, 251, 268, 280, 290; Drake's *Hubbard*, ii: 139.]

[40] Brackett's farm lay on the W. fhore of Back Cove, above the creek, on the ground now occupied by the manfion of James Deering, and the orchard extended toward the point. [Willis's *Hift. Port.* 278.] The Indians had gone round, under cover of the darknefs of the night, with their canoes from Peak's Ifland up Cafco River or Back Cove; from either of which Brackett's farm was acceffible.

eral Casks of Bullets and they were all too big, being
Musket Bullets, and would not fit their Guns, and that if
he did not go back himself a great part of the Army would
be kept back from Service for want of suitable Bullets: He
run back and ordered every Veffel to fend a-fhore all their
Casks of Bullets; being brought, knock'd out their heads,
and turn'd them all out upon the green by the Fort, and fet
all the People in the Town that were able to make flugs;
being moſt of them too large for their ufe, which had like
to have been the over-throw of their whole Army: He
finding fome fmall Bullets and what flugs were made, and
three Snapfacks of Powder, went immediately to the
Army, who were very hotly in[62]gag'd; but coming to
the River,[41] the Tide was up; he call'd to his men that
were ingag'd, incouraging them, and told them he had
brought more Ammunition for them. An *Indian* call'd
Capt. *Lightfoot*,[42] laid down his Gun, and came over the
River, taking the Powder upon his head and a Kittle of
Bullets in each hand, and got fafe to his Fellow Souldiers:
He[43] perceiving great firing upon that fide he was of, went
to fee who they were, and found them to be two of Maj.
Church's Companies, one of *Englifh* & the other of *In-
dians*, being in all about Fourfcore Men, that had not got
over the River, but lay firing over our Mens heads at the
Enemy; he prefently ordered them to Rally and come all

---

[41] This river was the prolongation into the neck, of the S. W. extremity of "Back Cove."

[42] See Part I. note 238.

[43] "He" — that is Church, not Lightfoot.

together; and gave the word for a *Casco* Man: So one *Swarton* [41] a *Jersey* man [45] appearing, who he could hardly underſtand; he ask'd him, How far it was to the head of the River? or whether there was any place they could get over? He ſaid, there was a Bridge [46] about three quarters of a Mile up where they might get over: So he calling to his Souldiers ingag'd on the other ſide, that he would ſoon be with them over the Bridge, and come upon the backs of the Enemy; which put new courage into them; ſo they immediately Mov'd up towards the Bridge, Marching very thin, being willing to make what ſhow they could, ſhouting as they March'd: they ſaw the Enemy running from the River-ſide, where they had made Stands with Wood to prevent any body from coming over the River; and coming to the Bridge, they ſaw on the other ſide that the Enemy had laid logs and ſtuck birch bruſh along to hide themſelves from our view. He ordered the

[41] Mather [*Magnalia*, Book VI. pp. 10-14] gives a narrative of the captivity of *Hannah Swarton*, who was taken by the Indians when Caſco Fort was taken, in 1690, with four children; her huſband being then ſlain. In November, 1695, ſhe reached Boſton, leaving two of her children behind her in Canada. She ſays ſhe lived in Beverly, Maſs., before going to Caſco; while Savage [*Gen. Dict.* iv: 237] gives the name of John Swarton as of Beverly, in 1672. In a liſt of Engliſh captives ranſomed from Quebec by Matthew Carey, in October, 1695, occurs the name of "Joſh. Swarton, boy, Caſcow," and "Johana Swarton, York"; while "Mary Swarton, girl, Dover," is named as remaining ſtill in captivity. [*N. E. Hiſt. & Gen. Reg.* vi: 87.]

It may, perhaps, be reaſonable to ſuppoſe that John Swarton was huſband of Hannah, father of theſe children, and the informant of Church on this occaſion.

[45] That is, an emigrant from the Iſle of Jerſey, — in Engliſh poſſeſſion, but in French neighborhood. Its native inhabitants ſpeak moſtly a French *patois*.

[46] "In the ſame place, probably, where one now ſtands, on Grove Street." [Willis's *Hiſt. Port.* 278.]

Company to come all together, ordering them all to run after him, who would go first, and that as soon as they got over the Bridge to scatter, that so they might not be all shot down together, expecting the Enemy to be at their Stands; so running up to the Stands, found none there, but were just gone, the ground being much tumbled with them behind the said Stands: He order'd the Captain with his Company of *English* to March down to our Men ingag'd, and that they should keep along upon the edge of the Marsh, and himself with his *Indian* Souldiers would March down thro' the brush:[47] and coming to a parcel of low ground which had been formerly burnt, the old brush being fallen down lay very thick, and young brush being grown up made it bad travelling; but coming near the back of the Enemy, one of his Men call'd unto him their Commander, and said, That the Enemy run *Westward*[48] to get between us and the Bridge, and he looking that way saw men running, and making a small stop, heard no firing, but a great chopping with Hatchets; so concluding the fight was over, made the best of their way to the Bridge again, left the Enemy should go over the Bridge into the Town. The men being most of them out (our Ammunition lay expos'd) coming to the Bridge where he had left Six *Indians* for an Ambofcade on the other side of the River, that if any Enemy offer'd to come over they

[47] Church's plan seems to have been to send his English soldiers along the curve of the edge of the marsh toward the battle-ground, while, with his Indians, he moved "across lots" due north, so as, if possible, to strike the enemy in the rear.

[48] By running westward, the enemy

should fire at them, which would give him Notice. [63] so would come to their assistance; (but in the way having heard no firing nor shouting, concluded the Enemy were drawn off) he asked the Ambuscade, whether they saw any *Indians?* They said, Yes, abundance. He ask'd them, Where? They answered, That they ran over the head of the River by the Cedar Swamp,[49] and were running into the Neck towards the Town: There being but one *English* man with him, he bid his *Indian* Souldiers scatter, run very thin to preserve themselves, and the better able to make a discovery of the Enemy: & soon coming to Lieut. *Clarks*[50] field on the South-side of the Neck, and seeing the Cattel feeding quietly, and perceiving no Track, concluded the Ambuscade had told them a false-

would be able to pass round Church's left flank, and get to the bridge, and into the town, in spite of, and before him.

[49] Church's Indians evidently supposed that the hostile party were running far enough west to flank the short river, and go around its swampy source into the neck and toward the town, instead of attempting to cross the defended bridge.

[50] *Thaddeus Clark* is said by Rev. Timothy Alden (who gives no authority) to have been born in Ireland [Alden's *American Epitaphs,* ii : 98.]; was at Falmouth, 1663, with his wife Elizabeth, then 18 years old, second daughter of Michael Mitton; lived on the bank of the Casco, just above the point which still bears his name; was Lieut. of a company of town soldiers: and, in an imprudent exposure of himself and his men, was killed, with thirteen of his company, by the Indians, when they attacked Falmouth in 1690, and buried 4 July. His widow died in Boston, in 1736, *æt.* 91. His eldest daughter, Elizabeth, married Capt. Edward Tyng; another married a Harvey, and was a widow in Boston 1719. His son Isaac settled in Framingham. Mass.; married Sarah Stow, of Marlborough; had seven children; commanded a company of troopers; and died 26 May, 1768, *æt.* 102, having lived 70 years with the wife of his youth. [Willis's *Hist. Port.* 139, 141. 232, 283, 292 ; Barry's *Hist. Fram.* 208; Savage's *Gen. Dict.* i : 400. *Me. Hist. Coll.* i : 203-214.]

hood; they haftily return'd back to the faid Bridge, perceiving there was no noife of the Enemy. He hearing feveral great Guns fire at the Town, concluded that they were either affaulted, or that they had difcover'd the Enemy: He having ordered that in cafe fuch fhould be, that they fhould fire fome of their great Guns to give him notice; he being a Stranger to the Country, concluded the Enemy had by fome other way got to the Town: whereupon he fent his Men to the Town, and himfelf going to the River, near where the fight had been; ask'd them [51] how they did? and what was become of the Enemy? who inform'd him that the Enemy drew off in lefs than an hour after he left them, and had not fired a Gun at them fince. He told them he had been within little more than a Gun fhot of the back of the Enemy, and had been upon them had it not been for the thick brufhy ground, &c. Now fome of his Men returning from the Town gave him the account, that they went while [52] they faw the Colours ftanding & Men walking about as not molefted. He prefently ordered that all his Army fhould purfue the Enemy: But they told him that moft of them had fpent their Ammunition, and that if the Enemy had engaged them a little longer they might have come & knock'd them on the head; and that fome of their Bullets were fo unfizeable that fome of them were forc'd to make flugs

---

[51] That is, having fent the Indians who had been with him to the town, he went back and hailed his Englifh troops, whom he had left near the original battle-field.

[52] "While — until." [*Bailey.*]

while they were ingag'd. He then order'd them to get over all the wounded and dead men, and to leave none behind: which was done by some Canoo's they had got. Capt. *Hall* and his men being firſt ingaged did great Service, and ſuffered the greateſt loſs in his Men. But Capt. *Southworth* [53] with his Company, & Capt. *Numpoſh* [54] with the *Seconit Indians*, and the moſt of the men belonging to the Town all coming ſuddenly to his relief, prevented him and his whole Company from being cut off, &c. By this time the day was far ſpent, and Marching into Town about Sun-ſet, carrying in all their wounded and dead men; [55] being all ſenſible of Gods goodneſs to them, in

---

[53] *William Southworth*, (probably youngeſt) ſon of Conſtant, was born 1659; ſettled in Little Compton; was ſelectman 1683-5; was commiſſioned Lieut. for Little Compton, 1689; was allowed (as Lieut., though Church forgot and called him Captain then) 25s. per week for his ſervice in this expedition; married (1) Rebecca ——, and had Benjamin, Joſeph, Edward, Elizabeth, Alice, Samuel, Nathaniel, Thomas, and Stephen; (2) ——, and had Gideon and Andrew. [*Plym. Col. Rec.* vi: 108, 129, 168, 223, 229; Savage's *Gen. Dict.* iv: 143.]

[54] See Part I. note 173.

[55] Church encloſed in his letter to the home authorities, the following "liſte of the men that was ſlain in a fite at Falmouth, and alſo how many was wounded in ſaid fite," under date of 21 Sept., 1689; which is ſtill preſerved in the Maſs. State Paper Office, as follows:—

"of Capt. Hall's ſoldiers, 6 ſlain,—
    Thomas Burton,
    Edward Ebens,
    Thomas Thaxter,
    Thomas Berry,
    John Maſon,
    David Homes.
of Capt. Davis's Company, 2 ſlain,—
    Giles Row,
    Andrew Alger (belonging to the fort of the town).
alſo, —— ——, 3 ſlain,—
    An Indian.
    A negro of Col. Tyngs,
    Capt. Brackett (carried away or ſlain).
Making 11 in all killed.
Wounded, 6 friend Indians, and of Capt Davis's Company James Freeze, Mr. Bramhall, Thomas Browne, Mr. Palmer,—inhabitants.
    Total, 21 ſlain and wounded."

Willis adds that Freeze, Bramhall, and one friend Indian, died of their wounds. [*Hiſt. Port.* 280.]

In relation to the enemy's loſs, Church

giving them the Victory, and causing the Enemy to fly with shame, who never gave one shout at their drawing off. The poor Inhabitants wonderfully rejoyced that the Almighty had favoured them so much: saying, That if Maj. *Church* with his Forces had not come at that juncture of time, they had been all cut off; and said further, That it was the first time that ever the *Eastward Indians* had been put to flight, and the said *Church* with his Volunteers were wonderfully preserved, having never a man kill'd out right, and but one *Indian* mortally wounded, who dy'd,[56] several more being badly wounded, but recovered.

After this ingagement Maj. *Church* with his Forces ranging all the Country thereabout, in pursuit of the Enemy; and visiting all the Garrisons, at [57]*Black Point*, [58]*Spur-*

---

wrote, 27 Sept., saying, "We know not yet what damage we did to the enemy in our last engagement, but several things that they left behind them on their flight we found yesterday, which was guncases and stockings and other things of some value, together with other signs that make us think that we did them considerable damage." [3 *Mass. Hist. Coll.* i: 92.]

[56] Mr. Drake [*Book of Ind.* 270.] states, on the authority of the MS. letter of Capt. Bassett, that the Indian who was killed was named *Sam Moses*. (See the letter. Drake's *Baylies's Plymouth*, p. 77.)

[57] *Black Point* lies in the town of Scarborough, on the shore E. of the mouth of the *Owaskoag* River, and between it and the *Spurwink*. Originally all the country between Saco and Spurwink was called Black Point. [*Me. Hist. Coll.* iii: 17.] In 1681 a strong fort was built "upon the plains between Moor's Brook and the South-east end of the great pond," at the instance of Capt. Joshua Scottow, the garrison of which, at this time, was under command of his son Thomas. [*Ibid.* 132, 133.]

[58] *Spurwink* settlement lay between the mouth of Spurwink River and Cape Elizabeth, in the southerly angle of the town of Cape Elizabeth. The garrison seems to have been at the house of Dominicus, son of Rev. Robert Jordan. [*Me. Hist. Coll.* iii: 137; Williamson's *Hist. Me.* i: 29.]

wink, and *Blew Point*;[59] and went up *Kennebeck* River,[60] but to little effect. And now Winter drawing near, he received orders from the Government of the *Massachusetts-Bay*, to settle all the Garrisons, and put in suitable Officers according to his best discretion, and to send home all his Souldiers the Volunteers and transports; which orders he presently attended.[61] Being oblig'd to buy him a Horse to

[59] *Blue Point* was in the S.-W. part of the town of Scarborough, on Saco line, not far W. of Black Point. The garrison appears to have been at Philip Foxwell's (son of Richard) house, nearly opposite to where Mill Creek flows into the *Owaskoug*.

[60] The mouth of the *Kennebec* is scarcely more than 30 miles N. E. from Falmouth. Williamson says Church ascended the river "several leagues." [*Hist. Me.* i: 617.]

[61] The following document — among the valuable additions recently made to Baylies's *Memoir of Plymouth Colony*, by Mr. S. G. Drake — demands a place here, describing, as it does, Church's action not merely, but disclosing, also, the names of so many of his companions, and the proportions in which they were distributed among the various garrisons: —

"Province of Maine

"Scarborough the 11th Nouember, 1689.

"Att a Councill of warr held at the point Garrison Present Major Benjemen Church, Capt Sylvanus Dauis, Capt. William Baffitt, Capt Simon Willard, with the rest of the Comission Offecers of Saco, Felmouth and Scarborough.

"Itt is Ordered that one hundred theire Majesties Horses now in this present Exspedition against the Coman Enimie, be detached out of the seuerall Companyes, which should number for the security of the Garrisons there Resident, and in Case any of the Enemie be discouered or Any tracks of them be made in this winter Season, untill further force be sent that may Advance to theire head Quarters.

"Souldiers Quartered in the towne Ship of Saco twenty men; in theire two Garrisons. In the township of Scarborough twenty men in theire Garrisons viz: three Sperwink Included.

"Felmouth the 13 Nouember: Att a Council of Warr held in persuance of what is above written, by Major Benjamen Church, and the officers abovesaid. Added Capt Nathaniel Hall, Leiut Thaddeus Clark, Leiut Elisha Andrews, Mr. Elisha Gallison, Leiut George Ingersoll, Leiut Ambrous Davis, Mr. Robert Lawrance, Mr. John Palmer and others &c.

"Itt is ordered that sixty souldjers be Quartered in Felmouth, besides the Inhabitants, and the Souldjers that shall Belonge to the sloart, which shall

go home by land, that fo he might the better comply with his orders. The poor People the Inhabitants of *Cafco* and Places Adjacent, when they faw he was going away from them, lamented fadly, & beg'd earneftly that he would fuffer them to come away in the Tranfports; faying if he left them there, that in the Spring of the Year the Enemy would come and deftroy 'em and their Families, *&c.* So by their earneft requeft the faid Maj. *Church* promifed them, that if the Governments that had now fent him, would fend him the next Spring, he would certainly come with his Volunteers and *Indians* to their relief: And that

be ffifteen Souldjers befides the Comander and Guñer, and the Remayner to be fent to Bofton, to be Ready to Returne Accordinge to Order.

"Itt is Ordered that there be A Sufficiant Garrifon Erected about Mr Gallifons houfe for a mayne Court of Guard, Together with Mr Robert Lawrance, his Garrifon, which two Garrifons are to be fupplyed with the Sixty Souldjers left for to guard the faid towne.

"Itt is Ordered that Capt Nathaniel Hall is to take Charge as Comander in Cheife of thofe fforces that are lefft for the defence of the Above faid three Townes, Thofe Souldjers that belong to Foart Loyall only to be under the Comander of faid Foart.

"Ordered that Leiut Richard Huniwell, is to Take the Charge and Conduct of the twenty Souldjers quartered at Blew-point Black point and Spurwinck Garrifons, as he the faid Leiut. Huniwell fhall Recaive orders from time to time from the faid Comander in Cheife.

"Itt is Ordered that Enfigne John Hill is to take the Care and Conduct of thofe twenty Souldjers Quartered at Saco Garrifon as the faid Enfigne Hill fhall Recaive orders from time to time, from his faid Comander in Cheife.

"Itt is Ordered that the fforty Souldjers pofted att Saco, Scarborough and Spurwinke are to be obedient unto the Comanders of the feverall Garrifons where they fhall be pofted whilft in Garrifon, but to Atend the Comands of Leiut. Huniwell and Enfigne John Hill refpectively as they are Concerned upon theire fcoutinge or marchinge out:

Given under my hand this 14th of Nouember: 1689:

"By Concent of faid: Councill
"p mee
"BENJAMIN CHURCH
Comander in Cheife."

[Drake's *Baylies's Hift. Mem. Plym. Col.* Part 5, p. 84.]

as soon as he had been at home, and taken a little care of his own bufinefs, he would certainly wait upon the Gentlemen of *Bofton*, and inform them of the Promife he had made to them; and if they did not fee caufe to fend 'em relief, to intreat their Honours feafonably to draw them off, that they might not be a prey to the barbarous Enemy. Taking his leave of thofe poor Inhabitants fome [62] of the chief men there waited upon him to *Black Point*, to Capt. *Scottaways* Garrifon; coming there they prevail'd with the faid Capt. *Scottaway* to go with him to *Bofton*, which he readily comply'd with, provided the faid *Church* would put another in to Command the Garrifon; which being done and taking their leaves one of another, they fet out and travelled thro' all the Country home to *Bofton*: (having imploy'd himfelf to the utmoft to fulfill his Inftructions laft received from *Bofton* Gentlemen, which coft him about a Months Service more and above what he had pay from *Plymouth* Gentlemen) and in his travel homeward feveral Gentlemen waited upon the faid Maj *Church* who was oblig'd to bare their Expences. When he came to *Bofton* Gentlemen, he inform'd them of the miferies thofe poor People were in by having their Provifions taken from

[62] *Thomas Scottow* (*Scottaway*) was fon of Jofhua, of Bofton and Scarborough; was born 30 June, 1659; graduated at Harvard College, 1677; was at Black Point, 1679; fwore allegiance, 1681; was appointed Regifter of Probate and County Commiffioner under Andros in 1688; in 1689 had command of the garrifon his father had built; fubfequently to the war, and his father's death, difgufted with the favage hoftilities incident to refidence there, he fold his Scarborough property to Timothy Prout, and left the place. [Savage's *Gen. Dict.* iv: 40; Williamfon's *Hift. Me.* i: 692; Willis's *Portland*, 220.]

them by order of the Prefident, &c.[63] Then went home; ftaid not long there before he return'd to *Bofton*,[64] where Capt. *Scottaway* waited for his coming, that he might have the determination of the Government of *Bofton* to carry home with him; and it being the time of the *Small Pox*[65] there (and Maj *Church* not having had it) taking up his Lodging near the Court-houfe,[66] took the firft opportunity [65] to inform thofe Gentlemen of the Court his bufinefs; who faid they were very bufy in fending home Sir *Edmund*, the Ship being ready to Sail.[67] The faid Maj.

[63] "Prefident Danforth, by requiring of them provifions for a fupply of the military, had brought them into great diftrefs." [Williamfon's *Hift. Me.* i: 618.]

[64] As, on the 6th Feb., he had been waiting in Bofton three weeks, the date of his "returning" to that city, here mentioned, muft have been about Wednefday, 16 Jan., 16$\frac{8}{9}\frac{9}{0}$.

[65] The fmall-pox raged in Bofton during the fpring and fummer of 1690; and this teftimony of Church's fhows that its ravages had commenced as early as January, 16$\frac{8}{9}\frac{9}{0}$. Samuel Green, jr., the printer, died, after an illnefs of three days with it, in July, 1690; and his wife followed him a few days after. In Auguft, 1690, a fon of Rev. John Cotton wrote to his father, "The fmall-pox is as bad as ever." [Thomas's *Hift. Printing*, i: 282.]

[66] The firft Bofton Court Houfe, or Town Houfe, was begun to be built about 1657. It ftood where the "old State Houfe" now ftands, in the head of State Street, and was burned in the great fire of 1711, being built of wood. [Drake's *Hift. Bof.* i: 350.]

[67] The exact date of the fhipping of Andros for England feems to have been fingularly unnoted in the records of the time; and is, perhaps, more nearly determined by what Church fays here than in any other way. Hutchinfon fays [*Hift. Mafs.* i: 349], "The firft opportunity (the beginning of February) after the arrival of the King's order, he, with Mr. Dudley and feveral others, embarked for England." Mr. Drake [*Hift. Bof.* i: 486] fays, "Some time in the winter following [that of 16$\frac{8}{9}\frac{9}{0}$], an order was received from their Majefties to fend the prifoners over thence; and they were accordingly fent in the firft fhip bound to that country." The author of the Life of Andros [*Governors of Mafs. Bay*, 419] fays, "In February, 1690, they were fent home to England." Elliott [*New-Eng. Hift.* i: 380] fays, "In February, 1689, with Dudley and fome

Church still waiting upon them, and at every opportunity intreating those Gentlemen in the behalf of the poor People of *Casco,* informing them the necessity of taking care of them either by sending them relief early in the Spring, or suffer them to draw off, otherwise they would certainly be destroyed, *&c.* There answer was, They could do nothing till Sir *Edmund* was gone. Waiting there three weeks upon great expences, he concluded to draw up some of the circumstances of *Casco* and Places Adjacent, and to leave it upon the Council-Board, before the Governour & Council; having got it done, obtained liberty to go up where the Governour and Council was sitting, he inform'd their Honours, that he had waited till his Patience was wore out; so had drawn up the matter to leave upon the Board before them: which is as follows.

To the Honoured Governour and Council of the Massachusetts.

Gentlemen,

Whereas by vertue of Yours with Plymouths *desires and Commands, I went* Eastward *in the last Expedition against the Common* Indian *Enemy, where Providence*

others, he was sent away to England." Barry [*Hist. Mass.* i : 508] says, "By the first opportunity the prisoners were sent to England in the ship 'Mehitabel,' Gilbert Baut, master," and places in the margin the date of "Feb. 9, 16$\frac{8 9}{9 0}$." The date of Church's communication to the Governor and Council seems to make it clear, that, so far as he was informed, as late as the 6th Feb., 16$\frac{8 9}{9 0}$ there was no immediate probability that the ship would sail; as, had he seen such a probability, having waited three weeks, he would have been likely to have waited at least a very few days longer in hope to secure his end.

so ordered that we Attack'd their greatest body of Forces, coming then for the Destruction of Falmouth, which we know March'd off Repul'st with confiderable Damage, leaving the ground, and never since seen there, or in any Place Adjacent: the time of the Year being then too late to profecute any further design, and other Accidents falling contrary to my expectation, Impeeding the defired Succefs. Upon my then Removal from the Province of Maine, the Inhabitants were very Solicitous that this Enemy might be further Profecuted, willing to venture their Lives and Fortunes in said Enterprize, wherein they might serve God, their King and Country, and injoy Quiet & Peaceable Habitations; Upon which I promised to signifie the same to Your Selves, and willing to ventue that little which Providence hath betrusted me with on the said account. The Season of the Year being such if some speedy Action be not performed in Attacking them, they will certainly be upon us in our Out Towns (God knows where) and the Inhabitants there being not able to Defend themselves, without doubt many Souls may be cut off, as our last Years Experience wofully hath declared; The Inhabitants there trust to your Protection, having undertaken Government and your Propriety; [68] If nothing be performed on the said account (The best way under Correction [69]) is to Demolish the Garrison, and draw off the Inhabitants, that they may not be left to a Mercilefs Enemy; and that the Arms and Ammunition may not be there left for the

---

[68] "Propriety — property." [Bailey.]
[69] That is — "the best way, in my judgment. holding myself liable to correction by your superior wisdom."

ſtrengthning of the Enemy; who without doubt have uſed enough, having exhauſted their greateſt Store in this Winter Seaſon: I have performed my Promiſe to them, and acquitted my ſelf in Specifying the ſame to your ſelves: Not that I deſire to be in any Action (altho' willing to ſerve my King & Country) and may paſs under the cenſure of Scandalous Tongues in the laſt Expedition, which I hope they will amend on the firſt opportunity of Service. I leave to the Mature Conſideration, the loſs of [66] *Trade and Fiſhery, the War brought to the Doors; what a Triumph will it be to the Enemy, deriſion to our Neighbours, beſides diſhonour to God and our Nation, and grounds of frowns from our Prince, the fruſtration of thoſe whoſe eyes are upon you for help, who might have otherwiſe applyed themſelves to their King.* Gentlemen, *this I thought humbly to propoſe unto you, that I might diſcharge my ſelf in my truſt from your Selves, and Promiſe to the Inhabitants of the Province, but eſpecially my Duty to God, His Majeſty and my Nation, Praying for Your Honours Proſperity, Subſcribe,*

 A true Copy given in at *Boſton*,   Your Servant,
  this 6th of *February* 1689.   Benj. Church.

 At the Council Board.   *Atteſt T. S.*

Maj. *Church* ſaid moreover that in thus doing he had comply'd with his Promiſe to thoſe poor People of *Caſco*, and ſhould be quit from the guilt of their bloud: the Governour was pleaſed to Thank him for his care & pains taken. Then taking his leave of them went home, and left Capt. *Scottaway* in a very sorrowful condition, who return'd home sometime after with only a Copy of what was left on the Board by the said *Church*. Maj. *Church* not hearing any thing till *May* following and then was inform'd, That those poor People of *Casco* were cut off by the barbarous Enemy: and that altho' they made their terms with Monsieur *Casteen*, who was Commander of those Enemies, yet he suffered those Merciless Salvages, to Massacre & Destroy the most of them.[70] To conclude this first Expedition, *East*; I shall just give you a hint how Maj. *Church* was treated (altho' he was Commander in Chief of all the Forces out of *Plymouth* and *Boston* Government) after he came home, for *Plymouth* Gentlemen paid him but *Forty two Pounds*;[71] telling him, He must go to *Boston* Gentlemen for the rest, who were his imployers as well as they. Of whom he never had one Peny for all Travel and Expences in Raising Volunteers, and Services done; except *Forty Shillings* or there about, for going from *Boston* to *Rhode-Island* on their business, and back to

---

[70] *Frontenac* sent a body of French and Indians with a large company of *Tarratines* under *Castin*, early in May, against Falmouth. They made their attack 16 May, and 20 May. *Castin* having "lifted his hand and sworn by the great and everliving God" to keep the articles of surrender, the garrison of Fort Loyall surrendered: to find every article violated, with insult. abuse, and the most fiendish atrocities. [3 *Mass. Hist. Coll.* i: 101-112.]

[71] Plymouth Colony voted, 25 Dec., 1689, to pay Major Church "£10. (besides what he hath received from the Bay) more than his wages by the weeke, and that his weekly wages as Major in ye late expedition be 40 s.": and "that Major Church shall have £5. cash, and Capt. Baffitt £3. cash, part of what is due to them from the Colony paid to them by the Constables of Plimouth out of the last rate." [*Plym. Col. Rec.* vi: 229.]

[67]

Boston again: Alſo for ſending a Man to *Providence* for Capt. *Edmunds*[72] (who raiſ'd a Company in thoſe Parts) and went *Eaſt* with them.

The Second Expedition, *Eaſt*.

IN the Year 1690. was the Expedition to *Canada*, and Maj. *Walley* often requeſted Maj *Church* that if he would not go himſelf in that expedition, that he would not hinder others: He anſwered the ſaid *Walley*, That he ſhould hinder none but his old Souldiers, that us'd to go along with him, *&c*. And the ſaid Church going down to *Charleſtown* to take his leave of ſome of his Relations,[73] and Friends, who were going in that Expedition, promiſed his Wife and Family not to go into *Boſton*, the Small Pox being very brief[74] there.[75] Coming to *Charleſtown*, ſeveral of his Friends in *Boſton* came over to ſee him; and the next day after the ſaid *Church* came there, Maj. *Walley* [67] came to him, and inform'd him, That the Governour

---

[72] See Part I, note 116.

[73] John Walley wrote, 21 Apr., 1690, to Gov. Hinckley, "The Indians of Dartmouth and Seaconnet — which are about 100 men, 50 or more armed — have had a meeting: choſe Lieut. Southard for their Captain or Commander, and one Daniel Eaton; under whom they are willing to ſerve the Engliſh, if we ſhould be aſſaulted. They have choſe Captain *Numpas* and another Indian for their Indian Commanders." [Hinckley Papers, 4 *Maſs. Hiſt. Coll.* v: 247.] This "Lieut. Southward" was doubtleſs Church's brother-in-law, William Southworth [see note 53, *ante*]; and, if he went to the war, he was probably one of the "relations" here referred to. Mr. Drake thinks he was (by his nickname *Bill*) the "B. Southworth" of Part I. page 35.

[74] An evident miſprint for "riſe" which Dr. Stiles corrected.

[75] See note 65, *ante*.

and Council wanted to fpeak with him: He anfwered him, That he had promis'd his Wife and Family not to go into *Bofton*; faying, If they had any bufinefs, they could Write to him, and that he would fend them his anfwer. Soon after came over two other Gentlemen with a Meflage, that the Governour & Council wanted to have fome difcourfe with him: The anfwer return'd was, That he intended to lodge that Night at the *Gray-hound* in *Roxbury*, and that in the Morning would come to *Pollards* at the South End of *Bofton*;[76] which accordingly he did: foon after he came thither received a letter from the Honourable Capt. *Sewall*[77] to requeft him to come to the Council;

---

[76] *William Pollard* was fon of William and Ann (who was wont to boaft that fhe went over in the firft boat that croffed Charles River, in 1630, and was firft to jump afhore at what is now Bofton), b. 20 Mar., 1653; m. Margaret ————; had William, b. 21 Dec., 1687 William again, 2 Apr., 1690, and Jonathan. Joined the Ancient and Honorable Artillery Co., 1679. He kept an "ordinary," as I learn from the record, (through J. Wingate Thornton, Efq., from the kindnefs of W. I. Bowditch, Efq.,) a little over 100 ft. juft fouth of Eliot St., on Wafhington St. [Savage's *Gen. Dict.* iii: 449; Whitman's *Hift. Anct. & Hon. Art. Co.* 211.]

[77] *Samuel Sewall*, fon of Henry, was born at Horton, near Bafingftoke, Eng., 28 March, 1652; came to New England with his mother 1661; graduated at Harvard Coll. 1671: was Captain of militia in Bofton, and Major of the regiment 1675-6; admitted freeman 1678; joined the Ancient and Honorable Artillery Co., 1679; was Captain of it 1701; Superintendent of the prefs 1681: Affiftant 1684-6, and again 1689-92; Judge of Superior Court 1692, and one of fpecial Commiffion to try the witches; Judge of Probate for 1715; Chief-juftice 1718-1728; died in Bofton, 30 Jan., 1730, *æt.* 78. He was a bookfeller at one time, and printed an edition of the catechifm with his own hand. He is now chiefly remembered for his copious notes of the facts of the time, in journals, almanacs, &c., &c. He married (1) 28 Feb., 1676, Hannah, only furviving child of John Hull, mint-mafter, by whom he had John, Samuel, Hannah, Elizabeth, Hull, Henry, Stephen, Jofeph, Judith, Mary, Sarah, Judith (again), and another: (2) 29 Oct., 1719, Abigail, daughter of Jacob Mel-

the answer he return'd by the bearer was, That he thought there was no need of his hazarding himself so much as to come & speak with them; not that he was afraid of his Life, but because he had no mind to be concern'd any further, by reason they would not hearken to him about the poor People of *Casco.* But immediately came Mr. *Maxfield*[78] to him, saying, That the Council bid him tell the said *Church,* That if he would take his Horse and ride along the middle of the Street there might be no danger, they were then sitting in Council: He bid him go and tell his Masters, Not to trouble themselves, whether he came upon his head or feet, he was coming: however thinking the return was something rude, call'd him back to drink a Glass of Wine, and then he would go with him. So coming to the Council, They were very thankful to him for his coming; and told him that the occasion of their sending for him was, That there was a Captive come in who gave them an account, That the *Indians* were come down and had taken possession of the Stone Fort at *Pejepscot,*[79] so that they wanted his advice & thoughts about the matter; whither

yen, and widow of William Tilley and James Woodmansey; (3) 29 Mar., 1722, Mary, daughter of Henry Shrimpton, and widow of Robert Gibbs. [Savage's *Gen. Dict.* iv : 55; *Hist. Antt. & Hon. Art.* 208; Washburn's *Judic. Hist. Mass.* 258-263.]

[78] *James Maxwell* was doorkeeper for the Governor and Council and Court in 1693, and was probably the man Church here had in mind. Indeed, Savage admits that the name may be the same as Maxfield. He was a member of the " Scot's Charitable Society," in Boston, in 1684. [Savage's *Gen. Dict.* iii : 183; Drake's *Hist. Bost.* i : 455.]

[79] *Pejepscot* fort was situated on the western side of what are now known as *Pejepscot* Lower Falls, or Brunswick falls, on the *Androscoggin.* [Williamson's *Hist. Me.* i : 46, 590, 624.]

they would tarry and keep in that Fort or not? and whither it was not expedient to fend fome Forces to do fome fpoil upon them; and further to know whither he could not be prevail'd with to Raife fome Volunteers and go, to do fome fpoil upon them? He anfwer'd them, he was unwilling to be concern'd any more; it being very difficult and chargeable to Raife Volunteers, as he found by experience in the laft Expedition. But they ufing many arguments prevail'd fo far with him, That if the Government of *Plymouth* faw caufe to fend him (he would go) thinking the Expedition would be fhort. Took his leave of them & went home. And in a fhort time after there came an Exprefs from Governour *Hinkley*, to requeft Maj *Church* to come down to *Barnftable* to him: he having received a Letter from the Government of *Bofton* to raife fome Forces to go *Eaft*; whereupon the faid Maj. *Church* went the next day to *Barnftable*, as ordered; finding the Governour and fome of the Council of War there,[80] dif-

---

[80] The Council of War at this time, by law of 1671, was compofed of the Governor and Affiftants as annually chofen, "and a like number of other trufty and able men chofen alfo by the General Court, and from year to year filled up, if by death removed, or otherwife any of them be wanting, or incapacitated to perform their truft." The Governor and Affiftants this year were: —

Thomas Hinckley, Gov.,	(Barnftable,)
William Bradford, Dep. Gov.,	(Plymouth,)
John Freeman,	(Eaftham,)
John Thacher,	(Yarmouth,)
John Walley,	(Barnftable,)
John Cufhing,	(Scituate.)

To thefe were added, in 1689, to make up the Council of War, the following, viz: —

Nathaniel Byfield,	(Briftol,)
Capt. Jonathan Sparrow,	(Eaftham,)
Lieut. Ifaac Little,	(Marfhfield.)

Who, of the number formerly appointed, held over to complete the number, we are not informed. [Brigham's *Laws of Col. of New Plym.* 285; *Plym. Col. Rec.* vi: 205, 212.]

cous'd him, concluding that he should take his *Indian* Souldiers, and two *English* Captains with what Volunteers as could be raised; and that one Capt. should go out of *Plymouth* and *Barnstable* County, and the other out of *Bristol* County,[81] with [68] what Forces he could raise, concluding to have but few Officers, to save Charge: the said *Church* was at great Charge & Expence in raising of Forces. Governour *Hinkley* promised that he would take care to provide Vessels to transport the said Army with Ammunition & Provisions, by the time prefixt by himself, for the Government of *Boston* had oblig'd themselves by their Letter, to provide any thing that was wanting; so at the time prefixt Major *Church* March'd down all his Souldiers out of *Bristol* County to *Plymouth*, as ordered; and being come, found it not as he expected, for there was neither Provisions, Ammunition nor Transports; so he immediately sent an Express to the Governour who was at *Barnstable*, to give him an account that he with the Men were come to *Plymouth*, and found nothing ready; in his[82] return to the said *Church*, gave him an account of his disappointments; and sent *John Lathrop*[83] of *Barnstable* in a

[81] The Plymouth Records show that the Court, which met 5 June, 1690, took action in regard to co-operating with the Mass. Colony in the proposed expedition to Canada, and appointed Capt. Joseph Silvester (of Scituate) and Mr. John Gorham (of Barnstable) to be Captains, with Jabez Snow (of Eastham) and Samuel Gallop (of Boston?) Lieutenants. [*Plym. Col. Rec.* vi: 250.]

[82] That is, Gov. Hinckley, in his reply to Church's message, "gave him an account, &c."

[83] *John Lothrop* was youngest son of Rev. John, of Barnstable; married 3 Jan., 1672, at Plymouth, Mary Cole; had John, Mary, Martha, Elizabeth, James, Hannah, Jonathan, Barnabas, Abigail, and Experience; died 17 Sept., 1727, æt. 85. [Savage's *Gen. Dict.* iii: 120.]

Veffel with fome Ammunition and Provifion on board, to him at *Plymouth*; alfo fent him word that there was more on board of *Samuel Alling*[81] of *Barnftable*, who was to go for a Tranfport, and that he himfelf would be at *Plymouth* the next day: but *Alling* never came near him, but went to *Billings-gate* at *Cape-cod*,[85] as he was inform'd. The Governour being come, faid to Maj. *Church* that he muft take fome of the open Sloops, and make Spar-Decks to them, and lay Platforms for the Souldiers to lye upon; which delays were very Expenfive to the faid *Church*; his Souldiers being all Volunteers, daily expected to be treated by him, and the *Indians* always begging for Money to get drink: but he ufing his utmoft diligence, made what difpatch he could to be gone. Being ready to Imbark, received his Commiffion and Inftructions from Governour *Hinkley*, which are as followeth, *viz.*

The Council of War of their Majefty's Colony of New-Plymouth *in* New-England. *To Major* Benjamin Church *Commander in Chief,* &c.

WHereas *the* Kenebeck *and* Eaftward *Indians, with the* French *their Confederates have openly made War*

---

[81] *Samuel Allyn* of Barnftable, eldeft fon of Thomas of the same, born 10 Feb., 165¾; was Lieut., and Town Clerk; was Deputy 1682-4; married Hannah, daughter of Rev. Thomas Walley; had Thomas, Samuel, Jofeph, Hannah, and Elizabeth; died 25 Nov., 1726, *æt.* 82. [Freeman's *Hift. Cape Cod.* ii: 274.]

[85] "Billingfgate Point is on the weft fide of the town [Eaftham], about 6 miles from the main land, with which it was formerly connected; but for many years it has been an ifland, the fea having broken over and wafhed it away in two places, where is fufficient water for fmall veffels to pafs through." [Pratt's *Hift. Eaftham,* 2.)

[68]

upon their Majesty's Subjects of the Provinces of Maine, New-Hampshire *and of the* Massachusetts *Colony, having committed many Barbarous Murders, Spoils and Rapines upon their Persons and Estates. And whereas there are some Forces of Souldiers* English & Indians *now raised and detached out of the several Regiments and Places within this Colony of* New-Plymouth,[86] *to go forth to the Assistance of our Neighbours and Friends of the aforesaid Provinces & Colony of the* Massachusetts, *Subjects of one and the same Crown. And whereas you* Benjamin Church *are appointed to be Major and Commander in Chief of all the Forces* English & Indians *detached within this Colony, together with such other of their Majesty's Subjects as else where shall List themselves, or shall be orderly put under your Command for the Service of their Majesties as aforesaid. These are in their Majesties Name to Authorize and Require You to take into your Care & Conduct all the said Forces* English & Indians, *and diligently to Intend that Service, by Leading*

---

[86] The proportion fixed by the Plymouth Court, on which these soldiers were to be raised and armed, was as follows:—

	Men.	Armes.		Men.	Armes.
Plimouth,	13	4	Falmouth,	2	1
Duxbury,	7	2	Monamoy,	2	1
Marshfield,	7	2	Rochester,	2	1
Scituate,	16	5	Bristol,	6	2
Bridgewater,	8	2	Swansey,	7	3
Middleborough,	3	1	Little Compton,	4	2
Barnstable,	12	4	Dartmouth,	8	3
Sandwich,	10	3	Taunton,	14	4
Yarmouth,	10	3	Rehoboth,	10	3
Eastham,	10	3	Freetown,	2	1

It was ordered, also, that there be raised 50 Indians,— 22 in the county of Barnstable, 22 in the county of Bristol, and 6 in that of Plymouth. Also, Plymouth County was to "provide armes and other necessaries" for 18 men, Barnstable County for 15, and Bristol County for 17. [*Plym. Col. Rec.* vi: 249.] The debt incurred by the Plymouth Colony for its share of the expenses of this campaign amounted to £1,350. The entire ratable estate of that Colony, then, was £35,900.

& *Exercising of your Inferiour Officers and Souldiers, Commanding them to Obey* [69] *you as their Chief Commander. And to pursue, fight, take, kill or destroy the said Enemies their Aiders and Abettors by all the ways and means you can, as you shall have opportunity, & to accept to Mercy or grant Quarter & Favour to such or so many of said Enemies as you shall find needful for promoting the design aforesaid. And you to observe and obey all such Orders and Instructions, as from time to time you shall receive from the Commissioners of the Colonies, or the Council of War of the said Colony of* New-Plymouth, *or from the Governour and Council of the* Massachusetts. *In Testimony whereof is affixed the Publick Seal of this Colony. Dated in* Plymouth *the Second day of* September, *Anno Domi.* 1690. *Annoque Regni Regis* et *Reginæ* Willielmi *et* Mariæ &c. Secundo. Tho. Hinkley *President.*

Instructions *for Major* Benjamin Church *Commander in Chief of the* Plymouth *Forces, with other of the* Massachusetts *put under his Command.*

'IN pursuance of the Commission given you for their
' Majesty's Service in the present Expedition against
' the Common Enemy, *Indian & French* their Aiders and
' Abettors, on the request of our Brethren and Friends of
' the *Massachusetts* Colony, Subjects of one and the same
' Crown of *England*; for our Assistance of them therein.
' Reposing confidence in your Wisdom, Prudence, Proness

'and Faithfulness in the trust under God committed to you
'for the Honour of His Name, the Interest of Christ in
'these Churches, and the good of the whole People; Pray-
'ing and Expecting that in your dependance on Him, you
'may be helped and Assisted with all that Grace, Wisdom
'and Courage necessary for the carrying of you on with
'Success in this difficult Service; and tho' much is and
'must be left to your discretion, with your Council of Offi-
'cers, as Providence & Opportunity may present from time
'to time in Places of action. Yet the following Instruc-
'tions are commended to you to be observed & attended
'by you, so far as the State and Circumstances of that affair
'will admit.

'You are with all possible speed to take care that the
'*Plymouth* Forces both *English* & *Indians* under your
'Command be fixed & ready on the first opportunity of
'Wind & Weather, to go on board such Vessels, as are
'provided to transport you to *Piscataqua*;[87] and there take
'under your care & command such Companies of the
'*Massachusetts* Colony, as shall by them be ordered and
'added to you there, or else where from time to time; all
'which you are to improve in such way, and from place to
'place, as with the advice of your Council, consisting of the
'Commission Officers of the *Massachusetts* Colony, and
'*Plymouth* under your conduct, shall seem meet, for the
'finding out, pursuing, taking or destroying of said com-
'mon Enemy, on all opportunities, according to Commis-

[87] Portsmouth, N.H.

'fion, and fuch further Orders & Inftructions as you have
'or may receive from the Governour & Council of the
'*Maffachufetts*, the Commiffioners for the United Colonies,
'or the Governour & Council of *Plymouth*; fo far as you
'may be capable, Intending what you can the preferving
'of the near Towns from the Incurfions and [70] deftruc-
'tion of the Enemy: But chiefly to intend the finding out,
'purfuing, taking and deftroying the Enemy abroad, and if
'poffible to attack them in their head quarters and principal
'Randezvouz, if you are in a rational capacity of fo doing;
'and for the better enabling you thereunto, We have ap-
'pointed the Veffels that tranfport you, and the Provifions,
'*&c.* to attend your motion & order, until you fhall fee
'caufe to difmifs them, or any one of them, which is
'defired to be done the firft opportunity that the Ser-
'vice will admit. You are to fee that your Souldiers
'Armes be always fixt, and they provided with Ammu-
'nition, and other neceffaries, that they may be always
'ready to repel and attack the Enemy. You are to take
'fpecial care to avoid danger in the purfuit of the Enemy's
'by keeping out Scouts, and a forlorn,[88] to prevent the
'Ambufhments of the Enemy on your main body in their
'Marches. And by all poffible means to furprize fome of
'the Enemy, that fo you may gain better Intelligence.

'You are to take effectual care that the worfhip of God

---

[88] "*Forlorn* — men detached from feveral regiments, or otherwife appointed to give the firft onfet in battle, or to begin the attack of a befieged place." [*Bailey.*] "Forlorn-hope" comes from it, as implying fpecial danger.

' be kept up in the Army, that Morning and Evening Prayer
' be attended, and the holy Sabbath duly Sanctified, as the
' Emergency of your affairs will admit.

'You are to take strict care to prevent or punish Drunk-
' enness, Curfing, Swearing and all other Vice; leaft the
' anger of God be thereby provoked to fight againft you.
' You are from time to time to give Intelligence and advice
' to the Governour of the *Maffachufetts*, and to us of your
' proceeding and occurances that may attend you. And in
' cafe of a failure of any Commiffion Officers, you are to
' appoint others in their ftead. And when with the advice
' of your Council aforefaid, you fhall after fome tryal fee
' your Service not like to be advantageous to the accom-
' plifhment of the Publick end aforefaid: That then you
' return home with the Forces; efpecially if you fhall
' receive any orders or directions fo to do from the *Maffa-*
' *chufetts*, or from us   *Given under my hand at* Plymouth,
' *the 2d day of* September, *Anno Domi* 1690.

'*Tho. Hinckley* GOV. *&* Prefident.

Now having a fair Wind Maj *Church* foon got to *Pifcataqua*,[89] who was to apply himfelf to Maj. *Pike*[90] a worthy

---

[89] If Church failed from Plymouth immediately on receipt of his commiffion and inftructions, he probably got off on Tuefday, 2 Sept., 1690. On the following Tuefday he received his inftructions at Portfmouth from Major Pike, and fpeaks of being delayed about 9 days. He probably reached *Pifcataqua* on Wednefday, 3 Sept., and received the Major's inftructions two or three days before he was ready to move upon *Pejepfcot*.

[90] *Robert Pike*, of Salifbury, fon of John, of Newbury: was freeman 17

Gentleman, who said, He had advice of his coming from *Boston* Gentlemen; also he had received directions that what Men the said *Church* should want must be raised out of *Hampshire*; out of their several Towns and Garrisons: Maj. *Pike* ask'd him, How many Men he should want? He said enough to make up his Forces that he brought with him, 300 at least, and not more than 350. And so in about Nine days time he was supply'd with two Companies of Souldiers. He having been at about *Twenty Shillings* a day charge in expences while there. Now he received Maj. *Pike's* Instructions: which are as followeth,

Portsmouth in *New-Hampshire, Sept.* 9, 1690.
To Maj. Benjamin Church *Commander in Chief of their Majesty's Forces now designed upon the present Expedition Eastward, & now Resident at* Portsmouth. [71]

THe Governour and Council of the Massachusetts *Colony reposing great trust and confidence in your Loyalty & Valour from experience of your former Actions, and of Gods presence with you in the same. In pursuant of an Order received from them, Commanding it. These are in their Majesty's Names to Impower and Require you as Commander in Chief, to take into your care and conduct these Forces*

May, 1637; Representative from S., 1648. and some following years; Assistant 1682 and 1691; Councillor 1689 and 1691; was Major in one of the Essex regiments. He married, 3 April, 1641, Sarah Sanders, and had Sarah, Mary, Dorothy, Mary (again), Elizabeth, John, Robert, and Moses; died 12 Dec., 1706, æt. 91. He was early a church member. [Savage's *Gen Dict*. iii: 436.]

now here prefent at their Randezvouz at Portfmouth ; *and they are alike required to obey you : and with them to Sail Eaftward by the firft opportunity to* Cafco, *or Places Adjacent, that may be moft commodious for Landing with fafety and fecrefy, and to vifit the Enemy* French & Indians *at their head quarters at* Ameras-cogen,[91] Pejepfcot, *or any other Plat, according as you may have hope or intelligence of the Refident of the Enemy ; ufing always your utmoft indeavour for the prefervation of your own Men, and the killing, deftroying and utterly rooting out the Enemy wherefoever they may be found ; as alfo as much as may poffibly be done for the redeeming or recovering of our Captives in any Places.*

You being then arrived, & underftanding your way, to take your Journey back again either by Land or Water, as you fhall judge moft convenient for the accomplifhing of the end intended ; and to give intelligence always of your motions whenfoever you can with fafety and convenience.

Laftly, in all to confult your Council the Commanders or

---

[91] *Androfcoggin.* On a rude pen-drawn map [in the Connecticut Archives, *War. Vol. III. Doc.* 86 (for a copy of which I am indebted to the kindnefs of the Hon. J. Hammond Trumbull)], bearing notes in the handwriting of Hon. William Pitkin, who was one of the two Connecticut Commiffioners at the meeting in Bofton, which declared war with the Eaftern Indians, and appointed Church commander (fee note 27, *ante*), — which map is clearly contemporaneous, and may have been traced by Church to affift their deliberations, — this is written in two words, thus, *Ambrofs Cogan,* and is ftated to be " about 80 myle from the fea." It was fituated upon a territory which ufed to be called by the Indians *Roccamecco,* and was the headquarters of the *Androfcoggin* tribe, and feems to have been near the great *Pennacook* falls on the *Androfcoggin* river, in Rumford. [*Me. Hift. Coll.* iii : 323.]

Commiſſion Officers of your ſeveral Companies, when it may be obtained, the greater part of whom to determine, and ſo the Lord of Hoſt the God of Armies go along with you, and be your Conduct. Given under my hand the day and year aboveſaid. *Per* Robert Pike.

Being ready,[92] they took the firſt opportunity and made the beſt of their way to *Pejepſcot* Fort,[93] where they found nothing. From thence they March'd to *Ameras-cogen*,[94]

[92] Church's letter to Gov. Hinckley, of date 30 Sept., 1690, narrating the events of this expedition — lately printed by Mr. S. G. Drake in his additions to Baylies's *Plymouth* [pp. 90-97] — ſays, "We ſett ſaile from Piſcataqua upon the 10th inſtant, at 2 in the afternoon, and came the 11th in the night amongſt the Iſlands in Caſco Bay." He proceeds as follows : —

"Laid the veſſells cloſe out of ſight — went on ſhore at breake of day, upon an Iſland that had been inhabited by the Engliſh, called *Capoag* [*Chebeague*, or *Chebacco*, now known as Great *Gebeag*, and called "*Sheab*" on the "Ancient Plan."] We ranged about, found where the enemie had lately been, but were drawn off. This was the twelfth day. In the evening we wayed and came down to *Macquait* [*Maquoit*, or *Marquoit*, the N. E. termination of *Magocook* bay, in Freeport, Me.], and the 13th day about 2 : of the clocke in the morning we landed our men ſilently upon the Maine; and leaveing ſouldiers on board to keep the veſſells, we marched in the night up to *Pochipſcutt* [*Pejepſcot*] fort, — diuided the army into : 3 : companies, ſurrounded the fort, and when daylight appeared we found that the enemie were removed not long before we came there; alſo the ſouldiers found ſome little plunder, and a barn of corn."

[93] Williamſon [*Hiſt. Me.* i : 624] makes the careleſs miſtake of repreſenting the flight of Doney, the releaſe of the captives, &c., which really took place on the next day (Sabbath, 14 Sept., 1690) at the upper falls, as taking place here at Brunſwick Lower Falls.

[94] Church ſays in his letter [ſee note 92, *ante*] that he went up "on the S. W. ſide of the river altho the way was extream difficult: yet it was a more obſcure way : the enemie uſeing to march on the N. E. ſide." He further ſays [p. 91] that they marched on the ſame day (Saturday) on which they reached *Prjepſcot*, "above the middle falls, about 20 miles," when it rained hard, and they there encamped. This was at Lewiſton Falls, called by the Indians *Amityonpontook*. They marched

and when they came near the Fort Maj. *Church* made a halt, ordering the Captains to draw out of their several Companies 60 of their meanest men, to be a guard to the Doctor & Snapsacks;[95] being not a Mile from said Fort; and then Moving towards the Fort, they saw young *Doney*[96] and his Wife, with two *English* Captives: the said *Doney* made his escape to the Fort, his Wife was shot down, and so the two poor Captives releas'd out of their bondage. The said Maj. *Church* and Capt. *Walton*[97] made no stop, making the best of their way to the Fort with some of the Army, in hopes of getting to the Fort before young

the next day at dawn, and came within sight of the fort about 2 P. M. [*Me. Hist. Coll.* iii : 322.]

[95] "In short time came to the westerly branch of the Great River, and there left our baggage and those men that were tired, and made them up to *forty* men to guard the Doctor." Church's *Letter* [Drake's *Baylies*, Pt. v: 91.]

[96] In his *Book of the Indians* [p. 307], Mr. Drake gives it as his opinion that this *Doney*, or *Douy*, family were French residents among the Indians, like *Castin*, and that this son was a half-breed. Williamson [i : 624] says he was one of the *Sokokis* (or *Sockhigones*), who were the aborigines of the *Saco* valley. Sullivan [*Hist. Dist. Me.* 180] calls old *Doney* "a savage." Mather [*Magnalia*, B. vii: 86, 87] enumerates *Robin Doney* among the Sagamores who signed the "submission" at *Pemmaquid* in 1693, and says he was seized at Saco within a year after. He is thought to have been the "Old Doney" mentioned in a letter written by Church, and the father of this fugitive. Williamson refers to him [i. 642] with *Bomaseen*.

[97] *Shadrach Walton*, of Great Island (now Newcastle, N.H.), was second son of George and Alice, was b. 1658, was Captain in 1690; Major in the attack on Port Royal in 1707; Colonel of New-Hampshire troops in 1710; Colonel of the Rangers in active service the next winter; was made a Royal Counsellor in 1716; quieted the Eastern Indians in 1720; was senior member and President of the Council Board in 1733; was Judge C. C. P. 1695-1698; Judge S. C. 1698, 1699; and again Judge C. C. P. 1716-1737. He died 3 Oct., 1741, aged 83. He was father of George; Benjamin (H. U. 1729, a minister); Elizabeth (m. Keefe); Abigail (m. Long); Sarah (m. Sheafe); Mary (m. Randall, and became g. g. m. of the founder of the "Free-Will Baptist Connection.") [Rev. A. H. Quint, D.D., in *N. E. Hist. & Gen. Reg.* ix : 57.]

Doney;[98] but the River thro' which they muſt paſs being as deep as their Arm-pits; however Maj. *Church* as ſoon as he was got over ſtrip'd to his Shirt and Jacket, leaving his Breeches behind, ran directly to the Fort, having an eye to ſee if young *Doney*, who ran on the other ſide of the River ſhould get there before him: the Wind now blowing very hard in their Faces as they ran was ſome help to them; for ſeveral of our Men fired Guns, which they in the Fort did not hear; ſo that we had taken all in the Fort had it not been for young *Doney*, who got to the Fort juſt before we did, who ran into the South Gate, and out at the [72] North, all the Men following him except one, who all ran directly down to the great River and Falls. The ſaid *Church* and his Forces being come pretty near, he ordered the ſaid *Walton* to run directly with ſome Forces into the Fort, and himſelf with the reſt ran down to the River after the Enemy, who ran ſome of them into the River, and the reſt under the great Falls; thoſe who ran into the River

---

[98] The account which Church gives in his letter is this:—

"And looking over the brow of a hill by the river, eſpied two Engliſh captives and an Indian, moving towards the fort: ran after them, and ſoon took the Engliſh but the Indian got cleare. Then I feared he would informe the fort: gave order, that all with one conſent ſhould run throw the river and not mind any other forme: but he that could gett firſt to the fort, if they had opportunity, to offer them peace. If they would not accept it to fall on, and by that time they were well entred the reſt would be come up: alſo I gave order for 2 companies to ſpread between the woods and the fort to prevent the eſcape of the enemie that way — all which was attended. We were very wett running throw the river, but got up undiſcovered to the fort till within ſhott: few Indians we found there, but two men and a lad of about: 18: with ſome women and children: 5 ran into the river, 3 or 4 of which were killed. We killed 6 or 7, and took eleven." [Drake's *Baylies*, Pt. v: 91, 92.]

were kill'd, for he faw but one man get over, and he only crept up the bank, and there lay in open fight; and thofe that ran under the Falls they made no difcovery of, notwithftanding feveral of his men went in under the faid Falls, and was gone fome confiderable time; could not find them; fo leaving a Watch there, return'd up to the Fort, where he found but one Man taken & feveral Women & Children, amongft which was Capt. *Hakins* [99] Wife & *Worumbos*'s [100] Wife, the Sachem of that Fort, with their Children; the faid *Hakins* was the Sachem of *Pennacook*, who deftroyed Maj *Walden* and his Family, fome time before,[101] *&c.* The faid two Women, *viz. Hakins* and *Worumbos*'s Wives, requefted the faid *Church* that he would fpare them and their Children's lives, promifing upon that condition, he fhould have all the Captives that were taken, and in the *Indians* hands: He ask'd them, How many? they faid about fourfcore: So upon that condition he promis'd them their lives, *&c.* And in the faid Fort there was feveral *Englifh* Captives, who were in a miferable condition; amongft whom

---

[99] *Kankamagus* (alias *John Hogkins, Hawkins*, or *Hakins*) was a Pennacook Sachem. About 1685 he wrote feveral letters to Gov. Cranfield, of New Hampfhire, difclofing his fear of the Mohawks and his defire for Englifh protection. He fubfequently fled to the eaftward, and joined the *Androfcoggins*, where he became hoftile to the fettlers, and in 1689 headed the maffacre of Maj. Waldron. His wife and four children were here taken captive, and his fifter was among the flain. [*Book of the Indians*, 297-300; Drake's *Baylies*, Pt. v: 97.]

[100] *Worombo* (*Worumbos*) was a *Tarratine*, and Sachem of *Androfcoggin* [*Amos Coggen*, Church fpells it, in his letter, much as Pitkin wrote it (see note 91, *ante*)]. He had *two* children captured here. [Vid. Church's *Letter*, 97.]

[101] See notes 12 and 32, *ante*.

was Capt. *Huckings's* Wife of *Oyster-River*.[102] Maj. *Church* proceeded to examine the Man taken, who gave him an account that most of their fighting men were gone to *Winter-harbour*, to provide Provisions for the *Bay* of *Fondy Indians*, who were to come and joyn with them to fight the *English*.[103] The Souldiers being very rude would hardly spare the *Indians* life, while in examination, intending when he had done that he should be Executed: but Capt. *Huckings* Wife and another Woman down on their knees beg'd for him, saying, He had been a means to save their Lives and a great many more; and had helped several to opportunities to run away & make their escape; and that

---

[102] "We found a prety deal of corn in barnes under ground, and destroyed it; also we found guns and amunition a prety deal, with beauer, and we took 5 English captives, viz. Lieut. Robert Hookins his widow of Oyster River; Benjamin Barnards wife of Salmon Falls; Ann Heard of Cochecho; one Willises daughter of Oyster Riuer, and a boy of Exeter." [*Ibid*. 92.] *Oyster River* was originally a part of Dover, N.H., now Durham. *James Huckins* was son of Robert, Constable 1683; had eldest son Robert; was killed in the onslaught of the Indians in August, 1689. [Farmer's *Belknap's New Hamp*. 131; Savage's *Gen. Dict*. ii: 487.]

[103] Dictating to his son Thomas a quarter of a century afterwards, it is not strange that some particulars should have faded from the memory of Capt. Church. He here represents his haste to make the best of his way back to Winter-Harbor to be for the purpose of intercepting and capturing these Indians, who were gone thither for provisions. But in his letter, written at the time, he informs Gov. Hinckley that —

"Both Indians and English informed us that the enemy had lately had a consultation. Many of them were for peace and many against it, and had hired and procured about 300, and intended for Wells with a flagg of truce and offer them peace. If they could not agree then to fall on. If they could not take Wells, then they resolved to attack *Piscattaqua*." [p. 92].

He adds [p. 93]: "We made all haste imaginable, *for fear some of our towns should be attacked before we came home*."

This would seem to be the true explanation of his hurried march back; that he feared a massacre in his absence.

never since he came amongst them had fought against the *English*, but being related to *Hakins* Wife kept at the Fort with them, he having been there two Years; but his living was to the westward of *Boston*. So upon their request his life was spared, *&c.* Next day the said *Church* ordered that all their Corn should be destroy'd, being a great quantity, saving a little for the two old *Squaws* which he design'd to leave at the Fort to give an account who he was, and from whence he came: the rest being knock'd on the head, except what afore-mentioned, for an example, ordering them to be all buried.[104] Having enquired where all their best Bever was? They said, it was carried away to make a present to the *Bay* of *Fondy Indians*, who were coming to their Assistance. Now being ready to draw off from thence, he call'd the two old Squaws to him, and gave each of them a Kittle and some Biskets, biding them to tell the *Indians* when they came home, [73] that he was known by the Name of Capt. *Church*, and liv'd in the Westerly part of *Plymouth* Government; and that

---

[104] There is a tinge of barbarity in the narrative here, which is absent from the letter, and which leads us to imagine that the doughty old warrior, roughly telling his tale so long after, was scarcely just to himself in some of the motives which he intimates. The letter thus narrates it [p. 93], saying nothing about "knocking on the head" for "example," which would have been a most unlikely procedure where the aim was to secure "the like to ours": "We left two old squaws that were not able to march; gave them victuals enough for one week of their own corn boiled, and a litle of our prouisions, and buried their dead, and left them clothes enough to keep them warme, and left the wigwams for them to lye in, — gave them orders to tell theire friends how kind we were to them, — bidding them doe the like to ours."

thofe *Indians* that came with him were formerly King *Philips* Men, and that he had met with them in *Philips* War, and drew them off from him, to fight for the *Englifh* againft the faid *Philip* and his Affociates, who then promifed him to fight for the *Englifh* as long as they had one Enemy left; and faid, that they did not queftion but before Indian Corn was ripe to have *Philips* head, notwithftanding he had twice as many men as was in their Country; and that they had kill'd and taken one thoufand three hundred and odd of *Philips* Men, Women & Children, and *Philip* himfelf, with feveral other Sachems, *&c.* and that they fhould tell *Hakins* & *Worumbo*, That if they had a mind to fee their Wives & Children they fhould come to *Wells* Garrifon, and that there they might hear of them, *&c.*[105] Maj. *Church* having done, Mov'd with all his Forces down to *Mequoyt*,[106] where the tranfports were (but in the way fome of his Souldiers threatned the *Indian* man Prifoner, very much, fo that in a thick Swamp he gave them the flip and got away) and when they all got on board the tranfport; the Wind being fair made the beft of their way for *Winter Harbour*,[107] and the next

---

[105] The letter fays [p. 93]:—

"Alfo, if they were for peace to come to goodman Smalls [?] att Barwick within 14 dayes, who would attend to difcourfe them."

[106] "Returned in that day, and one more, to our veffells at *Macquait*." [*Ibid.*]

[107] *Winter-Harbor* was the earlieft known Englifh name for the "Pool" at Saco, Me., near the mouth of the Saco River, above Wood Ifland, and the fettlement which grew up near it. Williamfon [*Hift. Me.* i: 26] fays it was "fo called after an ancient inhabitant there by the name of Winter." But John Winter lived at Richman's Ifland, or at the mouth of the *Spurwink*.

Morning [108] before day, and as foon as the day appear'd they difcovered fome Smokes rifing towards *Skamans* Garrifon: [109] He immediately fent away a Scout of 60 Men, and follow'd prefently with the whole body; [110] the Scout coming near a River difcovered the Enemy to be on the other fide of the River: [111] But three of the Enemy was come over the River to the fame fide of the River which the Scout was of; ran haftily down to their Canoo, two of which lay at each end of the Canoo, and the third ftood up to paddle over: The Scout fired at them, and he that paddled fell down upon the Canoo and broke it to pieces, fo that all three perifhed; [112] the firing put the Enemy to the

[Willis's *Portland*, 16.] A better fuggeftion of the origin of the name is that of Folfom [*Hift. Saco*, 24]: "We have the tradition of the inhabitants of that part of Biddeford, that an Englifh veffel wintered in the Pool before the fettlement of the country, and that the fhelter thus afforded gave rife to the name of *Winter Harbor*."

[108] This would appear to have been *Wednefday*, 17 *Sept.* The fort was taken on Sunday; Monday "and one more" brought them to *Maquoit*, and "the wind being fair," they feem to have failed immediately, and reached their deftination the next morning.

[109] Scammon's Garrifon was "on the eaft fide of the Saco, 3 miles below the falls." [*Williamfon*, i: 625.] *Humphrey Scammon* (*Scamman*, *Scammond*) was born 1640; m. Elizabeth, dau. of Dominicus Jordan, of *Spurwink*; lived at Kittery Point and Cape Porpoife (Kennebunk-port) before he went to Saco; where he received a town grant, in 1679, and the fame year purchafed of Henry Waddock's widow his 200 acres, extending "from the lower part of the river acrofs to Goofe-fair brook, and fo down to the fea." He died 1 Jan., 1727. Had Humphrey, (b. 10 May, 1677); Elizabeth (m. 1697, Andrew Haley, of Kittery); Mary (m. Puddington); Rebecca (m. Billings); Samuel, (b. 1689.) [Savage's *Gen. Dict.* iv: 34; Folfom's *Hift. Saco*, 188.]

[110] "I fent out a fcout of 60 men to Saco Falls to make difcouery; the reft in arms ready on fhore: intending at their returne to march by land to Wells." [*Letter*, p. 93.]

[111] "The fcout met with a fmall pty. upon the riuer, making fifh and other prouifions, viz. old Dony and his crue, — about 40, in all." [*Ibid.* p. 94.]

[112] In the letter, Capt. Church repre-

run,[113] who left their Canoo's and Provisions to ours;[114] and old *Doney*,[115] and one *Thomas Baker* an *English* Man who was a Prisoner amongst them, were up at the Falls and heard the Guns fire, expected the other *Indians* were come to their Assistance, so came down the River in a Canoo, but when they perceived that there was *English* as well as *Indians*, old *Doney* run the Canoo a shore, and ran over *Bakers* head and followed the rest, and then *Baker* came to ours; and gave an account of the Bever hid at *Pejepscot* plain: and coming to the place where the plunder was, the Major sent a Scout to *Pejepscot* Fort, to see if they could make any discovery of the Enemies Tracks, or could discover any coming up the River; who return'd and said they saw nothing but our old Tracks at said Fort, *&c.*[116]

---

sents the enemy as being all upon the other side. He says:—

"The enemie being on the other side the riuer, ours could not come at them: they made shot at them: killed one Dicks, a baco [Mr. Drake suggests *Abaco* (the largest of the Bahamas); but is *Sebago* (a nearer and so likelier word) impossible?] man, and got him on shore: 2 more men sank in the riuer: some of ours swam ouer the riuer, took their cannoos and plunder." [*Ibid.*]

[113] The letter states that "at this scirmish Lt. Hunniwell was shot thorrow the thigh." [*Ibid.*] This was Richard Hunniwell, concerning whose famous adventures as an Indian killer, see *Me. Hist. Coll.* iii: 144-148.

[114] "There we took a pretty deale of powder, shot and lead, and other plunder, and 8 or 9 cannoos." [*Ibid.*]

[115] *Thomas Baker*, Folsom says (on the authority of the Scarborough records), was "an inhabitant of Scarborough, in 1681." [*Hist. Saco*, 194.] Willis [*Hist. Portland*, 286] enumerates among those taken prisoners by the Indians, at the fall of Falmouth, 20 May, 1690, "Thomas Baker (a boy)."

[116] "The man we took from them at Salco, told us that the enemie from Cape Sables and all quarters were looked for by that time to rendevouze att Pechepscutt: also that he knew that the enemie had brought beauer and other goods to Pechepscutt Plaine, and hid them: he supposed it was a gratuity for the eastward Indians: also, that he

[74]

Now having got some Plunder,[117] One of the Captains said it was time to go home, and several others were of the same mind; and the Major being much disturb'd at the Motion of theirs, expecting the Enemy would come in a very short time where they might have a great advantage of them, &c. Notwithstanding all he could say or do, he was oblig'd to call a Council, according to his [74] Instructions, wherein he was out-voted. The said Commander seeing he was put by of his intentions profer'd if 60 Men would stay with him he would not imbark as yet; but all that he could say or do could not prevail;[118] then they Mov'd to the Vessels and Imbark'd, and as they were going in the Vessels on the back side of *Mayr-point* they discovered 8 or 9 Canoo's, who turn'd short about, and went up the River; being the same *Indians* that the Major expected, and would have waited for; and the aforesaid Captain being much disturb'd at what the Major had said to him, drew off from the Fleet, and in the Night run aground;[119] in the Morning *Anthony*

himselfe knew within half a mile where it was hid. This made us alter our former intention; and took ship and sailed to a place more eastward then *Macquait* (called Mare Point [the south extremity of Brunswick, Me.]) Landed our men by daylight, about 250: marched round in the woods: some upon the eastward of *Pechepscutt*." *Letter* [*Ibid.* p. 94.]

[117] "When we got upon the Plaine we parted into 3 companies: found none of the enemie; but we found the plunder: of which a pretty deale of powder and shot." *Letter* [*Ibid.*]

[118] The only paragraph in Church's letter which can be construed into any reference to this conflict between him and his subordinates is this: "Many cross things falling out to frustrate the designe, too long here to relate: but from Major Pike your honors will hear more at large." [*Ibid.* p. 97.]

[119] The letter says: —

"As god would have it one of our vessells run aground, which we did not

[74]

Brakit[120] having been advis'd and directed by the *Indian* that made his escape from our Forces, came down near where the aforesaid Vessel lay a-ground, and got aboard; who has proved a good Pilot and Captain for his Country. The next day it being very calm and misty, so that they were all day getting down from *Maquait* to *Perpodack*; and the Masters of the Vessels thinking it not safe putting out in the Night, so late in the Year,[121] Anchor'd there at *Perpodack*; the Vessels being much crouded, the Major ordered three Companies should go on shore, and no more, himself with Capt. *Converse*[122] went with them to order their lodging, and finding just Housing convenient for them, *viz.* Two Barns and one House; so seeing them all settled and their Watches out, the Major and Capt. *Converse* return'd to go aboard, and coming near where the Boat was,

---

understand (being in the night) and haueing left her we soon mist her, Capt. Alden concluding she had run aground. And before she came clear, there escaped one Anthony Brackett of Casco, who was informed by the lad that escaped from Amoscoggin aforesaid, of our army: he [Bracket] made his escape, got into our track, and came to Macquait, hollowed to the vessell, that heard him, and gladly took him on board." [*Ibid.* p. 93.]

[120] *Anthony Brackett*, jr. (eldest son of Anthony, note 39, *ante*), was afterwards serviceable as Lieut. and Capt. He finally settled in Boston. [Willis's *Hist. Portland*, 290.]

[121] "Came there [to Casco, or *Purpooduck*, opposite to what is now Portland] in the evening, being the 20th instant." [*Letter*, p. 94.]

[122] *James Converse* was son of James of Woburn, who was son of Edward, who, with wife Sarah, came in the fleet with Winthrop, 1630; he was of Woburn, freeman, 1671, rep. 1679, 1684-6, 1689, 1692, and Speaker in 1699, 1702-3. He married 1 Jan., 1669, Hannah Carter; had James, John, Elizabeth, Robert, Hannah, Josiah, Josiah, Patience, and Ebenezer. He was distinguished as a Captain and Major in the Indian wars, and was mixed up with an ecclesiastical difficulty just before his death. [Savage's *Gen. Dict.* i : 444; Mather's *Magnalia*, vii : Appendix, 16; Hutchinson's *Hist. Mass.* ii : 67, 72; *Hist. and Gen. Reg.* xiii : 31.]

it was pretty dark, they difcovered fome Men, but did not know what or who they were; the Major ordered thofe that were with him all to clap down and cock their Guns, and he call'd and afk'd them, Who they were? and they faid, *Indians*: he afk'd them, Whofe Men they were? they faid Capt. *Southworth*'s: he afk'd them where they intended to lodge? They faid in thofe little Hutts that the Enemy had made when they took that Garrifon. The Major told them they muft not make any fires; for if they did the Enemy would be upon them before day. They laugh'd, and faid, Our Major was afraid. Having given them their directions, he with Capt. *Converfe* went on board the *Mary Sloop*; defigning to Write home, and fend away in the Morning the two Sloops which had the Small Pox on board, *&c.* But before day our *Indians* began to make fires and to Sing and Dance; fo the Major call'd to Capt. *Southworth* to go a-fhore & look after his Men, for the Enemy would be upon them by'nd by. He order'd the Boat to be hall'd up to carry him a-fhore, and call'd Capt. *Converfe* to go with him, and juft as the day began to appear, as the Major was getting into the Boat to go a-fhore, the Enemy fired upon our Men the *Indians*, notwithftanding that one *Philip* an *Indian* of ours, who was out upon the Watch, heard a man cough, and the fticks crack; who gave the reft an account, that he faw *Indians*; which they would not believe; but faid to him, You are afraid: his anfwer was, that they might fee them come creepping: they laugh'd and said, they were Hogs: Ay, (said he) and they [75] will bite you by'nd by. So prefently they did fire upon our Men; but the Morning being mifty their Guns did not go off quick, fo that our Men had all time to fall down before their Guns went off, and faved themfelves from that Volley, except one man, who was kill'd. This fudden firing upon our *Indian* Souldiers furprized them that they left their Arms, but foon recover'd them again, and got down the bank which was but low: the Major with all the Forces on board landed as faft as they could; the Enemy firing fmartly at them; however all got fafe a-fhore. The Enemy had a great advantage of our Forces, who were between the Sun rifing & the Enemy, fo that if a man put up his head or hand they could fee it, and would fire at it: However fome with the Major got up the bank behind ftumps and rocks, to have the advantage of firing at the Enemy; but when the Sun was rifen the Major flip'd down the bank again where all the Forces were order'd to obferve his Motion, *viz.* That he would give three fhouts and then all of them fhould run with him up the bank: fo when he had given the third fhout, ran up the bank, and Capt. *Converfe* with him, but when the faid *Converfe* perceived that the Forces did not follow as commanded, call'd to the Major and told him the Forces did not follow; who notwithftanding the Enemy fired fmartly at, yet got fafe down the bank again, and Rallying the Forces up the bank, foon put the Enemy

[75]

to flight;[123] and following them so close, that they took 13 Canoo's,[124] and one Lusty Man, who had *Joseph Ramsdle*'s[125] Scalp by his side, who was taken by two of our *Indians*, and having his deserts was himself Scalp'd. This being a short and smart fight, some of our Men were kill'd, and several wounded.[126] Some time after an *English* Man who

---

[123] Church's account in his letter varies a little:—

"I landed the most part of the men and went on shore and ordered them where they should lodge; but the Indians in particular I ordered to such a house, or else to goe on board again; but they, contrary to my order, took up their lodge on the riuer by Papooducke side, where the enemie had lately randeuouzed. All the rest of the comandes and companies were where I ordered them to be. The enemie discouered the Indians fires,—came in the night and discouered where the Companies lay, and ambushed them at day-light: made a shot upon our Indians; it being the 21st instant, and the Sabbath day. Our English arose to the succour of the Indians, friends; being all ready at break of day, pr. my order, and drawing up towards them, many were wounded and slain: the enemie haveing great advantage of ours; for the light of the day, and stares reflecting upon the waters gave them advantage to see us, when as we could not see them att all, against the dark woods: espcially we could not se to distinguish between our Indians and theirs. Whereupon I ordered to lie still under the sea banck, till day-light: I coming on shore the second boat, and see the difficulty: but the enemie fired hard upon the veffells and boats coming on shore: and when the day was light enough, I ordered the men to arise from the banks, and run all upon them at once; the which we did, and soon put them to the flight,—followed them hard thorrow a swamp, firing briskly. They knowing where there cannoos were, got their wounded men into them before we came up, and most of them put off. Our men affirmed but two that they see killed." [*Letter,* p. 95.]

[124] "We took 2 guns and many blankets and gun-cafes, and 4 cannoos." [*Ibid.* p. 96.]

[125] "A company of soldiers from Lynn were impressed by order of the Governor, and sent out against the Indians in the depth of winter. One of the soldiers from Lynn, Mr. Joseph Ramsdell, was killed by them at Cafco Bay, in 1690." [Lewis's *Hist. Lynn,* 177; Newhall's *Annals of Lynn,* 289.]

[126] The letter gives a more particular statement, as follows:—

"We went on board sent away two veffells with the captiues and sick and wounded men, and buried our dead, which was 3 English and 4 Indians. The wounded were 17 English and 7 Indians. Them that were slain were

was Prisoner amongst them, gave an account that our
Forces had kill'd and wounded several of the Enemy, for
they kill'd several Prisoners according to their Custom &c.
After this action was over our Forces imbark'd for *Piscataqua*, and the Major went to *Wells*,[127] and remov'd the Captain there, and put in Capt. *Andras*,[128] who had been with
him and knew the Discourse left with the two old Squaws
at *Ameras-cogen*, for *Hakins* & *Worumbo* to come there in
14 days, if they had a mind to hear of their Wives & Children: Who did then or soon after come with a Flag of
Truce to said *Wells* Garrison, and had leave to come in,
and more appearing came in, to the number of Eight,
(without any terms) being all Chief Sachems; and was
very glad to hear of the Women and Children, *viz.*
Hakins and *Worumbo*'s Wives and Children; who all
said three several times that they would never fight

chiefley Plimouth. The wounded of
Capt. Counyerse, 6; Capt. Floid, 3;
Capt. Southworth, 4; Capt. Waltons,
3; of Capt. Andrews, one, (since that);
one Englishman of Plimouth is dead of
his wounds, and an Indian: also an
Indian and Englishman both of Plimouth dead of the small-pox." [*Letter*, p. 96.]

[127] The letter particularizes:—
"We embarked and came to Cape
Neddicke, the 22d day, and marched
with about 200 men, (all we had fitt for
service,) to Wells: Sent a scout the next
day to Saleo and Winter Harbour,—
about 24 miles: made no discoverie of
the enemie later than we were there
before. Then we returned and come
to Portsmouth the 26th instant, because
our doctor was gon home with the
wounded men, and our men were several of them sick and lame, and wanted
shoose and other recruits; or else we
would have gon furder before we had
com home." [*Ibid.* p. 96.]

[128] *Elisha Andros* [*Andrews, An-
drows*] was son of James, (who was
son of Samuel, and was born probably
in Saco, 1635, and who married Sarah,
dau of Michael Mitton, and Margaret
——,) and survived his father, who
removed to Boston and died in 1704.
[Savage's *Gen. Dict.* i: 53; Willis's
Hist. Portland, 289.]

againſt the *Engliſh* any more, for the *French* made fools of them, *&c.* They ſaying as they did, the ſaid *Andras* let them go. Maj *Church* being come to *Piſcataqua*,[129] and two of his tranſports having the Small Pox on board; and ſeveral of his Men having got great Colds by their hard Service, pretended they were going to have the Small Pox, thinking by that means to be ſent home ſpeedily; the Major being willing to try them, went to the Gentlemen there and deſired them to provide an Houſe, for ſome of his Men expected they ſhould have the Small Pox; who readily did, and told him, That the People belonging to it was juſt recover'd of the Small Pox, and had been all at Meeting, *&c.* The Major returning to his Officers order'd them to draw out all their men that were going to have the Small Pox, for he had provided an Hoſpital for them: So they drew out 17 Men, that had as they ſaid, all the ſymptoms of the Small Pox; he ordered them all to follow him, and coming to the Houſe, he ask'd them, How they liked it? they ſaid very well. Then he told them that the People in ſaid Houſe have all had the Small Pox, and was recovered; and that if they went in they muſt not come out till they all had it: Whereupon they all preſently began to grow better, and to make excuſes, except one Man who deſired to ſtay out till Night before he went in, *&c.* The Major going to the Gentlemen, told them,

---

[129] The letter fixes the date of arrival: —
"And we returned to Portſmouth the 26th inſtant." The letter bears date, Sept. 30, 1690, which puts the arrival, Sept. 26. [*Letter*, p. 97.]

That one thing more would work a perfect cure upon his
Men, which was to let them go home: Which did work a
cure upon all, except one, and he had not the Small Pox.
So he ordered the Plunder should be divided forthwith, and
sent away all the *Plymouth* Forces. But the Gentlemen
there desired him to stay and they would be assisting to
him in raising new Forces to the number of what was sent
away; and that they would send to *Boston* for Provisions:
which they did, and sent Capt. *Plaisted*[130] to the Governour
and Council at *Boston*, &c. And in the mean time the
Major with those Gentlemen went into all those Parts and
raised a sufficient number of Men, both Officers & Souldiers; who all met at the bank[131] on the same day that Capt.
Plaisted return'd from *Boston*; whose return from *Boston*
Gentlemen was, That the *Canada* Expedition had dreen'd
them so that they could do no more: So that Maj. *Church*
notwithstanding he had been at considerable Expences
in raising said Forces to Serve his King and Country was
oblig'd to give them a Treat and dismiss them: Taking
his leave of them came home to *Boston* in the *Mary* Sloop
Mr. *Alden*[132] Master, and Capt. *Converse* with him, of a Sat-

---

[130] *Capt. Ichabod Plaisted*, of Kittery, 1674? [*Hist. & Gen. Reg.* xv: 272.]

[131] *Strawberry Bank, i.e.* Portsmouth. "Whereas the name of this plantation att present being Straberry Banke, accidentally soe called, by reason of a banke where straberries *was* found in this place, now we humbly desire to have it called Portsmouth, being a name most suitable for this place, it being the river's mouth, and good as any in this land, and your petit'rs shall humbly pray." [Petition to General Court for change of name. Brewster's *Rambles about Portsmouth*, p. 23.]

[132] *Capt. John Alden*, eldest son of Pilgrim John, was born in 1622; removed to Boston as early as December, 1659; was well known as a naval com-

[77]

urday; and waiting upon the Governour, and some of the Gentlemen in *Boston*, they look'd very strange upon them, which not only troubled them but put them into some consternation what the matter should be, that after so much toyl & hard Service could not have so much as one pleasant word, nor no Money in their Pockets; for Maj *Church* had but *Eight Pence* left, and Capt. *Converse* none, as he said afterwards. Maj. *Church* seeing two Gentlemen which he knew had Money, ask'd them to lend him *Forty Shillings*, telling them his necessity: Yet they refused. So being bare of Money was oblig'd to lodge at Mr. *Aldens* three Nights;[133] and the next Tuesday Morning Capt. *Converse* came to him (not knowing each others circumstances as yet) and said he would walk with him out of Town; so coming near *Pollards* at the South End, they had some Discourse; that it was very hard that they should part with dry lips: Maj. *Church* told Capt. *Converse* that he had [77] but *Eight Pence* left, and could not borrow any Money to carry him home. And the said *Converse* said, that he had not a *Peny* left; so they were oblig'd to part without going in to *Pollards*, *&c*. The said Capt.

mander; was in danger in the witchcraft delusion [Winsor (*Hist. Duxbury*, 215) wrongly says it was his son John; but the documents call him "John Aldin, *Senior*, of Boston, Marriner,"] in 1692, and was committed to jail, but ran away, and was ultimately cleared, in 1693, "by proclamation, none appearing against him." He died in Boston, 14 March, 1702, *æt*. 82, leaving upwards of £2000. [Drake's *Hist. Boston*, i: 499; Drake's *Witchcraft Delusion in New England*, iii: 26; Alden's *American Epitaphs*, iii: 266.]

[133] Capt. Alden lived on an alley leading from Cambridge to Sudbury Streets, from him called Alden's Lane, and, since 1846, Alden Street; now the headquarters of less useful persons. [Drake's *Hist. Boston*, i: 500.]

[77]

Converse returned back into Town, and the said *Church* went over to *Roxbury*; and at the Tavern he met with *Stephen Braton*[134] of *Rhode-Island*, a Drover; who was glad to see him the said *Church*, and he as glad to see his Neighbour: whereupon Maj. *Church* call'd for an *Eight-Peny* Tankard of drink, and let the said *Braton* know his circumstances, ask'd him whether he would lend him *Forty Shillings?* He answered, Yes: *Forty Pounds*, if he wanted it. So he thank'd him, and said, he would have but *Forty Shillings*; which he freely lent him: and presently after Major *Church* was told that his Brother *Caleb Church*[135] of *Watertown* was coming with a spare Horse for him, having heard the Night before that his Brother was come in; by which means the said Maj. *Church* got home. And for all his travel & expences in raising Souldiers, and Service done, never had but 14 *l.* of *Plymouth* Gentlemen, & not a *Peny* of *Boston*: notwithstanding he had wore out all his Clothes, and run himself in debt, so that he was oblig'd to Sell half a-share of Land in *Tiverton* for about

---

[134] *Stephen Brayton* was son of Francis, of Portsmouth, R.-I.; freeman, 1678; on the grand jury, 1687; married, 8 March, 1679, Ann, dau. of Peter Tolman, of Newport, and had Mary, Elizabeth, Ann, Preserved, and Stephen. [Savage's *Gen. Dict.* i: 240; *R.-I. Col. Rec.* iii: 4, 233.]

[135] *Caleb Church* appears to have been the sixth child of Richard — being the youngest son of at least nine children, as Benjamin was the oldest; admitted freeman 4 March, 1689-1690; kept a tavern from 1686 to 1711 [see Drake's *Book of the Indians*, p. 263]; lived first in Dedham, and afterwards in Watertown; Representative, 1713; married, 16 Dec., 1667, Joanna, dau. of William Sprague, of Hingham; had eight children, viz.: Richard, Ruth, Lydia, Caleb, Joshua, Isaac, and Rebecca. The last two were twins; and, after giving them birth, their mother died, 11 July, 1678. [Bond's *Hist. Watertown*, 158; *N. E. Hist. & Gen. Reg.* xi: 154; Part I. of this edition, p. xxx.]

60 *l.* which is now worth 300 *l.* more and above than what he had.[136]

Having not been at home long before he found out the reason why *Boston* Gentlemen look'd so disaffected on him; as you may see by the sequel of two Letters Maj. *Church* sent to the Gentlemen in the Eastward parts: which are as followeth.

Bristol, Novemb. 27. 1690.

Worthy Gentlemen,

'ACcording to my promise when with you last, I waited
'upon the Governour at *Boston* upon the Saturday,
' Capt. *Converse* being with me. The Governour informed
' us that the Council was to meet on the Monday follow-
' ing in the afternoon, at which time we both there waited
' upon them, and gave them an account of the State of
' your Country, and great necessities. They informed us,
' that their General Court was to Convene on the Wednes-
' day following; at which time they would debate & con-
' sider of the matter; my self being bound home, Capt.
' *Converse* was ordered to wait upon them, and bring you
' their resolves. I then took notice of the Council that

---

[136] It is my impression, that the good Col. Church got a little mixed in his recollections of these events, when, in his old age, he dictated this narrative. The County Records contain no trace, which I have been able to discover, of any such sale of half a share of land in Tiverton by him at this time, or for years afterward; while the fact that he was almost constantly purchasing land — buying £170 worth within a year of this date — scarcely favors the idea of pecuniary distress. He did sell, however, in June, 1691, to Nathaniel Byfield, £50 worth of land (43 acres) on *Poppasquash* neck, in *Bristol*. He owned, at this time, largely in Tiverton, and in what is now the city of Fall River. [See Part I., *Introductory Memoir*, pp. xxix., xxx.]

'they look'd upon me with an ill afpect, not judging me
'worthy to receive thanks for the Service I had done in
'your parts; nor as much as ask me whether I wanted
'Money to bare my Expence, or a Horfe to carry me
'home. But I was forc'd for want of Money (being far
'from friends) to go to *Roxbury* on foot; but meeting there
'with a *Rhode-Ifland* Gentleman, acquainted him of my
'wants, who tendered me *Ten Pounds*,[137] whereby I was
'accommodated for my Journey home: And being come
'home, I went to the Minifter of our Town,[138] and gave him
'an account of the tranfactions of the great affairs I had
'been imploy'd in, and of the great [78] favour God was
'pleafed to fhew me, and my Company, and the benefit I

[137] He doubtlefs refers to Mr. Brayton [note 134, *ante*], but he ftates the amount of the loan differently from his former account of it.

[138] *Samuel Lee* was born in London, 1625; the fon of Samuel, who was a merchant of large eftate; took M. A. at Oxford, 1640; had a Wadham fellowfhip, and, in 1656, was Proctor, and Lecturer at Great St. Helen's, London; in 1677 was affociated with Theophilus Gale, in Holborn; in 1679 was fettled at Bignal, near Bicefter, in Oxfordfhire; was afterwards at Newington Green, near London; in the fummer of 1686, he landed here; went foon to Briftol, R.-I., and became paftor of the church at its organization, 8 May, 1687; in 1691, moved by the hope of better times under William and Mary in England than he had left there, and greatly to the regret of his people and of the miniftry and churches who knew him here, he failed for England on the Dolphin; was captured by a French privateer and carried into St. Malo, where he died of prifon fever, leaving a wife and daughter, and was buried outfide the walls as a heretic. Cotton Mather faid of him, "It muft be granted that hardly ever a more univerfally learned perfon trod the American ftrand." He left a dozen or more volumes of printed works. While in Briftol, he lived on the eaft fide of Thames St. (which was then the fhore of the harbor), a fhort diftance north of the "Old Walley houfe." His houfe was afterwards the refidence of Jeremiah Finney, and of his fon Jofiah. [Sprague's *Annals*, i: 209; Palmer's Calamy's *Nonconformift's Memorial*, i: 95; Wood's *Ath. Oxon.* ii: 882, 883; Shepard's *Difcourfes at Briftol, R.-I.*, pp. 11, 50.]

[78]

'hoped would accrue to your felves; and defired him to
'Return Publick Thanks: but at the fame interim of time
'a Paper was prefented unto him from a Court of *Ply-*
'*mouth*, which was holded before I came home,[139] to Com-
'mand a day of Humiliation thro' the whole Government,
'becaufe of the frowns of God upon thofe Forces fent
'under my Command, and the ill fuccefs we had, for want
'of good conduct. All which was caufed by thofe falfe
'Reports which were pofted home by thofe ill affected
'Officers that were under my Conduct; efpecially one
'which your felves very well know,[140] who had the advan-
'tage of being at home a Week before me, being fick of
'Action, and wanting the advantage to be at the Bank,[141]
'which he every day was mindful of more than fighting the
'Enemy in their own Country. After I came home, being
'inform'd of a General Court at *Plymouth*,[142] and not forget-
'ting my faithful Promife to you, and the duty I lay under,
'I went thither, where waiting upon them, I gave them an
'account of my Eaftward tranfactions, and made them
'fenfible of the falfenefs of thofe reports that were pofted
'to them by ill hands, and found fome fmall favourable
'acceptance with them, fo far that I was credited. I pre-
'fented your Thanks to them for their feafonable fending

[139] I find no record of this court, or of any fuch appointment of a day of humiliation. "A publique day of humiliation and faft" was appointed at the December court, to be held on the "fecond Wednefday of January next."

[140] Doubtlefs the "Captain" before referred to [p. 59] as having "faid it was time to go home;" but I have not been able to identify him.

[141] *Strawberry Bank.*

[142] Held 4 Nov., 1690. See record of fome things done then on the next page (note 143). [*Plym. Col. Rec.* vi: 252.]

'thofe Forces to relieve you, with that expence and
'charge they had been at; which Thanks they gratefully
'received; and faid a few Lines from your felves would
'have been well accepted. I then gave them an account
'of your great neceffities by being imprifoned in your
'Garrifons, and the great mifchief that would attend the
'Publick concerns of this Country by the lofs of their
'Majefty's Intereft, and fo much good Eftate of yours &
'your Neighbours, as doubtlefs would be on the deferting
'of your Town. I then moved for a free Contribution for
'your relief, which they with great forwardnefs promoted;
'and then ordered a day of Thankfgiving thro' the Govern-
'ment upon the 26th. day of this Inftant. Upon which
'day a Collection was ordered for your relief (and the
'Places near Adjacent) in every refpective Town in this
'Government; and for the good management of it that it
'might be fafely convey'd unto your hands, they appointed
'a Man in each County for the reception & conveyance
'thereof.[143] The perfons nominated and accepted thereof,
'are: For the County of *Plymouth*, Capt. *Nathanael Thomas*
'of *Marfhfield*:[144] For the County of *Barnftable*, Capt.

---

[143] The record is as follows: —

"Cap! Nath!! Thomas apointed in ye county of Plimouth to receive & take care for conveyance of the contribution propofed for the relief of ye town of Wells & parts adjacent.

"Cap! Jofeph Lothrop, ye like for ye county of Barnftable, & Major Benjamin Church for ye county of Briftol.

"The Court apoint the 26th inftant to be kept and obferved as a publick day of thankfgiving throughout ye colony." [*Plym. Col. Rec.* vi: 255.]

[144] *Nathaniel Thomas* was fon of Nathaniel of Marfhfield; was born 1643; married, 19 Jan., 1664, Deborah, dau. of Nicholas Jacobs, of Hingham; had Nathaniel, Jofeph, Deborah, Dorothy, William, Elifha, Jofhua, Caleb, Ifaac, and Mary; 3 Nov., 1696, he married

[79]

'*Joseph Lathrop* of *Barnstable*:[145] And for the County of
'*Bristol*, my self. Which when gathered you will have a
'particular account from each perfon, with orders of advice
'how it may be difpofed of for your beft advantage, with a
'Copy of the Courts order. The Gentlemen the effects
'are to be fent to are your felves that I now Write to, *viz.*
'*John Wheelwright* Efq;[146] Capt. *John Littlefield*,[147] and
'Lieut. *Joseph Story*.[148] I defer'd writing expecting every
'day to hear from you concerning the *Indians* coming to
'treat about their Prifoners that we had taken. The
'difcourfe I made with them at *Ameras-cogen*, I knew
'would have that Effect as to bring them to a treaty, which
'I fhould have thought my felf happy to have been im-
'proved in, knowing that it would have made much for
'your good. But no intelligence coming to me from any

Elizabeth, widow of Captain William Condy; he was Reprefentative 1672, and feven years more, and alfo at Bofton under the new charter; ferved in Philip's War; died 22 Oct., 1718. [Savage's *Gen. Dict.* iv: 281; Thomas's *Memorials of Marshfield*, p. 54.]

[145] *Joseph Lothrop* was third fon of Rev. John, of Barnftable; born in England; married 11 Dec., 1650, Mary Anfell; licenfed to keep an ordinary, 1653; ranked as Lieut., 1670; was Deputy from, and Selectman at, Barnftable for various years, and was of the Council of War; had Jofeph, Mary, Benjamin, Elizabeth, John, Samuel, John, Barnabas, Hope, Thomas, and Hannah. [Savage's *Gen. Dict.* iii: 120; Freeman's *Hift. Cape Cod*, ii: 262, 271; *Plym. Col. Rec.* vi: 10, 67, 85, 106, 128, 169, 240, 251.]

[146] *John Wheelwright* was probably fon of Samuel, of Wells; was Colonel and Deputy, and "a gentleman of a character above fufpicion"; died 1745. Little feems to be known of him that can be accurately ftated. [Savage's *Gen. Dict.* iv: 503; Allen's *Biog. Dict.* p. 846.]

[147] *John Littlefield* was fon of Edmund, of Exeter and Wells; was at Wells, 1656; Conftable, 1661; Lieut., 1668; had a dau. Mary, who married Matthew Auftin. [Savage's *Gen. Dict.* iii: 100.]

[148] Was he fon of William, of Dover, 1637-1658? (*N. E. Hift. & Gen. Reg.* viii: 130.]

'Gentlemen in your parts, and hearing nothing but by
'accident, and that in the latter end of the week by some
'of ours coming from *Boston*, informed me that the *Indians*
'were come in to your Town to seek for Peace; and that
'there was to be a treaty speedily;[149] but the time they
'knew not. I took my Horse, and upon the Monday set out
'for *Boston*, expecting the treaty had been at your Town,
'as rationally it should but on Tuesday Night coming to
'*Boston*, there met with Capt. *Elisha Andros*,[150] who in-
'formed me that the Place of treaty was *Sacaty-hock*,[151] and
'that Capt *Alden* was gone from *Boston* four days before I
'came there, and had carryed all the *Indian* Prisoners
'with him, and that all the Forces were drawn away out
'of your parts, except 12 men in your Town, and 12 in
'*Piscataqua*, which news did so amuse me, to see that wis-
'dom was so taken from the wise, and such imprudence in
'their actions, as to be deluded by *Indians*; and to have a
'treaty so far from any *English* Town, and to draw off the
'Forces upon what pretence soever, to me looks very ill.
'My fear is that they will deliver those we have taken,
'which if kept would have been greatly for your Security,
'it keeping them in awe, and preventing them from doing
'any hostile action or mischief, I knowing that the *English*
'being a broad are very earnest to go home, and the *In-*
'*dians* are very tedious in their discourses, and by that
'will have an advantage to have their Captives at a very

[149] See Williamson's *Hist. Me.* i: 626.
[150] See note 128, *ante*.
[151] *Sagadahoc*, the site of Popham's convict-colony, of 1607.

'low rate to your great damage. *Gentlemen*, as to *Rhode-*
'*Island*, I have not concern'd my self as to any relief for
'you, having nothing in writing to fhow to them, yet upon
'difcourfe with fome Gentlemen there, they have fignified
'a great forwardnefs to promote fuch a thing. I lying
'under great reflections from fome of yours in the Eaft-
'ward parts, that I was a very Covetous Perfon, and came
'there to enrich my felf, and that I kill'd their Cattel and
'Barrel'd them up and fent them to *Bofton*, and Sold them
'for Plunder, and made Money to put into my own Pocket;
'and the owners of them being poor People beg'd for the
'Hides and Tallow, with tears in their eyes; and that I
'was fo cruel as to deny them; which makes me judge
'my felf uncapable to Serve you in that matter: yet I do
'affure you that the People are very charitable at the *If-*
'*land*, and forward in fuch good actions, and therefore advife
'you to defire fome good fubftantial Perfon to take the man-
'agement of it, and write to the Government there, which I
'know will not be labour loft.[152] As for what I am accufed
'of, you all can witnefs to the contrary, and I fhould take it
'very kindly from you to do me that juft right, as to vindi-
'cate my Reputation; for the wife man fays, *A good Name*
'*is as precious Oyntment*. When I hear of the effect of the

---

[152] Williamfon fays Church "magnanimoufly collected a confiderable contribution in Plymouth Colony, which he tranfmitted to the Eaftern Provinces, accompanied by an addrefs to Major Froft, John Wheelwright, Efq., and others, encouraging their expectations of ftill further relief." [*Hift. Me.* i: 626.] If his authority is this letter of Church, — and I know of no other on which he could have relied, — he overftates the facts.

[80]

'Treaty, and have an account [80] of this Contribution, I
' intend again to Write to you, being very defirous, &
' fhould think my felf very happy, to be favoured with a
' few lines from your felves, or any Gentlemen in the Eaft-
' ward parts. Thus leaving you to the protection & gui-
' dance of the Great God of Heaven and Earth, who is able
' to protect and fupply you in your great difficulties, and to
' give you deliverance in His own due time.

I Remain, Gentlemen,
Your moft affured Friend to Serve you to my utmoft power,
Benjamin Church.

Poftfcript.

' Efq; *Wheelwright*, Sir, I intreat you, after your perufal
' of thefe lines, to communicate the fame to Capt. *John*
' *Littlefield*, Lieut. *Jofeph Story*; and to any other Gentle-
' men, as in your judgment you fee fit: With the tenders of
' my refpects to you, *&c.* and to Maj. *Vaughan*,[153] and his
' good Lady & Family. To Capt. *Fryer*[154] & good Mrs.
' *Fryer*, with hearty thanks for their kindnefs whilft in thofe
' parts, and good Entertainment from them. My kind Re-

---

[153] *William Vaughan* was born probably in Wales; lived in Portfmouth; freeman, 1669; 1672 was Lieut. of cavalry under Capt. Robert Pike; Counfellor of Province of N. H. and Chief-Juftice of Sup. Court; died 1719. He married 8 Dec., 1668, Margaret, dau. of Richard Cutt; had Eleanor, Mary, Cutt, George, Bridget, Margaret, Abigail, and Elizabeth. [Savage's *Gen. Dict.* iv: 368.]

[154] *Nathaniel Fryer* was of Bofton, where he had, by wife Chriftian, James, Sarah, and Elizabeth; removed to Portfmouth; married, as fecond wife, Dorothy Woodbridge; Deputy, 1666; Captain and Counfellor, 1683; died 13 Aug., 1705. [*Ibid.* ii: 214.]

[80]

'fpects to Maj. *Froſt*,[155] Capt. *Walton*,[156] Lieut. *Honeywel*,[157]
'and my very good friend little Lieut. *Plaiſted*:[158] with due
'reſpects to all Gentlemen my friends in the Eaſtward
'parts, as if particularly named.   *Farewell.*   B. C.

Briſtol, Novemb. 27. 1690.

To Major Pike.[159]   Honoured Sir,

THeſe *come to wait upon you, to bring the tenders of my hearty Service to your Self & Lady, with due acknowledgment of thankfulneſs for all the kindneſs and favour I received from you in the Eaſtward parts, when with you. Since I came from thoſe parts, I am informed by Capt.* Andros, *that your Self, and moſt of all the Forces are drawn off from the Eaſtward parts; I admire at it, conſidering that they had ſo low Eſteem of what was done, that they can apprehend the Eaſtward parts ſo ſafe before the Enemy was brought into better Subjection. I was in*

---

[155] *Charles Froſt*, born in Tiverton, Eng., 1632; came over with his father Nicholas about 1637; Deputy, 1658-61; Counſellor, 1693; Captain and Major, commanding the Yorkſhire militia; was Judge of the Common Pleas when he was ſhot by the Indians, 14 July, 1697, æt. 65. [Savage's *Gen. Dict.* ii: 210; Williamſon's *Hiſt. Me.* i: 674; *N. E. Hiſt. & Gen. Reg.* iii: 249-262.]

[156] See note 97, *ante*.

[157] *Richard Hunniwell* was ſon of Roger, who lived on Parker's neck, near the entrance to the Pool, Saco; was of Black Point, 1681; Enſign, 1680; Lieut., 1689; was put by Church in charge of the Blue Point, Black Point, and Spurwink garriſons, in the winter of 1689 [ſee note 61, *ante*]; earned the *ſoubriquet* of "the Indian killer"; and was himſelf murdered by the ſavages, with circumſtances of great atrocity, 6 Oct., 1703 [Savage ſays 1703, Southgate's *Hiſt. Scarborough* ſays 1713]. He married Sarah, dau. of Nathaniel Adams (ſee note 113, *ante*). [Savage's *Gen. Dict.* ii: 499; Folſom's *Hiſt. Saco*, p. 182; *N. E. Hiſt. & Gen. Reg.* iii: 25; *Me. Hiſt. Coll.* iii: 144-48.]

[158] See note 130, *ante*.

[159] See note 90, *ante*.

hopes when I came from thence, that those that were so
desirous to have my room, would have been very brisk in
my absence to have got themselves some Honour, which they
very much gapped after, or else they would not have spread
so many false reports to defame me. Which had I known
before, I left the Bank, I would have had satisfaction of
them. Your Honour was pleased to give me some small
account before I left the Bank, of some things that were ill
resented to you, concerning that Eastward Expedition, which
being rowled home like a Snow-ball thro' both Colonies, was
got to such a bigness that it over-shadow'd me from the
Influence of all comfort, or good acceptance amongst my
friends in my Journey homeward. But thro' Gods goodness am come home finding all well, and my self in good
Health, hoping that those Reports will do me that favour,
to quit me from all other Publick Action: That so I may
the more peaceably & quietly wait upon God, and be a comfort unto my own Family in this dark time of trouble, being
as on that is [160] hid, till His Indignation is over past: I
shall take it as a great favour to hear of your Honours well-
fare.   Subscribing my self as I am, Sir,
    Your most assured Friend and Servant.
                              Benjamin Church. [81]

Major *Church* did receive after this, Answers to his Letters, but hath lost them, except it be a Letter from several
of the Gentlemen in those parts in *June* following: which
is as followeth.

[160] Southwick's edition omits "that is."

[81]

Portsmouth June 29 1691.

Major *Benj. Church.*   Sir,

*Y*Our *former readiness to expose your self in the Service of the Country against the Common Enemy; and particularly the late Obligations*[161] *you have laid upon us in these Eastern parts, leaves us under a deep & grateful sense of your favour therein*: *And forasmuch as you were pleased when last here, to signifie your ready inclination to further Service of this kind, if occasion should call for it*; *We therefore presume confidently to promise our selves complyance accordingly*; *and have sent this Messenger on purpose to you, to let you know that notwithstanding the late overture of Peace the Enemy have approved themselves as perfidious as ever, and are almost daily killing and destroying upon all our Frontiers*; *The Governour & Council of the* Massachusetts *have been pleased to Order the Raising of* 150 *Men to be forthwith dispatch'd into these parts*; *and as we understand have Writ to your Governour & Council of* Plymouth *for further Assistance, which we pray you to promote, hoping if you can obtain about* 200 *Men* English *&* Indians, *to visit them at some of their Head-quarters up* Kenebeck *River, or else-where, which (for want of necessaries) was omitted last Year, it may be of great advantage to us*: *We offer nothing of advice as to what Methods are most proper to be taken in this affair, your acquaintance with our Circum-*

---

[161] This perhaps refers to the contributions, which had before this reached them, from the committee of which Church was a member.

stances as well as the Enemies, will direct you therein, We leave the Conduct thereof to your own discretion: But that the want of Provision, &c. may be no Remora *to your Motion, you may please to know Mr.* Geafford [162] *One of our principal Inhabitants now residing in* Boston, *hath promised to take care to supply to the value of two or three hundred Pounds, if occasion require: We pray a few lines by the bearer to give us a prospect of what we may expect for our further Encouragement, and remain,*

  Sir, Your Obliged Friends and Servants,

Will. Vaughan Charles Frost William Fernald [166]
Francis Hooke [163] Nathanael Fryer Robert Elliott. [167]
Richard Martyn [164] John Wincol [165]

 A True Copy of the Original Letter; which Letter was presented to me by Capt. Hatch,[168] *who came Express.*

---

[162] I find no trace of this man, unless he were William Gifford, who was a bricklayer, admitted to inhabit at Boston 28 Feb., 1654. [Drake's *Hist.*

[163] *Francis Hooke* was son of Humphrey, Alderman of the city of Bristol, Eng.; lived at Kittery, Me.; was Magistrate, 1666; Captain; Treasurer of

[164] *Richard Martin* (*Martins*) was at Portsmouth, N.H.; was made "overseer" of John Cutt's will, 6 May, 1680; had the first place in "the front seat

[165] *John Wincol* (*Wincoln, Wincall, Winkell, Winkle*) was son of Thomas, of Watertown; freeman there 6 May, 1646; selectman, 1649, 56, 61, 62; Depu-

[166] *William Fernald* was eldest son of Reginald (or, as he himself, at least, sometimes wrote it, Renald), who was the first surgeon among the New-Hamp-

[167] *Robert Eliot* (*Eliott, Eliot, Elliott*) seems to have been of Portsmouth, 1660; of Casco, before 1670; of Scarborough soon after, where he was

[168] *Philip Hatch*, who was freeman, 1652, York, Me., or one of his sons? [Savage's *Gen. Dict.* ii: 375.]

Maj. *Church* sent them his Answer: the Contents whereof was, That he had gone often enough for nothing; and especially to be ill treated with scandals and false Reports, when last out, which he could not forget. And signifyed to them, That doubtless some amongst them thought they could do without him, *&c.* And to make short of it, did go out, and meeting with the Enemy at *Maquait*, were most shamefully beaten: as I have been inform'd.[169]

Boston, i : 334.] There was time enough for him to grow to be a "principal inhabitant" by 1690, as many another had done in less time.

Province of Maine under Pres. Danforth, 1680; of the Council, 1684, and again, under the new charter, 1693; died 10 Jan., 1695, "much lamented."

He married Mary (Maverick), widow of John Palfgrave, and dau. of Samuel Maverick, of Noddle's Island. [Savage's *Gen. Dict.* ii : 457.]

before the minister" in "seating the meeting-house" (he being chairman of the committee to do that work), 3 April, 1693. Was he Richard, whose son ty, 1658; soon moved to Piscataqua, and then to Kittery (at *Newichawannock*, or So. Berwick); came thence Deputy to Boston, 1675, 7, 8; during 1676-85 was connected with the government as Councillor and otherwise; fought the shire settlers. He resided at Kittery; and, in 1688, deeded to his sister Sarah, then the wife of Richard Waterhouse, Selectman, 1682, and Deputy, 1685; Counsellor, 1688, when he lived at Portsmouth. He died in 1720, leaving his estates in Scarborough to his son-in-

Richard, Coffin says, was born 8 Jan., 1674? [Brewster's *Rambles about Portsmouth*, 36, 63; Coffin's *Hist. Newbury*, 309.]

Indians bravely at Saco, in 1675; had wife Elizabeth; and died, by a fall from his horse, 22 Oct., 1694. [Savage's *Gen. Dict.* iv : 592; Bond's *Hist. Watertown*, 654; Williamson's *Hist. Me.* i : 349, 524, 565, 566.]

of Portsmouth, tanner, what is now Pierce's Island, and One Tree Island. [Brewster's *Rambles, &c.* 370.]

law, Col. Geo. Vaughan. [Savage's *Gen. Dict.* ii : 111; Willis's *Hist. Portland*, 139; Brewster's *Rambles, &c.* 25; *Me. Hist. Coll.* iii : 210.]

[169] Cotton Mather makes the following statement in regard to this expedition here referred to : —

" About the latter end of *July* we sent out a small Army under the Command of Captain *March*, Captain *King*, Cap-

[82] The Third Expedition, *East*.

THis was in the Year 1692. In the time of Sir *William Phip*'s[170] Government: Major *Walley*[171] being at tain *Sherburn*, and Captain *Walten* (*Convers* lying *Sick* all Summer had this to make him yet more *Sick* that he could have no part in these Actions) who landing at *Macquoit*, marched up to *Pechypscot*, but not finding any signs of the enemy, *marched down again*. While the *Commanders* were waiting *Ashore* till the *Soldiers* were got aboard, such great Numbers of *Indians* poured in upon them, that tho' the *Commanders* wanted not for Courage or Conduct, yet they found themselves obliged, with much ado, (and not without the Death of worthy Captain *Sherburn*) to retire into the Vessels which then lay aground. Here they kept pelting at one another all Night; but unto little other purpose than *this*, which was indeed Remarkable, That the Enemy was at this time *going* to *take* the Isle of *Shoales*, and no doubt had they *gone* they would have *taken* it, but having exhausted all their Ammunition on this Occasion, they desisted from what they designed." [*Magnalia*, Book VII: 77.]

[170] *Sir William Phips* (*Phipps*) was son of James, gunsmith, from Bristol, Eng.; was born at what is now Phipsburg, Me.; became a ship-carpenter; married Mary, widow of John Hull (not the mint-master); with her money set up a shipyard at Sheepscot, and then in Boston when "driven in" by Indian hostilities; thence went to sea, 1677; at the Bahamas heard of the wreck of a Spanish treasure-laden galleon, and went to England and offered his services to the king to recover the gold; his project was approved, and he went to the spot with two frigates in 1683; failed for want of proper instruments; returned to England, and persuaded Monk, Duke of Albemarle, to furnish him for the work again; went back, fished up £300,000, of which £16,000 fell to him, and he was knighted by James II., 28 June, 1687; Andros made him Sheriff of New England; joined Second Church, 8 March, 1690; May, 1690, conducted the attack on Nova Scotia; was chosen Assistant, projected the silly expedition, in the August following, against Quebec; went to London, 1691, was appointed Governor on Increase Mather's recommendation; arrived back 14 May, 1692; sanctioned the witchcraft delusion in 1693, flogged Collector William Brenton, and, 1694, caned Capt. Short of the Nonsuch Frigate, and, through the trouble thence arising, was recalled to London, where he died 18 Feb., 1695, and was buried in St. Mary, Woolnoth, in Lombard St., where John Newton lies. [Savage's *Gen. Dict.* iii: 420; Palfrey's *Hist. N. E.* iii: 590; Hutchinson's *Hist. Mass.* ii: 76; Sparks's *Amer. Biog.* vii: 5-102; Mather's *Magnalia*, Book II: 15-75.]

[171] See note 24, *ante*.

Boſton, was requeſted by his Excellency to treat with Maj. *Church* about going Eaſt with him. Maj. *Walley* coming home, did as defired; and to incourage the faid Maj *Church*, told him, That now was the time to have recompence for his former great Expences; ſaying alſo, That the Country could not give him leſs than Two or three hundred Pounds. So upon his Excellency's requeſt Maj *Church* went down to *Boſton*, and waited upon him; who ſaid he was glad to ſee him, *&c.* And after ſome difcourfe told the ſaid *Church*, That he was going Eaſt himſelf, and that he ſhould be his Second, and in his abfence Command all the Forces: And being requeſted by his Excellency to raiſe what Volunteers of his old Souldiers in the County of *Briſtol*, both *Engliſh* & *Indians*. Receiving his Commiſſion: which is as followeth.

SIR William Phips Knight, Captain General and Governour in Chief in and over their Majeſty's Province of the Maſſachufetts-Bay *in* New-England. *To* Benjamin Church *Gent. Greeting.*

'R Epofing ſpecial Truſt and Confidence in your Loy-
' alty, Courage and good Conduct. I do by theſe
' preſents Conſtitute & Appoint You to be Major of the
' ſeveral Companies of Militia, detached for their Majeſty's
' Service againſt their *French* and *Indian* Enemies. You
' are therefore Authorized and Required in their Majeſty's
' Names, to difcharge the duty of a Major, by Leading
' Ordering and Exerciſing the ſaid ſeveral Companies in

'Arms, both Inferiour Officers & Souldiers, keeping them
' in good Order & Difcipline, Commanding them to Obey
' you as their Major: And diligently to intend the faid
' Service, for the profecuting, purfuing, killing and deftroy-
' ing of the faid Common Enemy. And your felf to ob-
' ferve and follow fuch Orders & Directions as you fhall
' from time to time Receive from my Self, according to
' the Rules & Difcipline of War, purfuant to the Truft
' repofed in you for their Majefty's Service. Given under
' my Hand and Seal at *Bofton*, the Twenty-fifth day of
' *July* 1692. In the Fourth Year of the Reign of our
' Soveraign Lord & Lady *William* and *Mary*, by the
' Grace of GOD King & Queen of *England*, *Scotland*,
' *France* and *Ireland*, Defender of the Faith, *&c.*

WILLIAM PHIPS.

By his Excellency's Command,
    Ifaac Addington, Secr.

Returning home to the County aforefaid, he foon raifed a fufficient Number of Volunteers both *Englifh & Indians* and Officers fuitable to Command them, March'd them down to *Bofton*. But there was one thing I would [83] juft mention; which was, That Maj *Church* being fhort of Money, was forc'd to borrow Six Pounds in Money of Lieut. *Woodman*[172] in *Little Compton*, to diftribute by a

---

[172] *John Woodman*, of Little Compton, perhaps fon of John, a prominent citizen of Newport; Church bought land of him, 30 Oct., 1702; and his oldeft fon, Thomas, married Woodman's fecond daughter, Edith. [*R.-I. Col. Rec.* iii: 106, 150, 168, 185, 231; Part I. of this work, pp. xxxiii. xliv.]

Shilling, and a Bit [173] at a time to the *Indian* Souldiers; who without such Allurements would not have March'd to *Boston*. This Money Major *Church* put into the hands of Mr. *William Fobes*,[174] who was going out their Commissary in that Service, who was order'd to keep a just accompt of what each *Indian* had that so it might be subducted out of their wages at their return home. Coming to *Boston*, his Excellency having got things in a readiness, they Embark'd on board their transports, his Excellency going in Person with them, being bound to *Pemequid*: [175] But in their way stop'd at *Casco*, and buried the bones of the dead People there,[176] and took off the great Guns that were there; then went to *Pemequid* : [177] Coming there his Excellency ask'd Maj. *Church* to go a-shore & give his judgment about Erecting a Fort there? He answer'd, That his Gen-

---

[173] "*Bitt*, a piece of silver in *Barbadoes* current for seven pence half-penny. [*Bailey*.] The name was applied later, especially at the South, to the *ninepence*, or one-eighth of a dollar. [Bartlett's *Dictionary of Americanisms*, 33.] Mr. Drake says it was *sixpence*. [*Church*, (ed. 1827,) 209.]

[174] See note 242, Part I.

[175] "*Pemaquid*, like *Acadia*, appears to have been of indefinite extent; but under this general name there seems to have been embraced, at a later date, *Monhegan*, and its companion, the islet of *Monanis*, the cluster of the *Damariscove* islands, and territory somewhat beyond the limits of the peninsula of *Pemaquid* proper." [*Me. Hist. Coll.* v : 181.] "The river of *Pemaquid* is ten miles east of *Damariscotta*. There is a large bay through which we pass to enter *Pemaquid* harbor or river. The bay is full of islands, the greater part of which are settled. The fort, called Fort George, was on a point at the mouth of the river, and on the east side of it. The remains of the fortress are there at this day (1795)." [Sullivan's *Hist. Dist. Me.* 35.]

[176] That is the bones of those — over 100 persons — who had been destroyed there by the savages under the *Sieur Hertel*, 17 May, 1690. [Holmes's *Annals*, i : 431 ; Belknap's *Hist. N. Hamp.* i : 257-9; Hutchinson's *Hist. Mass.* i : 353.]

[177] This was early in August, 1692. [*Me. Hist. Coll.* v : 282.]

[83]

ius did not incline that way, for he never had any value for them, being only Nefts for Deftructions:[178] His Excellency faid, He had a fpecial Order from their Majefties King *William* and Queen *Mary* to Erect a Fort there, *&c.* Then they went a-fhore and fpent fome time in the projection thereof.[179] Then his Excellency told Maj. *Church* that he might take all the Forces with him, except one Company to ftay with him and work about the Fort; the Major anfwered that if his Excellency pleas'd he might keep two Companies with him, and he would go with the reft to *Penobfcot,* and Places Adjacent. Which his Excellency did, and gave Maj. *Church* his Orders: which are as followeth.

---

[178] Recall Church's previoufly expreffed opinions in regard to the forts at *Mount Hope* and *Pocaffet.* [pp. 25, 47, Part I.]

[179] This fort was built of over 2000 cartloads of ftone, in a quadrangular figure, 737 feet in circumference outfide the outer wall, and 108 feet fquare within the inner walls. The fouthern wall, fronting the fea, was 22 feet high, and more than 6 feet thick at the ports, which were 8 feet from the ground. The great flanker or round tower at the weft end of the fouthern wall was 20 feet high; the wall on the eaft line 12 feet high; that on the north 10 feet, and on the weft 18. It had 28 ports, and 18 guns mounted, fix of which were eighteen-pounders. The ftructure ftood back 20 rods from high-water mark, and was garrifoned by 60 and fometimes 100 men. [*Magnalia*, Book VII: 81; *Me. Hift. Coll.* v: 282.] This fort was not intended to operate againft Indians merely, but againft piratical rovers who infefted the fea, and againft the French, who intended repoffeffion. That which Maj. Andros had built in 1677, and which the Indians took in 1690, was a mere ftockade; "un Fort, qui n'étoit à la vérité que de pieux, mais affez regulierement conftruit." [Charlevoix, *Nouv. France*, i: 557.]

By his Excellency Sir William Phips *Knight, Captain General and Governour in Chief in and over their Majesties Province of the* Massachusetts-Bay *in* New-England, *&c.* **Instructions** *for Major* Benjamin Church.

'Whereas you are Major and so Chief Officer of a
' body of Men detached out of the Militia appointed
' for an Expedition against the *French & Indian* Enemy;
' you are duely to observe the following Instructions.

' *Impri.* You are to take care that the Worship of God
' be duely & constantly maintained and kept up amongst
' you, and to suffer no Swearing, Cursing, or other pro-
' phanation of the Holy Name of God; and as much as in
' you lyes to deter and hinder all other Vice amongst your
' Souldiers.

' *2ly.* You are to proceed with the Souldiers under your
' Command to *Penobscot*, and with what privacy & undis-
' coverable Methods you can, there to Land your men,
' and take the best measures to surprize the Enemy.

' *3ly.* You are by killing, destroying, and all other means
' possible to endeavour the destruction of the Enemy in
' pursuance whereof, being satisfyed of your Courage &
' Conduct, I leave the same to your discretion.

' *4ly.* You are to indeavour the taking what Captives
' you can either Men, Women or Children, and the same
' safely to keep and convey them unto, me. [84]

' *5ly.* Since it is not possible to judge how affairs may
' be circumstanced with you there, I shall therefore not

'limit your return, but leave it to your Prudence, only
'that you make no longer ſtay than you can improve for
'advantage againſt the Enemy, or may reaſonably hope
'for the ſame.

'6*ly*. You are alſo to take care and be very induſtruous
'by all poſſible means to find out and deſtroy all the Ene-
'mies Corn, and other Proviſions in all Places where you
'can come at the ſame.

'7*ly*. You are at your return from *Penobſcot* and thoſe
'Eaſtern Parts, to make all diſpatch hence for *Kenebeck*
'River, and the Places Adjacent, and there proſecute all
'advantages againſt the Enemy as aforeſaid.

'8*ly*. If any Souldier, Officer or other ſhall be diſobe-
'dient to you as their Commander in Chief, or other their
'Superiour Officer, or make or cauſe any Mutiny, commit
'other offence or diſorders, you ſhall call a Council of
'War amongſt your Officers, and having tryed him or
'them ſo offending, inflict ſuch puniſhment as the merit
'of the offence requires, Death only excepted, which if
'any ſhall deſerve, you are to ſecure the perſon, and ſig-
'nify the Crime unto me by the firſt opportunity.

Given under my hand this 11*th day of* Auguſt, 1692.

WILLIAM PHIPS.

Then the Major and his Forces embark'd and made the beſt of their way to *Penobſcot*; and coming to an Iſland in thoſe Parts [180] in the evening, landed his Forces at one end

---

[180] *Seven Hundred Acre Iſland.* [Williamſon's *Hiſt. Me.* i: 71, 636.]

of the faid Ifland: Then the Major took part of his Forces and mov'd toward Day to the other end of the faid Ifland, where they found two *French Men*, and their Families in their houfes; and that one or both of them had *Indian* Women to their Wives, and had Children by them. The Major prefently examining the *French men*, Where the *Indians* were? They told him, That there was a great company of them upon an Ifland juft by:[181] and fhowing him the Ifland, prefently difcover'd feveral of them. Maj. *Church* and his Forces ftill keeping undifcover'd to them, ask'd the *French men* where their paffing Place was? Which they readily fhew'd him; fo prefently placed an Ambafcade to take any that fhould come over. Then fent orders for all the reft of the Forces to come; fending them an account what he had feen & met withal; ftrickly charging them to keep themfelves undifcovered by the Enemy. The Ambafcade did not lye long before an *Indian* Man and a Woman came over in a Canoo to the Place for landing, where the Ambafcade was laid: who haul'd up their Canoo, and came right into the hands of our Ambafcade, who fo fuddenly furprized them that they could not give any notice to the others from whence they came; the Major ordering that none of his fhould offer to meddle with the Canoo, left they fhould be difcovered, hoping to take the moft of them if his Forces came as order'd, he expecting them to come as directed. But the firft news he had of them was, That they were all coming,

[181] Long Ifland. [*Ibid.* 636.]

[85]

tho' not privately [85] as ordered; but in the Veffels fair in fight of the Enemy, which foon put them all to flight; and our Forces not having Boats fuitable to purfue them, they got all away in their Canoo's, &c. (which caufed Maj *Church* to fay, He would never go out again without fufficient number of Whale-boats) which for want of, was the ruine of that action. Then Maj. *Church* according to his inftructions rang'd all thofe parts, to find all their Corn, and carried aboard their Veffels what he thought convenient, and deftroy'd the reft. Alfo finding confiderable quantities of Plunder, *viz* Bever & Moofe skins, &c. Having done what Service they could in thofe parts,[182] he returned back to his Excellency at *Pemequid*;[183] where being come, ftaid not long: they being fhort of Bread, his Excellency intended home for *Bofton*, for more Provifions; but before, going with Maj. *Church* & his Forces to *Kenebeck* River, and coming there, gave him his further Orders; which are as followeth.

By his Excellency the Governour.

To *Major* Benjamin Church.

'YOu having already received former Inftructions, are
' now further to proceed with the Souldiers under
' your Command for *Kenebeck* River, and the Places Adja-

---

[182] Mather fays he "took five Indians" here; Hutchinfon fays "three or four." It is certain that he took but few. [*Magnalia*, Book VII: 81; Hutchinfon's *Hift. Mafs.* ii: 69.]

[183] His inftructions were to "make all defpatch" thence "for *Kenebeck* River"; but in doing fo he muft naturally touch at *Pemaquid*, which lay between.

'cent, and ufe your utmoft indeavours to kill, deftroy and
'take Captive the *French* & *Indian* Enemy wherefoever
'you fhall find any of them; and at your return to *Peme-*
'*quid* (which you are to do as foon as you can conveni-
'ently; after your beft indeavour done againft the Enemy,
'and having deftroyed their Corn and other Provifions)
'you are to ftay with all your Souldiers and Officers, and
'fet them to work on the Fort, and make what difpatch
'you can in that bufinefs, ftaying there until my further
'order.   *WILLIAM PHIPS.*

Then his Excellency taking leave went for *Bofton*;[184]
and foon after Maj. *Church* and his Forces had a fmart
fight with the Enemy in *Kenebeck*-River, Purfued them fo
hard that they left their Canoo's & ran up into the woods,
ftill purfued them up to their Fort at *Taconock*,[185] which

[184] The witch trials were in progrefs in Bofton during his abfence, and it is not unlikely that it was while he was gone on this bufinefs that the incident occurred, which Hutchinfon mentions, on the authority of a *MS.* letter; that Mrs. Phips, being applied to for interpofition in the cafe of a lady accufed of witchcraft, took the refponfibility of figning a difcharge for her, upon which document the jailor took the refponfibility of fetting the accufed free, — to his own harm, it was faid. Whether this had any thing to do with that accufation of the Governor's lady herfelf as a witch, which Calef afferts and Douglafs hints, and which it was believed had fome influence in opening the Governor's eyes, and ftaying the delufion with its plague of blood, is not obvious. [Hutchinfon's *Hift. Mafs.* ii: 61; Drake's *Witchcraft Delnfion, &c.* iii: 159; Douglafs's *Summary*, i: 450.]

[185] *Teconnet* falls are on the *Kennebec*, oppofite the village of Waterville. On the point of land above the confluence of the *Sebafticook* with the *Kennebec*, and below thefe falls, ftood the old *Teconnet* fort of the Indians, here referred to, and, in 1754, Fort Halifax of the Englifh. The fite of the fort itfelf is in Winflow, and the block-houfe was lately ftanding. [Williamfon's *Hift. Me.* i: 50; Minot's *Hift. Mafs.* i: 186.]'

the Enemy perceiving fet fire to their Houfes in the Fort, and ran away by the light of them, and when Maj. *Church* came to the faid Fort found about half their Houfes ftanding and the reft burnt; alfo found great quantities of Corn, put up into Indian Cribs, which he and his Forces deftroyed, as ordered. Having done what Service he could in thofe parts return'd to *Pemequid*, and coming there imploy'd his Forces according to his Inftructions:[166] being out of Bread, his Excellency not coming, Maj. *Church* was oblig'd to borrow Bread of the Captain of the Man of War that was then there, for all the Forces under his Command, his Excellency not coming as expected. But at length his Excellency came and brought very little Bread more than would pay what was borrowed of the Man of War: So that in a fhort time after Maj. *Church* with his Forces return'd home to *Bofton*, and had their Wages for their good Service done. Only one thing by the way I will but juft mention, that is, about the Six Pounds Maj. *Church* borrowed as afore-mention'd, and put in-to the hands of Mr. *Fobes*, who diftributed the faid Money, all but 30 *s.* to the *Indian* Souldiers as directed, which was deducted out of their Wages, and the Country had Credit for the fame; and the faid *Fobes* kept the 30 *s* to himfelf, which was deducted out of his Wages. Whereupon Maj *Walley* and the faid *Fobes* had fome words. In fhort, Maj. *Church* was forc'd to pay the Six Pounds he borrowed out of his own Pocket, befides which

---

[166] In the hateful bufinefs of fort-building.

the said *Church* was oblig'd to expend about Six Pounds of his own Money in Marching down the Forces both *Englifh* and *Indians* to *Bofton*, having no drink allow'd them upon the Road, *&c.* So that in ftead of Maj *Church*'s having the allowances afore-mentioned by Maj. *Walley*, he was out of Pocket about Twelve Pounds more and above what he had;[187] all which had not been, had not his Excellency been gone out of the Country.[188]

The Fourth Expedition, *Eaft*.

IN 1696. Maj *Church* being at *Bofton*, and belonging to the Houfe of Reprefentatives,[189] feveral Gentlemen requefting him to go Eaft again, and the General Court having made Acts of Incouragement, *&c.* He told them, if they would provide Whale Boats, & other neceffaries convenient, he would: Being alfo requefted by the faid General Court, he proceeded to raife Volunteers, and made it his whole bufinefs Riding both Eaft and Weft in our Province[190] and *Connecticut*, at great charge and expences; and in about a Months time raifed a fufficient

---

[187] Walley told him in the outfet (p. 83), that "the country could not give him lefs than two or three hundred pounds"; fo that, at the loweft calculation, Church made a lofs of £188 upon his expectations "aforementioned."

[188] He means that Gov. Phips's abfence when this fettlement took place was the caufe of the wrong which he fuffered.

[189] I have found no trace of his appointment as Deputy this year, on the Briftol Town Records. This would feem, from various confiderations, to have been juft about as he was removing to Fall River. [See Part I. xxxi.]

[190] Plymouth and Maffachufetts Colonies had been confolidated into the new "Province of Maffachufetts Bay" by the new Charter of 1692.

number out of thofe Parts, and March'd them down to *Bofton*; where he had the promife that every thing fhould be ready in three Weeks or a Months time, but was oblig'd to ftay confiderable longer. Being now at *Bofton* he received his Commiffion and Inftructions; which are as followeth.

William Stoughton, *Efq*;[191] *Lieutenant Governour and Commander in Chief in and over His Majefties Province of the* Maffachufetts-Bay *in* New-England. *To Major* Benjamin Church, *Greeting.*

W*Hereas there are feveral Companies raifed, confifting of Englifh-Men & Indians for His Majefties Service, to go forth upon the Encouragement given by the Great and General Court or Affembly of this His Majefties Province, convened at* Bofton *the* 27th *Day of* May 1696. *to profecute the French and Indian Enemy,* &c. *And you having offered your felf to take the command and conduct of the faid feveral Companies. By vertue therefore of the Power and Authority in and by His Majefties Royal Commiffion to me*

---

[191] *William Stoughton*, fon of Ifrael, of Dorchefter, graduated at Harvard, and then at Oxford, Eng.; became a preacher; is named by Calamy among thofe ejected; came back, and preached the election fermon of 1668; became Selectman, Affiftant, Commiffioner of the United Colonies; went to England in 1677 with Bulkley as agent of the colonies; was one of Andros's Council; was chofen Lieut. Gov. under the new Charter; and became Chief-Juftice; died 7 July, 1701. The recall of Sir William Phips left him in chief command until Bellamont's arrival in 1699. He was on the witch bench, and, unlike Sewall, never expreffed penitence for the part he took. He built Stoughton Hall at Harvard. [Savage's *Gen. Dict.* iv: 215; Palmer's *Noncon. Mem.* i: 197; Quincy's *Hift. Har. Un.* i: 178, 9; Eliot's *Biog. Dict.* 444.]

Granted, repofing fpecial truft and confidence in your Loyalty, Prudence, courage and good conduct. I do by thefe Prefents Conftitute and Appoint you to be Major of the faid feveral Companies, both Englifh-Men and Indians, raifed for His Majefties Service upon the Encouragement aforefaid. You are therefore carefully and diligently to perform the duty of your place, by Leading, Ordering, and Exercifing the faid feveral Companies in Arms, both Inferiour Officers and Soul-[87]diers, keeping them in good Order and Difcipline, commanding them to obey you as their Major. And your felf diligently to intend His Majefties Service for the profecuting, purfuing, taking, killing or deftroying the faid Enemy by Sea or Land; And to obferve all fuch Orders and Inftructions as you fhall from time to time receive from my Self or Commander in chief for the time being, according to the Rules and Difcipline of War, purfuant to the truft repofed in you. Given under my Hand & Seal at Arms at Bofton, the Third Day of Auguft, 1696. In the Eighth Year of the Reign of Our Soveraign Lord William the Third by the Grace of God of England, Scotland, France and Ireland, King, Defender of the Faith, &c.

Wm. STOUGHTON.

By Command of the Lieut. Governour, &c.

    Ifaac Addington, Secr.

Province of the Maffachufetts-Bay.

By the Rt. Honourable the Lieutenant Governour and Commander in Chief.

𝕴𝖓𝖘𝖙𝖗𝖚𝖈𝖙𝖎𝖔𝖓𝖘 *for Maj.* Benjamin Church, *Commander of the Forces raised for His Majesties Service against the French and Indian Enemy and Rebels.*

Pursuant to the Commission given you, you are to Embark the Forces now furnished and equipped for His Majesties Service on the present Expedition to the Eastern parts of this Province, and with them and such others as shall offer themselves to go forth on the said Service to Sail unto Piscataqua, *to joyn those lately dispatched thither for the same Expedition, to await your coming. And with all care and diligence to improve the Vessels, Boats and Men under your command in search for, prosecution and pursuit of the said Enemy, at such places where you may be informed of their abode or resort, or where you may probably expect to find or meet with them, and take all advantages against them which Providence shall favour you with.*

You are not to list or accept any Souldiers that are already in His Majesties pay and posted at any Town or Garrison within this Province, without special Order from my self.

You are to require and give strict Orders that the duties of Religion be attended on board the several Vessels, and in the several companies under your command, by daily Prayers unto God and reading His Holy Word, and Observance of the Lords Day to the utmost you can.

You are to see that your Souldiers have their due allow-

[88]

ance of Provisions and other necessaries, & that the Sick or Wounded be accommodated in the best manner your circumstances will admit. And that good order and command be kept up & maintained in the several companies, and all disorders, drunkenness, prophane cursing, swearing, disobedience to Officers, mutinies, omissions or neglect of duty, be duly punished according to the Laws Martial. And you are to require the Captain or chief Officer of each company with the Clerk of the same, to keep an exact Journal of all their proceedings from time to time.

In case any of the Indian Enemy and Rebels offer to submit themselves, you are to receive them only at discretion. But if you think fit to improve any of them or any others which you may happen to take Prisoners, you may encourage them to be faithful by the promise of their lives, which shall be granted upon approbation of their fidelity. [88]

You are carefully to look after the Indians which you have out of the Prison,[192] *so that they may not have opportunity to escape, but otherwise improve them to what advantage you can, and return them back again to this place.*

You are to advise as you can have occasion with Capt. John Gorham [193] *who accompanies you in this Expedition, and is to take your command in case of your Death. A*

[192] In pursuance of the policy by which, in the time of Philip's war, Cornelius the Dutch pirate, and others, had been taken out of Boston jail, and "allowed" to march against the Indians, the Province seems now to have swelled the ranks of its volunteers by a similar resource. [Drake's *Hist. Bost.* i: 402; Part I. note 56.]

[193] *John Gorham* (*Gorum, Goram, Gorrum, Goaram*) was son of Capt. John, of Barnstable; was born at Marshfield, 20 Feb., 165½; was a tanner, like his father; was with his father in

copy of thefe Inftructions you are to leave with him, and to give me an account from time to time of your proceedings.
Bofton, Auguft 12*th.* 1696. *Wm. STOUGHTON.*

In the time Maj. *Church* lay at *Bofton*, the News came of *Pemequid* Fort being taken,[194] it came by a Shallop[195] that brought fome Prifoners to *Bofton*, who gave account alfo that there was a French Ship at Mount-*Defart*,[196] who

Philip's war; 5 June, 1690, was made captain in the Canada Expedition, and was afterwards Lieut. Col.; later was much employed as a conveyancer; died 9 Dec., 1716, and lies buried at the N.E. corner of the Unitarian meeting-houfe in Barnftable. He married, 24 Feb., 1674, Mercy, daughter of John Otis; had John, Temperance, Mary, Stephen, Shubael, John, Thankful, Job, Mercy; left a real eftate of £2000, and perfonal of £322. [Otis's *Hift. Barnftable*, i: 217-222.]

[194] The French conceived that Fort William Henry, at *Pemaquid*, had importance in controlling the weftern portion of Acadia, and determined to reduce it. Iberville was fent from Quebec with two fhips of war, with arrangements to co-operate with Villebon and 50 *Mickmacks*, and Caftine with 200 of his favages; on the way, met and captured one of an Englifh fleet, and then invefted and attacked *Pemaquid*. The fort was at the time in command of Capt. Pafcoe Chubb (of Andover), who had fhown his incompetence by treachery toward fome Indian envoys in the previous February; and was bafely furrendered without any determined effort at defence, — though Charlevoix fuggefts, through the cowardice of the garrifon compelling the captain againft his will, — 15 July, 1696. The fort was moftly demolifhed, after a hiftory of four years fully juftifying Church's fcruples in the beginning. Chubb was cafhiered, and was not forgotten by the Indians, who fucceeded in murdering him and his wife Hannah (Faulkner) at Andover, 5 March, 1698. [Williamfon's *Hift. Me.* i: 642-4; Hutchinfon's *Hift. Mafs.* ii: 88; Charlevoix's *Hift. Nouv. France.* iii: 260-2; Abbott's *Hift. Andover*, 43.]

[195] Hutchinfon fays it was "a French fhallop belonging to St. John's, with 23 foldiers under *Villeau*, their captain." [*Hift. Mafs.* ii: 91.]

[196] *Mount Defert* Ifland lies juft eaft of the *debouchure* of Union river, — fay 25 miles eaft of the centre of Penobfcot Bay, and is the largeft ifland in the State, being 15 miles long by about 7 in mean width, and containing fome 60,000 acres. A third part of this fhoots up into 13 high and rugged peaks, vifible 20 leagues at fea, and giving to it its French name, *Monts Deferts* (the defolate mountains — not, as Mr. Drake

had taken a Ship of ours;[197] so the discourse was that they would send the Man of War,[198] with other Forces to take the said French Ship and retake ours. But in the mean time Maj. *Church* and his Forces being ready, imbark'd, and on the 15th day of *August* set Sail for *Piscataqua*, where more Men were to joyn them (but before they left *Boston*, Maj *Church* discours'd with the Captain of the Man of War, who promised him, if he went to Mount-*Desart* in pursuit of the said French Ship, that he would call for him and his Forces at *Piscataqua*, expecting that the *French* & *Indians* might not be far from the said French Ship, so that he might have an opportunity to fight them while he was ingag'd with the French Ship:) Soon after the Forces arrived at *Piscataqua* the Major sent his *Indian* Souldiers to Col. *Gidney*[199] at *York*,[200] to be assist-

---

suggests, named by Champlain in honor of *De Monts*).

[197] The "ship of ours" was the Newport, Capt. Paxton, which was cruising off the Bay of Fundy (to intercept French stores supposed to be on their way from Quebec to Villebon) with the Sorlings, Capt. Eames, and the Province tender. The two latter escaped in a fog. Iberville refitted the Newport, and took her with him to help reduce *Pemaquid*.

[198] The Sorlings.

[199] *Bartholomew Gedney (Gidney)* was son of John, of Salem; was baptized 14 June, 1640; became a practising physician; freeman, 1669; 1680-83, Assistant and Counsellor; joined Bradstreet and others when they assumed the government on Andros's overthrow; was named as Counsellor in the new charter; 1690, commanded in the French and Indian Expedition; 3 Oct., 1692, was made Judge of Probate for Essex County; same year was made Judge of Court of Com. Pleas for the same County. He was constantly engaged in civil and military life until his death, 28 Feb., 169⅘. He married Hannah Clark, and had Jonathan, Bartholomew, Hannah, Lydia, Bethia, Deborah, Samuel, Deborah and Martha (twins), Priscilla, and Ann. He was one of the seven "witch" judges. [Savage's *Gen. Dict.* ii: 240; Washburn's *Judicial Hist. Mass.* 141, 147.]

[200] "16 Aug., 1696, Col. Gedney marches with 460 of his regiment for

ing for the defence of thofe Places; who gave them a
good Commend for their ready & willing Services done, in
Scouting, and the like Lying at *Pifcataqua* with the reft
of our Forces near a Week, waiting for more Forces who
was to joyn them to make up their complement;[201] in all
which time heard never a word of the Man of War. On
the 22d of *Auguft* they all imbark'd from *Pifcataqua*, and
when they came againft *York*, the Major went a fhore,
fending Capt. *Gorham* with fome Forces in the two Briganteens and a Sloop to *Winter Harbour*, ordering him to
fend out Scouts to fee if they could make any difcovery of
the Enemy, and to wait there till he came to them: Maj.
Church coming to *York*, Col. *Gidney* told him his opinion
was, That the Enemy was drawn off from thofe parts, for
that the Scouts could not difcover any of them, nor their
Tracks. So having done his bufinefs there, went with
what Forces he had there to *Winter Harbour*, where he
had the fame account from Capt. *Gorham*, That they had
not difcovered any of the Enemy, nor any new Tracks:
So concluding they were gone from thofe Parts towards
Penobfcot; the Major ordered all the Veffels to come to
Sail and make the beft of their way to *Monhegin*,[202] which
being not far from *Penobfcot*,[203] where the main body of

Kittery. He is accompanied by a troop under Capt. John Turner." [Felt's *Annals of Salem*, ii: 509.]

[201] The "complement" was 500 men. [Hutchinfon's *Hift. Mafs.* ii: 91.]

[202] *Monhegan* (*Monchiggon, Monhiggon, Morattigon*) lies 9 miles S. of George's Iflands, 5 leagues E. S. E. of Townfend, and 3 leagues W. of *Metinic*, on the coaft of Maine; and contains more than 1000 acres of good land, with a bold fhore. [Williamfon's *Hift. Me.* i: 61.]

[203] It is perhaps 14 miles S. E. from

our Enemies living was; being in great hopes to come up with the Army of *French* & *Indians*, before they had scattered and were gone past *Penobscot* or Mount-*Desart*, which is the chief place of their [89] departure from each other after such actions; and having a fair wind made the best of our way, and early next Morning they got into *Monhegin*, and there lay all day fitting their Boats, and other necessaries to imbark in the Night at *Mussel neck*[204] with their Boats; lying there all Day to keep undiscovered from the Enemy; at Night the Major ordered the Vessels all to come to Sail and carry the Forces over the Bay near *Penobscot*; but having little Wind,[205] he ordered all the Souldiers to imbark on board the Boats with eight days Provision, and sent the Vessels back to *Monhegin*, that they might not be discovered by the Enemy; giving them orders when and where they should come to him. The Forces being all ready in their Boats, rowing very hard, got a-shore at a Point near *Penobscot*[206] just as the day broke, and hid their Boats, and keeping a good look-out by Sea, and sent Scouts out by Land; but could not discover neither Canoo's nor *Indians*; what Tracks and fire places they saw were judg'd to be 7 or 8 days before they

---

Pemaquid, and 25 miles S. W. of the entrance of *Penobscot* bay.

[204] I am not clear whether the reference here is to a point of that name on *Monhegan*, or to the *Mussel Ridges*, which is a cluster of about a dozen islands, not far off.

[205] The boats, of course, were with the ships; and so, finding that the wind was too light to make progress by sails, he put his men into the boats, and sent the ships back.

[206] At *Owl's Head*, in the N. E. corner of Thomaston. [Sewall's *Anc. Dom. of Me.* 215; Eaton's *Hist. Thomaston, Rockland, and So. Thom.* i: 29.]

came: As soon as Night came that they might go undiscovered got into their Boats and went by *Muffel-neck*, and so amongst *Penobscot* Islands,[207] looking very sharp as they went for fires on the shore, and for Canoo's, but found neither; getting up to *Mathebestucks* hills,[208] day coming on, landed, and hid their Boats; looking out for the Enemy, as the day before, but to little purpose. Night coming on, to their Oars again, working very hard, turn'd the Night into Day; made several of their new Souldiers grumble: but telling them they hoped to come up quickly with the Enemy put new life into them; and by day-light they got into the Mouth of the River, where landing, found many Randezvous and fire Places where the *Indians* had been; but at the same space of time, as before mentioned. And no Canoo's passed up the River that day. Their Pilot *Joseph York*[209] inform'd the Major that 50 or 60 Miles up that River at the great Falls, the Enemy had a great Randezvous,[210] and planted a great quantity of

---

[207] A large cluster of islands lie off in the mouth of Penobscot bay. Among them are Long, Seven Hundred Acre, Billy Job's, Marshall's, Laffell's, Mark, Saddle, Lime, Ensign, two Mouse, Spruce, and Fox islands, with some unnamed.

[208] These are Camden heights — as the crow flies, about 10 miles N. W. from Owl's Head, in the town of Camden. They are five or six in number, the highest being some 1500 feet above the sea level. They can be seen 20 leagues at sea. [See Williamson's *Hist. Me.* i : 95.]

[209] Williamson [*Hist. Me.* i : 645] calls this pilot *John* York, but gives no authority for differing from Church. A family of Yorks was among the earliest settlers of these regions, who were probably descendants of Richard, who lived in Dover, N.H., 1648. John York was one of the trustees of No. Yarmouth, 1685; and *James*, Thomas, and Samuel purchased land of the Indians, in July, 1670, on the east side of the Androscoggin. [Willis's *Hist. Portland*, 302; Sullivan's *Hist. Me.* 146.]

[210] Supposed to be the present *Oldtown*, 12 miles above Bangor.

Corn, when he was a Prifoner with them, four Years a goe, and that he was very well acquainted there; this gave great incouragement to have had fome confiderable advantage of the Enemy at that Place; fo ufing their utmoft endeavours to get up there undifcovered: and coming there found no Enemy nor Corn Planted, they having deferted the Place. And ranging about the Falls on both fides of the River, leaving Men on the Eaft fide of the faid River, and the Boats juft below the Falls,[211] with a good guard to fecure them, and to take the Enemy if they came down the River in their Canoo's: The weft fide being the Place where the Enemy lived and beft to travel on, they refolved to range as privately as they could, a Mile or two above the Falls, difcovered a birch Canoo coming down with two *Indians* in it, the Major fent word immediately back to thofe at the Falls to lye very clofe, and let them pafs down the Falls, and to take them alive, that he might have Intelligence where the Enemy was (which would have been a great advantage to them:) but a foolifh [90] Souldier feeing them paffing by him, fhot at them, contrary to orders given, which prevented them going into the Ambafcado that was laid for them; whereupon feveral more of our Men being near, fhot at them; fo that one of them could not ftand when he got a-fhore, but crept away into the brufh, the other ftep'd out of the Canoo with his Paddle in his hand, and ran about a rod, and then threw

---

[211] Williamfon fays they left their boats at the "Bend," in what is now Eddington. [*Hift. Me.* i: 645.]

down his Paddle and turn'd back & took up his Gun, and
so escaped: One of our *Indians* swom over the River and
fetch'd the Canoo, wherein was a considerable quantity of
bloud on the Seats, that the *Indians* sat on; the Canoo
having several holes shot in her: They stopt the holes, and
then Capt. *Brackit*[212] with an *Indian* Souldier went over
the River, who Track'd them by the bloud about half a
Mile, found his Gun, took it up, and seeing the bloud no
further, concluded that he stopt his bloud, and so got away.
In the mean time another Canoo with three Men were
coming down the River were fired at by some of our
Forces, ran a-shore and left two of their Guns in the Canoo, which were taken, and also a Letter from a Priest to
Casteen,[213] that gave him an account of the *French* and
Indians returning over the Lake[214] to *Mount-Royal*,[215] and
of their little Service done upon the *Maquas Indians* westward, only demolishing one Fort and cutting down some
Corn, &c.[216] He desiring to hear of the proceedings of

---

[212] See note 120, *ante*.

[213] See note 34, *ante*.

[214] The *Oneida* or *Onondaga* lake. [1 *New York Hist. Coll.* iv: 121.]

[215] *Montreal*. "Ils admirèrent la beauté des alentours, comme aussi le cours majestueux & la largeur du grand fleuve, qu'ils suivaient des yeux au-tant que leur vue pouvait s'etendre; enfin l'imp tuosit du saut où leurs barques étaient restées; ce qui fut cause que Cartier, charmé des' points de vue qu'il découvrait de là, nomma cette montagne le *Mont-Royal*, d'où est venu le nom de *Montreal* donné a l'île où cette petite montagne est assise." [*Histoire de la Col. Française en Canada*, i: 24.]

[216] The *Maquas* (*Mingos*) were the *Five Nations* of the English, and the *Iroquois* of the French. The expedi-tion to which reference is here made was that of *Frontenac*, who added to all his own French regulars as many Indians as he could collect, and left *Lachine*, 7 July, 1696, with light *batteaux* for river portage, &c., with a powerful force to attack the Five Nations. After 12 days'

Deborahuel,²¹⁷ and the French Man of War; and informed him that there were several Canoo's coming with workmen from *Quabeck*, to Saint *John*'s,²¹⁸ where since we concluded it was to build a Fort at the Rivers Mouth, where the great Guns were taken, *&c*. It being just Night, the Officers were call'd together to advise, & their Pilot *York*

march, they arrived at *Cadaracqui*, and scattered the *Onondagas*, but only captured a little corn and a Sachem 100 years old, whom they tortured in a way which extorted from Charlevoix the remark, that "never was a man treated with more cruelty, nor ever did any man bear torture with greater firmness and magnanimity." Frontenac marched back, with no further results for this expensive campaign than the treacherous capture of 35 confiding *Oneidas*, who were taken by the Chevalier *Vaudrueil*. [1 *New-York Hist. Coll.* ii: 44; iv: 121; Bancroft's *Hist. U. S.* iii: 190; Hildreth's *Hist. U. S.* ii: 193; Dunlap's *Hist. New York*, i: 227; Colden's *Hist. Five Ind. Nations*, 188–194.]

²¹⁷ This is a curious illustration of the ease with which names are changed by passing from one language into another. Between Col. Church's way of pronouncing the name of this French admiral, and his son Thomas's way of writing it, the very respectable *D'Iberville* was metamorphosed into the abnormal, if not neutral, certainly peculiar, "*Deborahuel*."

Lemoine D'Iberville was born in Montreal, 1642; was one of seven brothers active in Canadian affairs; went early to sea; distinguished himself for bravery and ability; commanded the expedition which recovered Fort Nelson to the French, 1686; successfully invaded Newfoundland, and gained victories in Hudson's Bay, 1697; was reputed to be the most skilful naval officer in the French service; was commissioned to explore the mouth of the Mississippi, and sailed from *Rochefort* for that purpose, 17 Oct., 1698; entered the river, 2 March, 1670; returned to France, but was again ordered to the river; captured Nevis, 1706; died at Havana, on board his ship, on the eve of an expedition against Jamaica, 9 July, 1706. Hutchinson is wrong in his note, "This was not the *Iberville* who laid the foundation of the French colony at Mississippi in 1690. He died in a year or two after that." The colony was founded in 1699, and D'Iberville lived seven years after that date. He was invading Newfoundland the next year after this expedition of Church, and there is no reason to doubt that he was the admiral in command of the French ships which captured and razed *Pemaquid*. [Hutchinson's *Hist. Mass.* ii: 88; *New Amer. Cyc.* ix: 430.]

²¹⁸ *Saint John* still stands — as the principal city and seaport of New Brunswick — on a rocky peninsula on the left bank of the picturesque river of the name.

[91]

inform'd them of a Fort up that River, & that it was built on a little Ifland in that River;[219] and that there was no getting to it but in Canoo's, or on the Ice in the Winter time: This with the certain knowledge that we were difcovered by the Enemy that efcaped out of the upper Canoo, concluded it not proper at that time to proceed any further up, and that there was no getting any further with our Boats; and the Enemy being Alarm'd would certainly fly from them (and to do as they did four Years ago at their Fort at *Taconock*, having fought them in *Kanebeck* River, and purfued them about 30 Miles to *Taconock*;[220] for they then fet their Fort on fire, and run away by the Light of it, ours not being able to come up with them at that Place.) Maj. *Church* then incouraging his Souldiers, told them, he hop'd they fhould meet with part of the Enemy, in *Penobfcot* bay, or at Mount-*Defart*, where the French Ships were. So notwithftanding they had been rowing feveral Nights before, with much toyl, befides were fhort of Provifions, they chearfully embark'd on board their Boats, and went down the River, both with and againft the Tide: and next Morning came to their Veffels, where the Major had ordered them to meet him, who could give him no intelligence of any Enemy. Where being come they refrefh'd themfelves; Meeting then with another difappointment, for their Pilot *York* [91] not being acquainted any further,

[219] See note 210, *ante*.   [220] See note 185, *ante*.

they began to lament the lofs of one *Robert Cawley*,[221] who they chiefly depended on for all the Service to be done now Eaftward: he having been taken away from them the Night before they fat Sail from *Bofton* (and was on board Mr. *Thorps*[222] Sloop) and put on board the Man of War, unknown to Maj *Church*; notwithftanding he had been at the charge and trouble of procuring him. Then the Major was oblig'd to one *Bord*,[223] procured by Mr. *William Alden*,[224] who being acquainted in thofe parts, to leave his Veffel and go with him in the Boats, which he readily complyed with, and fo went to *Nasket* point;[225] where being inform'd was a likely place to meet with the Enemy; coming there found feveral Houfing and fmall Fields of Corn, the fires having been out feveral days, and no

---

[221] *Robert Cawley* (*Caule*, *Caulie*), of *Pemaquid*, took the oath of fidelity to Maffachufetts, at the Court, 7 Oct., 1674; and was undoubtedly the perfon here referred to. He may have been a fon of Thomas, who was freeman, Cambridge, 1640; was "alowed to keepe victualing in his houfe for ftrang'rs" 14 May, 1645, and appears to have been at Marblehead, 1671. [*Mafs. Col. Rec.* ii: 98; v: 18; *N. E. Hift. and Gen. Reg.* iii: 187; Savage's *Gen. Dict.* i: 350.]

[222] There was a *Robert Thorpe* at York, 1660; and one of that name was admonifhed by the Court "not to adventure too many into any boate." [Savage's *Gen. Dict.* iv: 293; *Mafs. Col. Rec.* i: 249.]

[223] *Henry Boade* (*Bord*, *Bode*, *Boad*) fettled at Saco before 1636; was freeman at Wells, Me., 5 July, 1653; was Juftice there 1653; died 1657. This man of whom Church fpeaks, may have been his fon. [*N. E. Hift. and Gen. Reg.* iii: 193; Folfom's *Hift.* Saco, 119.]

[224] *Capt. John Alden* (see note 133, *ante*) had a fon William, born 10 Sept., 1669, who would now be 27 years old, and may have followed his father's feafaring trade, and been a member of this expedition, as "mafter of the Briganteen *Endeavour*." [Savage's *Gen. Dict.* i: 23.]

[225] *Nafkeag* point is the S. E. extremity of the prefent town of Sedgewick, Me.

new Tracks. But upon *Penobscot* Island [226] they found several *Indian* Houses, Corn & Turnips, tho' the Enemy still being all gone, as before mentioned. Then they divided and sent their Boats some one way and some another, thinking that if any straggling *Indians*, or *Casteen* himself should be there-about, they might find them, but it prov'd all in vain. Himself and several Boats went to Mount-*Desart*, to see if the French Ships were gone and whither any of the Enemy might be there, but to no purpose: The Ships being gone and the Enemy also. They being now got several Leagues to the Westward of their Vessels; and seeing that the way was clear for their Vessels to pass: And all their extream rowing and travelling by Land and Water, Night and Day to be all in vain. The Enemy having left those parts, as they judg'd about eight or ten days before. And then returning to their Vessels, the Commander calling all his Officers together, to consult and resolve what to do, concluding that the Enemy by some means or other had received some Intelligence of their being come out against them; and that they were in no necessity to come down to the Sea side as yet, Moose and Bever now being fat. They then agreed to go so far East, and imploy themselves, that the Enemy belonging to those parts might think they were gone home: having some discourse about going over to Saint *John*'s; but the

---

[226] Now called *Orphan* Island, containing some 5000 acres, and dividing the waters of the *Penobscot* into two branches. The island is taxed in Bucksport, and owned by descendants of an *orphan*, who inherited a part of the old Waldo patent. [Williamson's *Hist. Me.* i: 69.]

Masters of the Vessels said, he had as good carry them to old *France, &c.* which put off that design, they concluding that the French Ships were there. Then the Major mov'd for going over the Bay towards *Lahane*,[227] and toward the Gut of *Cancer*,[228] where was another considerable Fort of *Indians*, who often came to the assistance of our Enemy, the barbarous *Indians*; saying that by the time they should return again, the Enemy belonging to these parts would be come down again, expecting that we are gone home. But in short, could not prevail with the Masters of the open Sloops to venture a-cross the Bay; who said it was very dangerous so late in the Year, and as much as their Lives were worth, *&c.* Then they concluded and resolved to go to *Senactaca*,[229] wherein there was a ready compliance (but the want of their Pilot *Robert Cawley* was a great damage to them, who knew all those parts:) how-

---

[227] Misprint for *La Have*, a harbor of Nova Scotia on its S. E. coast, at the mouth of the Have, some 50 miles S. W. from Halifax. [Haliburton's *Hist. Nov. Scot.* i: 141.]

[228] The gut of *Canseau* is the narrow channel between Nova Scotia and Cape Breton, from the Atlantic into Northumberland Strait; averaging scarcely more than 2 miles in width, to a length of 17 miles. Almost the whole length of Nova Scotia lies between it and St. John, — making it at least four and a half degrees farther E. than that town. The saying above, of the masters, that "he had as good carry them to old *France*, &c.," must refer to their notion that St John was as full of enemies as "Old France," and not to the ocean distance; as is shown here by their reluctance even to cross the Bay.

[229] *Chiegnecto* Bay (*Beau Basin*) is an inlet between Nova Scotia and New Brunswick, being the tapering northern extremity of the Bay of Fundy. This is two degrees farther E. than St. John's, and a little farther north. The fort, or settlement, of *Beau Basin*, which Church was proceeding to attack, was situated at the extreme N. E. terminus of the bay, and just N. of the entrance of the river *La Planche*, on nearly the same spot where Fort Lawrence afterward stood.

[92] ever Mr. *John Alden* Mafter of the Briganteen Endeavour Pilotted them up the Bay to *Senaɛ́taca*; and coming to *Grinſton*-point,[230] being not far from *Senaɛ́taca*; then came too with all the Veſſels; and early next Morning came to Sail, and about Sun-riſe got into Town; but it being ſo late before we landed, that the Enemy moſt of them made their eſcape, (and as it happen'd landed where the *French & Indians* had ſome time before killed Lieut. *John Paine*,[231] and ſeveral of Capt. *Smithſons*[232] Men, that

[230] I know not how to explain this, except it refers to *Iſle des Meules* (Iſle of Grindſtones, or Millſtones), which is laid down on Charlevoix's Map of *Acadia*, a few miles N. W. of *Beau Baſin*, and juſt out of ſight from it round *Cape des Maringouins* (Moſquito Point).

[231] I find no ſatisfactory account of this *John Paine*. Mr. Drake [ed. of *Church* (1843), 228; ed. of *Hubbard*, ii: 212] intimates that this may have been the John Pain who had trouble with the government in 1669, in the matter of Thomas Dickinſon's murder at *Pennacook* in the previous ſummer, by an Indian beſide himſelf with rum, which Pain had furniſhed to him and others. But the records are perfectly explicit on the point that that man's name was "*Thomas* Payne, late trader among the Indians at *Pennicooke* upon *Merrimack* river." This Lieut. John may have been his ſon. [*Maſs. Col. Rec.* iv: Part II. 428; Bouton's *Hiſt. Concord, N.H.* 35.]

[232] I am equally unfortunate with regard to *Capt. Smithſon*. The name is a very uncommon one in early New-England annals. It does not appear in Savage's omnivorous pages; nor in the crowded indexes of the 20 vols. of the *N. E. Hiſt. and Gen. Regiſter*, except as the name of a paſſenger to Virginia in 1635; nor in thoſe of the 43 vols. of the Collections and Proceedings of the Maſs. Hiſt. Society; nor in that of Drake's *Founders of New England*; nor in the liſt of freemen of Maſs.; nor in the indexes of the *Maſs. Col. Records*; nor in the liſt of the freemen of Plymouth Colony, or the indexes of its records; nor in thoſe of the records of the Colonies of Rhode Iſland, Connecticut, and New Haven. Under theſe circumſtances I have little doubt that the name is a miſtake for another — what, I have no uſeful conjecture. Nor can I ſuggeſt in what ſkirmiſh theſe lives had been loſt, unleſs it were connected with Sir William Phips's Expedition in 1690, when he ſeems to have viſited *Beau Baſin*. [Haliburton's *Hiſt. Nov. Scot.* i: 77; Hutchinſon's *Hiſt. Maſs.* i: 352.]

was with said *Paine*) They seeing our Forces coming took the opportunity, fired several Guns, and so run all into the Woods, carryed all or most part of their goods with them. One *Jarman Bridgway*[233] came running towards our Forces with a Gun in one hand, and his Cartridg-box in the other, calling to our Forces to stop that he might speak with them; but Maj. *Church* thinking it was that they might have some advantage, ordered them to run on; when the said *Bridgway* saw they would not stop, turn'd and run, but the Major call'd unto him, and bid him stop, or he should be shot down; some of our Forces being near to the said *Bridgway*, said it was the General that call'd to him: he hearing that, stop'd and turn'd about, laying down his Gun, stood, till the Major came up to him, his desire was that the Commander would make haste with him to his house, lest the Salvages[234] should kill his Father and Mother, who were upward of fourscore Years of Age, and could not go. The Major ask'd the said *Bridgway* whither there was any *Indians* amongst them? and where they liv'd? he shak'd his head, and said, he durst not tell, for if he did they would take an opportunity and kill him and his: so all that could be got out of him was, that they were run into the Woods with

---

[233] "The English pursued, and soon met *Bourgeois* (Church calls him Bridg*man*) a principal inhabitant, coming to ask quarter for himself and family." [Hutchinson's *Hist. Mass.* ii : 92.] Haliburton calls him "one of the most respectable Acadians." [*Hist. Nov. Scot.* i : 77.]

[234] That is, Church's Indians, — among whom probably were still some of those faithful old *Saconets* who had followed him on so many war-paths.

the reft. Then orders were given to purfue the Enemy, and to kill what *Indians* they could find, and take the *French* alive, and give them quarter, if they ask'd it. Our Forces foon took three French Men, who upon examination faid, That the Indians were all run into the woods. The French firing feveral Guns at our Forces, and ours at them; but they being better acquainted with the woods than ours, got away. The Major took the above faid *Jarman Bridgway* for a Pilot, and with fome of his Forces went over a River,[235] to feveral of their houfes, but the People were gone and carryed their goods with them: In ranging the woods found feveral Indian-houfes, their fires being juft out, but no Indians. Spending that day in ranging to & fro, found confiderable of their goods, and but few People; at Night the Major writ a Letter, and fent out two French Prifoners, wherein was fignifyed, That if they would come in, they fhould have good quarters. The next day feveral come in, which did belong to that part of the Town where our Forces firft landed, who had encouragements given them by our Commander, That if they would affift him in taking thofe *Indians* which belong'd to thofe parts, they fhould have their goods return'd to them again, and their Eftates fhould not be damnify'd;[236] which they refufed. Then the Major and his [93] Forces purfued their defign and went further ranging their Coun-

[235] Probably the *Miffaquafh*; and the houfes were, moft likely, where was afterwards Fort Cumberland.

[236] "Damnified — to do damage to." — *Bailey*. "That the Commonwealth of learning be not *damnified*."— *Milton*.

try, found several more houses, but the People fled, and carried what they had away; but in a Crick [237] found a prize Bark that was brought in there by a French Privateer: in ranging the woods took some Prisoners, who upon examination gave our Commander an account that there was some *Indians* upon a Neck of Land towards *Menes*;[238] so a party of Men was sent into those woods, and in their ranging about the said Neck found some Plunder, and a considerable quantity of *Hurtleburies*, both green and dry, which were gathered by the *Indians*, and had like to have taken two *Indians*, who by the help of a birch Canoo got over the River [239] and made their escape. Also they found two Barrels of Powder, and near half a bushel of Bullets; the French denying it to be theirs, said they were the Salvages; but sure it might be a supply for our Enemies: Also they took from *Jarman Bridgway* several Barrels of Powder, with Bullets, Shot, Spears and Knives, and other supplies to relieve our Enemies; he owning that he had been a Trading with those *Indians* along *Cape Sable* Shore, with *Peter Assnow*, &c. in a Sloop our Forces took from him; and that there he met with the French Ships, and went along with them to St. *John*'s, and helped them to unload the said Ships and carryed up the River Provisions, Am-

---

[237] The mouth of *Tantamar* river, or the *Memramcook*?

[238] *Les Mines* was the name of the first bay running into the interior of Acadia, from the Bay of Fundy W. of Beau Basin; and the neck was that which terminated in Cape *Chiegnecto*, now known as Cumberland.

[239] *Riviere aux Pommes*: now Apple River?

munition, and other goods to *Vilboons* [240] Fort. The Major having ranged all Places as was thought proper, return'd back to the place where they firſt Landed, and finding ſeveral Priſoners come in, who were much troubled to ſee their Cattel, Sheep, Hogs & Dogs lying dead about their houſes, chop'd and hack'd with Hatches, (which was done without order from the Major [211]) however he told them, It was nothing to what our poor *Engliſh* in our Frontier Towns were forc'd to look upon, for Men, Women and Children were chop'd and hack'd ſo, and left half dead, with all their Scalps taken of, and that they and their *Indians* ſerved ours ſo; and our Salvages would be glad to ſerve them ſo too, if he would permit them; which cauſed them to be mighty ſubmiſſive, and beg'd the Major that he would not let the Salvages ſerve them ſo. Our *Indians* being ſome what ſenſible of the diſcourſe, deſired to have ſome of them to Roſt, and ſo make a dance; and dancing

---

[240] The *Chevalier Villebon* was ſent over from France to take the government of Nova Scotia, ſucceeding M. *Perot*. He made his fort at the mouth of the St. John the rallying point of French and Indians for their deſcents upon the Engliſh colonies. He participated with *D'Iberville* in the capture of *Pemaquid*, and was now back at his fort. Charlevoix makes the miſtake of confounding him with *Villeau* (ſee note 194, *ante*), and ſo repreſents him as having been captured and releaſed by the Engliſh. Haliburton copies the blunder, ſaying he " was captured with 23 others, and ſent to Boſton." [Charlevoix's *Hiſt. Nouv. France;* Haliburton's *Hiſt. Nov. Scot.* i: 77.]

[241] Charlevoix ſays that our ſoldiers plundered the Acadians until *Burgeois* produced a proclamation which had been given by Sir Wm. Phips, aſſuring them of protection ſo long as they remained faithful to King William; and that Church, being made acquainted with it, reſpected it, and ordered his ſoldiers to do the ſame, who however, he adds, ſtill "conducted themſelves as if they had been in a conquered country." [*Hiſt. Nouv. France.*]

in a hideous manner to terrify them, said, That they could eat any sort of flesh, and that some of theirs would make their hearts strong: stepping up to some of the Prisoners, said, They must have their Scalps, which much terrifyed the poor Prisoners, who beg'd for their lives. The Major told them he did not design the Salvages should hurt them; but it was to let them see a little what the poor *English* felt, saying, it was not their Scalps he wanted, but the Salvages, for that he should get nothing by them; and told them, That their Fathers the Fryers [242] and Governours incouraged their Salvages, and gave them Money to Scalp our *English*, notwithstanding they were with them; which several of our *English* there present did testify to their Faces, that their Fathers and Mothers were [94] served so in their sight. But the Major bid them tell their Fathers the Fryers and the Governours, That if they still persisted and let their wretched Salvages kill & destroy the poor *English* at that rate, he would come with some hundreds of Salvages, and let them loose among them, who would Kill, Scalp and carry away every French person in all those parts, for they were the root from whence all the branches came that hurt us; for the *Indians* could not do us any harm, if they did not relieve and supply them. The *French* being sensible of the Majors kindness to them, kifs'd his hand, & was very thankful to him for his favour to them in saving their lives; owned that their Priests was at the taking of *Pemaquid* Fort, and were now gone to

[242] The Acadians were bigoted Romanists.

Layhone²¹³ with some of the *Indians*, to meet the French Ships, but for what they would not tell. The Commander with his Forces having done all the Service they could in those parts, concluded to go to St. *John*'s River²¹⁴ to do further Service for their King and Country, Embark'd all on board their Transports,²¹⁵ and having a fair wind soon got to *Monogeneft*,²¹⁶ which lyes a little distance from the Mouth of St. *John*'s River. Next Morning early the Major with his Forces landed to see what discovery they could make, Travel'd a cross the woods, to the old Fort or Falls at the Mouth of St. *John*'s River, keeping themselves undiscovered from the Enemy; finding that there were several Men at work, and having inform'd themselves as much as they could, (the Enemy being on the other side of the River, could not come at them) Returned back, but Night coming on and dark wet Weather, with bad Travelling, was oblig'd to stop in the woods till towards day next Morning, and then went on board; soon after the Major ordered all the Vessels to come to Sail, and go into the Mouth of the River; being done, it was not long before the Major and his Forces landed on the

---

²¹³ *La Have* (see note 227, *ante*.)

²¹⁴ The scruples of those who thought "he had as good carry them to old France" as to St. John, when they were at *Penobscot*, were probably removed by finding that they would now be going near 150 miles toward home by repairing thither. It seems to have made a great difference in the valor of some of the party, whether they were heading E. or W.

²¹⁵ Hutchinson says they left *Beau Basin*, 20 Sept., 1696. [*Hift. Mafs.* ii : 94.]

²¹⁶ *Ifle de Menagoniche* (given on Haliburton's Map as *Meogenes*) lies off the shore, a little W. of the entrance of the river St. John, and of the site of an old fort. The new fort, which *Villebou* was building, was on the other (E.) side of the river, just above the *Ifle aux Perdraux* (now Partridge I.)

East side of the River, the *French* firing briskly at them, but did them no harm; and running fiercely upon the Enemy, they soon fled into the Woods. The Major ordered a brisk party to run a cross a Neck [247] to cut them off from their Canoo's, which the day before they had made a discovery of; so the Commander with the rest ran directly towards the New Fort they were a building, not knowing but they had some Ordnance mounted. The Enemy running directly to their Canoo's was met by our Forces, who fired at them and kill'd one and wounded Corporal *Canton*,[248] who was taken, the rest threw down what they had and ran into the woods; the said Prisoner *Canton* being brought to the Major, told him, if he would let his Surgeon dress his wound and cure him, he would be Serviceable to him as long as he liv'd: so being dress'd, he was Examin'd: who gave the Major an account of the Twelve great Guns which were hid in the beach below high water Mark (the Carriges, Shot and Wheelbarrows, some Flower & Pork, all hid in the Woods:) And the next Morning the Officers being all ordered to meet together, to consult about going up the River to *Vilboons* Fort,[249]

[247] The neck, apparently, between the St. John and the *Riviere de Cauibechis* (Haliburton gives it *Kennebeckasis*), the first Eastern confluent of the former above its mouth.

[248] It would be a hopeless task to conjecture what French name lies *perdu* under this cognomen.

[249] The fort which was the headquarters of *Villebon* was up the St. John at the *Gemsec*. Haliburton gives the following paper, which describes minutely its condition in 1670; and which may be worth the space it will occupy as hinting the fashion of these Indian forts, and their fittings in the earlier days:

"INVENTORY. — 1. At the entering in of said Fort, on the left hand we found a court of guard about 15 paces long, and 10 broad, having, upon the right

and none amongſt them being acquainted [95] but the *Aldens*, who ſaid the Water in the River was very low; ſo that they could not get up to the Fort, and the Priſoner *Canton* told the Commander, That what the *Aldens* ſaid was true. So not being willing to make a *Canada* Expedition,[230] concluded it was not practicable to proceed. Then ordered ſome of the Forces to get the great Guns on board the open Sloops, and the reſt to rang the woods for the Enemy, who took one Priſoner, and brought in; who in their ranging found there a Shallop haul'd into a Crick, and a day or two after there came in a Young Souldier to our Forces, who upon examination gave an account of

hand a houſe of the like length and breadth, built with hewn ſtone and covered with ſhingles, and above them there is a chapel of about 6 paces long and 4 paces broad; covered with ſhingles and built with terras, upon which there is a ſmall turret, wherein there is a little bell, weighing about 18 lbs.

"2. Upon the left hand as we entered into the Court, there is a magazine, having 2 ſtories built with ſtone, and covered with ſhingles, being in length about 36 paces long, and 10 in breadth; which magazine is very old and wanted much repair; under which is a little cellar, in which there is a well; and upon the other ſide of ſaid court, being on the right hand, there is a houſe of the ſame length and breadth the magazine is, being half covered with ſhingles, and the reſt uncovered and wanting much repair; upon the ramparts of the ſaid fort are 12 iron guns, weighing in all 21,122 lbs.

"3. We do find in the ſaid fort 6 murtherers, without Chambers, weighing 1200 lbs.

"4. 200 iron bullets, from 3 to 8 lbs.

"5. About 30 or 40 paces from the ſaid fort, there is a ſmall outhouſe, being about 20 paces in length, and 8 in breadth; built with planks and half covered with ſhingles, which do not ſerve for any uſe but to houſe cattle.

"6. About 50 paces from ſaid outhouſe there is a ſquare garden, encloſed with rails, in which garden there are 50 or 60 trees bearing fruit.

"Signed,
    LE CHEVALIER DE GRAND FONTAINE.
    JEAN MAILLARD.
    RICHARD WALKER.
    ISAAC GARNER.
    MARSHALL, Sec'y."

[Haliburton's *Hiſt. Nov. Scot.* i: 66.]

[230] Sir William Phips's attack upon Canada had ingloriouſly failed in 1690, partly becauſe of the lateneſs of the ſeaſon at which it was undertaken, and

[95]

two more which he left in the woods at some distance; so immediately the Major with some of his Forces went in pursuit of them, taking the said Prisoner with them, who convey'd them to the place where he left them, but they were gone. Then ask'd the Prisoner, Whither there were any *Indians* in those parts? Said, No, it was as hard for *Vilboon* their Governour to get an *Indian* down to the water side, as it was for him to carry one of those great Guns upon his back to his Fort: for they having had Intelligence by a Prisoner out of *Boston* Goal,[251] that gave them an account of Maj. *Church* and his Forces coming out against them. Now having with a great deal of pains and trouble got all the Guns, Shot and other Stores aboard, intended on our design which we came out first for, but the Wind not serving, the Commander sent out his Scouts into the woods to seek for the Enemy, and four of our *Indians* come upon three *French* Men undiscovered, who concluded that if the *French* should discover them would fire at them and might kill one or more of them, which to prevent fired at the *French*, kill'd one and took the other two Prisoners; and it happen'd that he who was kill'd was *Shanelere*,[252] the Chief Man there *&c*. The same Day they mended their Whale-boats, and the Shallop which they took, fitting her to Row with Eight Oars, that she might be helpful to their Prosecuting their intended design against the Enemy in their returning homewards. Then the

partly because of its inherent weakness. [Hutchinson's *Hist. Mass.* i: 352-6.]

[251] There was hardly time for this to be one of *Villeau's* men (see note 195, *ante*).

[252] See note 248, *ante*.

Commander ordering all the Officers to come together, Inform'd them of his intentions and ordered that no Veſſels ſhould depart from the Fleet, but to attend the Motions of their Commadore, as formerly, except they were parted by Storms or thick Fogs, and if ſo it ſhould happen that any did part, when they come to *Paſſamequady*,[253] ſhould ſtop there a while, for there they intended to ſtop, and do buſineſs with the help of their Boats againſt the Enemy, and if they miſt that to ſtop at *Machias*;[254] which was the next place he intended to ſtop at, having an account by the Priſoners taken, That Mr. *Lateril*[255] was there a trading with the *Indians* in that River: Incouraging them, ſaid, He did not doubt but to have a good booty there; and if they ſhould paſs thoſe two places, be ſure not to go paſt *Naskege*-point,[256] but to ſtop there, till he came, and not to depart thence in a Fortnight without his orders, having great Service to do in and about *Penobſcot*, &c. Then the Major diſcourſed with Capt. *Brackit*,[257] Capt. *Hunewell*[258] and Capt. *Larking*,[259] [96] (with their Lieutenants) Commanders of the Forces belonging to the Eaſtward parts, who were to diſcourſe their Souldiers about their proceeding, when they came to *Penobſcot*; and the Major himſelf

---

[253] The bay into which empties the St. Croix, the boundary between the United States and the Britiſh Provinces.

[254] The next port weſtward.

[255] Probably the Frenchman who is twice referred to ſubſequently (on p. 109 of the original paging) as "old *Lotriel*," and as being captured in the fifth expedition, with his family, ſome of whom were reported to be drowned.

[256] See note 225, *ante*.

[257] See note 120, *ante*.

[258] See note 157, *ante*.

[259] There was a Samuel Larkin among the early inhabitants of Portſmouth, N.H.

was to difcourfe his *Indian*-Souldiers, and their Captains; who with all the reft readily comply'd. The projection being fuch, That when they came to *Penobfcot* the Commander defign'd to take what Provifions could be fpared out of all the Sloops, and put on board the two Briganteens,[260] and to fend all the Sloops home with fome of the Officers and Men that wanted to be at home: and then with thofe Forces afore-mentioned (*to wit*) the Eaftward Men, and all the *Indians*; and to take what Provifions and Ammunition was needful, and to March with himfelf up into the *Penobfcot* Country, in fearch for the Enemy, and if poffible to take that Fort in *Penobfcot* River. Capt. *Brackit* informing the Major, That when the water was low they could waid over (which was at that time) the loweft that had been known in a long time. And being there to rang thro' that Country down to *Pemequid*, where he intended the two Briganteens fhould meet them; and from thence taking more Provifions (*viz.*) Bread, Salt & Ammunition fuitable (to fend thofe two Veffels home alfo) to travel thro' the Country to *Nerigiwock*,[261] and from thence to *Ameras cogen*-Fort, and fo down where the Enemy us'd to Plant, not doubting but that in all this Travel to meet with many of the Enemy before they fhould get to *Pifcataqua*. All which intentions were very acceptable to the

---

[260] "*Brigantine*, — a fmall, flat, open, light veffel, going both with fails and oars, either for fighting or for giving chafe." — *Bailey*.

[261] *Norridgewock* (*Narantfouat*) is a point in the bend of the *Kennebec* oppofite to the mouth of Sandy river, where was the ancient feat of the *Canibas* Indians. [Williamfon's *Hift. Me.* i: 467; *Father Druillettes's Journal*, 310.]

Forces that were to undertake it, who rejoycing, faid, They had rather go home by Land than by Water, provided their Commander went with them: (who to try their fidelity) faid, He was grown Ancient, and might fail them; They all faid they would not leave him, and when he could not Travel any further, they would carry him. Having done what Service they could at and about the Mouth of St. *John*'s River, Refolved on their intended defign; and the next Morning having but little Wind, came all to Sail, the Wind coming againft them they put into *Mufhquafh* Cove,²⁶² and the next day the Wind ftill being againft them, the Major with part of his Forces Landed, and imployed themfelves in ranging the Country for the Enemy, but to no purpofe; and in the Night the wind came pretty fair, and at 12 a Clock they came to Sail, and had not been out long before they fpy'd three Sail of Veffels; Expecting them to be *French*, fitted to defend themfelves, fo coming near, hail'd them: who found them to be a Man of War, the Province Galley, and old Mr. *Alden* ²⁶³ in a Sloop, with more Forces, Col. *Hathrone* ²⁶⁴ Commander. Maj. *Church* went aboard the

---

²⁶² The outlet of *Riviere de Mechecafcor*, the fecond ftream coming into the bay W. of the St. John; which Haliburton's map names Mufquafh river, — which would feem to be a tranflation of found rather than of fenfe.

²⁶³ See note 133, *ante*.

²⁶⁴ *John Hathorne* (*Hathorn, Hawthorne*) was fon of William, of Salem; born 4 Aug., 1641; freeman, 1677; Deputy, 1683; Affiftant or Counfellor, 1684-1712; Judge of Com. Pleas, 1692-1702; Judge of Supreme Court, 1702-15; Commiffioner to Eaftern Indians, and Commander, 1696; refigned his place on the bench on account of deafnefs, 1712; died 10 May, 1717, *æt.* 76. He had five fons. [Savage's *Gen. Dict.* ii: 377; Wafhburn's *Judic. Hift. Mafs.* 271.]

[97]

Commadore, where Col. *Hathrone* was, who gave him an account of his Commiffion & Orders, and read them to him. Then his Honour told Maj. *Church*, that there was a particular Order on board Capt. *Southack*[265] for him: which is as followeth. [97]

Sir,   Bofton, September. 9*th*. 1696.

H*Is Majefties Ship* Orford *having lately furprized a* French *Shallop with twenty three of the Soldiers belonging to the Fort upon* John's *River in* Nova-Scotia, *together with* Villeau *their Captain, Providence feems to encourage the forming of an Expedition to attack that Fort, and to difreft and remove the Enemy from that Poft, which is the chief Scource from whence the moft of our difafters do iffue, and alfo to favour with an opportunity for gaining out of their hands the Ordnance, Artillery and other Warlike Stores and Provifions lately fupplied to them from* France, *for erecting a new Fort near the Rivers mouth, whereby they will be greatly ftrengthened, and the reducing of them rendred more difficult. I have therefore ordered a Detachment of two new Companies confifting of about an Hundred Men*

---

[265] *Cyprian Southack* was commander of the Province galley; was with Church in his laft Eaftern Expedition, 1704; and went to Canada in 1714 on the Stoddard and Williams Expedition; lived on Tremont Street, which then embraced only that portion now included between School and Howard Streets; 19 Oct., 1733, was warned to secure "his hill near Valley acre, by rails, or otherwife, that people may not be in danger." Valley acre was the hill juft eaft of Beacon hill, occupying the fpace, nearly, of what is now Pemberton Square. Capt. Southack's hill probably adjoined his houfe, which feems to have ftood not far from the prefent fite of the *Albion*. [Drake's *Hift. Boft.* i: 529, 539, 593; *N. E. Hift. and Gen. Reg.* v: 39.]

to joyn the Forces now with you for that Expedition, and have commiſſionated Lieut. Colonel John Hathorne, one of the Members of His Majeſties Council, who is acquainted with that River, and in whoſe courage and conduct I repoſe ſpecial Truſt, to take the chief command of the whole during that Service, being well aſſured that your good affections and zeal for His Majeſties Service will induce your ready compliance and aſſiſtance therein, which I hope will take up no long time, and be of great benefit and advantage to theſe His Majeſties Territories if it pleaſe God to ſucceed the ſame. Beſides its very probable to be the fareſt opportunity that can be offered unto your ſelf and Men, of doing Execution upon the Indian Enemy and Rebels, who may reaſonably be expected to be drawn to the defence of that Fort. I have alſo ordered His Majeſties Ship Arundel, and the Province-Gally to attend this Service.

Colonel Hathorne will communicate unto you the contents of his Commiſſion and Inſtructions received from my ſelf for this Expedition, which I expect and order that your ſelf, Officers and Souldiers now under you yield obedience unto. He is to adviſe with your ſelf and others in all weighty attempts. Praying for a Bleſſing from Heaven upon the ſaid Enterprize, and that all engaged in the ſame may be under the ſpecial Protection of the Almighty. I am your Loving Friend, Wm. STOUGHTON.

The Major having read his laſt Orders, and conſidering his Commiſſion, found that he was oblig'd to attend, *All*

Orders, &c. was much concern'd that he and his were prevented in their intended projection, if carryed back to St. *John*'s. Then discoursing with Col. *Hathorne*, gave him an account of what they had done at St. *John*'s, *viz.* That as to the demolishing the New Fort they had done it, and got all their great Guns and Stores aboard their Vessels; and that if it had not been that the waters were so low would have taken the Fort up the River also before he came away. Told him also that one of the Prisoners which he had taken at St. *John*'s, upon examination concerning the *Indians* in those parts, told him, it was as hard for *Vilboon* their Governour to get one of their *Indians* down to the water side, as to carry one of those great Guns upon his back: and that they had an account of him and his Forces coming to those parts by a Prisoner out of *Boston* Goal. Also [98] told his Honour, That if they went back it would wholly disappoint them of their doing any further Service, which was that they came for to *Penobscot*, and Places Adjacent; but all was to no purpose, his Honour telling the Major that he must attend his Orders then received. And to incourage the Officers and Souldiers, told them, They should be wholly at the Majors Ordering & Command in the whole action: (and to be short did go back) and the event may be seen in Col. *Hathron*'s Journal of the said action.[266] Only I must ob-

---

[266] Church speaks as if Hathorn's Journal were public property; but I have not been able to find it. Mather sums up the issue thus: "But the Difficulty of the *Cold Season* so discouraged our Men, that after the making of some few Shot, the Enterprize found itself under too much *Congelation* to proceed any

ferve one thing by the way, which was, That when they drew off to come down the River again, Col. *Hathorne* came off and left the Major behind to fee that all the Forces were drawn off; and coming down the River in or near the Rear, in the Night heard a perfon hollow, not knowing at firft but that it might be a fnare to draw them into; but upon confideration fent to fee who or what he was, found him to be a Negro man belonging to *Marblehead*, that had been taken, and kept a Prifoner amongft them for fome time. The Major ask'd him, Whither he could give any account of the *Indians* in thofe parts? He faid, Yes, they were or had been all drawn off from the Sea Coaft up into the Woods near a hundred Miles having had an account by a Prifoner out of *Bofton* Goal; that Maj. *Church* and his Forces were coming out againft them

further." [*Magnalia*, Book VII: 90.] Hutchinfon fays, "*Villebon* had timely notice of the return and re-enforcement, and made the beft preparations he could for his defence. Four of the fmall veffels went up the river, and landed their men near the fort, October the 7th. They raifed a battery for two field pieces, and began to fire with them and with their mufketry the fame day; and the French made return. When night came on, which proved very cold, the Englifh lighted their fires to keep them from perifhing. This made them a mark for the French cannon, which difturbed them to that degree that they were obliged to put out their fires, and to be expofed all night to the inclemency of the weather. They were foon difcouraged, for the next night they re-embarked; and having joined thofe at the mouth of the river, made the beft of their way to Bofton. No notice was taken of any lofs on either fide, except the burning a few of the enemy's houfes; nor is any fufficient reafon given for relinquifhing the defign fo fuddenly.

It is probable that the forces were not provided with tents nor cloathing fufficient to defend them from the cold, which they had reafon to expect to increafe every day, and it is certain the old Colonel Church was offended at being fuperfeded in command." [*Hift. Mafs.* ii : 94.]

[98]

in four Briganteens, & four Sloops, with 24 Peraougers,[267] meaning Whale-boats, which put them into a fright, that notwithſtanding they were ſo far up in the Woods were afraid to make fires by Day left he and his Forces ſhould diſcover the Smokes, and in the Night left they ſhould ſee the light. One thing more I would juſt give a hint of, that is, How the *French* in the Eaſtward parts were much ſurpriz'd at the motion of the Whale boats; ſaid, There was no abiding for them in that Country: and I have been inform'd ſince, that ſoon after this Expedition, they drew off from St. *John*'s Fort & River But to return, Then going all down the River, Embark'd and went homeward; only by the way *Candid Reader*, I would let you know of two things that proved very prejudicial to Major *Church* and his Forces: The firſt was, That the Government ſhould miſs it ſo much as to ſend any Priſoner away from *Boſton* before the Expedition was over. Secondly, That they ſhould ſend Col. *Hathrone* to take them from the Service & buſineſs they went to do: Who with ſubmiſſion, doubtleſs thought they did for the beſt, tho' it prov'd to the contrary. So ſhall wind up with juſt a hint of what happen'd at their coming home to *Boſton*. After all their hard Service both Night & Day, the Government took away all the great Guns, and Warlike Stores, and gave them not a Peny for them, (except it was ſome Powder, and that they gave what they pleas'd for it) and beſide the Aſſembly paſt a Vote that they ſhould have but half

[267] *Pirogue*, boat of ſavages. — *Spiers and Sureune*.

pay. But his Honour the Lieut. Governour [268] being much disturb'd at their so doing went in to the Town-House where the Representatives were sitting, and told them except they did Re-assume that Vote, which was to cut Maj. *Church* [99] and his Forces off half their pay, they should sit there till the next Spring. Whereupon it was Re-assumed: So that they had just their bare Wages. But as yet never had any Allowance for the great Guns and Stores; neither has Maj *Church* had any Allowance for all his Travel and great Expences in Raising the said Forces Volunteers.

The Fifth and Last Expedition, *East*.

IN the Year 1703, 4. Major *Church* had an account of the miserable Devestations made on *Deerfield*,[269] a Town in the Westward parts of this Province, and the horrible Barbarities & Cruelties exercised on those poor Innocent People, (by the *French & Indians*) especially of their Cruelties towards that worthy Gentlewoman Mrs. *Williams*,[270] and several others, whom they March'd in that

---

[268] Lieut. Gov. William Stoughton. See note 191, *ante*.

[269] *Deerfield* was destroyed 29 Feb., 170¾; 38 were slain in the palisaded village and 9 in the meadow fight; and 112 were taken, of whom 2 soon escaped, 22 were slain or perished on their way to Canada, 28 remained in Canada, and 60 returned. A few of the captives and of the slain — 8 or 9 of each — belonged to other towns. [Judd's *Hist.* *Hadley*, 272.] Church probably had forgotten the exact sequence of events when dictating this, as his letter to Gov. Dudley is dated 5 Feb., 170¾ — 24 days before Deerfield fell.

[270] *Mrs. Eunice Williams* was daughter of Rev. Eleazer Mather of North-

extream Seafon; forcing them to carry great loads, and when any of them by their hard ufage could not bare with it, were knock'd on the head, and fo kill'd in cool Bloud. All which with fome other horrible Inftances done by thofe Barbarous Salvages, which Maj. *Church* himfelf was an eye witnefs to in his former Travels in the Eaftward parts, did much aftonifh him. To fee a Woman that thofe Barbarous Salvages had taken and kill'd, expofed in a moft bruitifh manner (as can be exprefs'd) with a Young Child feiz'd faft with ftrings to her breaft; which Infant had no apparent wound, which doubtlefs was left alive to fuck its dead Mothers Breaft, and fo miferably to perifh & dye. Alfo to fee other poor Children hanging upon Fences dead, of either Sex, in their own poor Rags, not worth their ftripping them of, in fcorn and derifion. Another Inftance was, of a ftraggling Souldier, who was found at *Cafco*, expos'd in a fhameful and barbarous manner; his body being ftaked up, his head cut off, and a hogs head fet in the room, his body rip'd up, and his heart and inwards taken out, and private Members cut off, and hung with belts of their own, the inwards at one fide of his body, and his private at the other, in fcorn & derifion of the *Englifh* Souldiers, *&c.* Thefe and fuch like Barbarities caufed Major *Church* to exprefs himfelf to this

ampton, and wife of Rev. John Williams of Deerfield (who was fon of Dea. Samuel, of Roxbury, who was eldeft fon of Robert); was married 21 July, 1687; taken captive, 29 Feb., 1703; was murdered on the road to Canada on the fecond day's march by her Indian captor. [Savage's *Gen. Dict.* iv: 563; Holland's *Hift. Weft. Mafs.* i: 153; Hoyt's *Antiq. Refearches*, 190.]

purpose, That if he were Commander in Chief of these Provinces, he would soon put an end to those barbarities done by the Barbarous Enemy, by making it his whole business to fight and destroy those Salvages, as they did our poor Neighbours; which doubtless might have been done if rightly managed, and that in a short time &c. So that these with the late Inhumanities done upon the Inhabitants of *Deerfield*, made such an Impression on his heart as cannot well be expressed; so that his Bloud boyl'd within him, making such Impulses on his Mind, that he forgot all former treatments, which were enough to hinder any Man especially the said Maj. *Church* from doing any further Service. Notwithstanding [100] all which, having a mind to take some Satisfaction on the Enemy, his heart being full. Took his Horse & went from his own Habitation near Seventy Miles,[271] to wait upon his Excellency, and offered his Service to the Queen, his Excellency & the Country; which his Excellency readily accepted of, and desired Maj. *Church* to draw a Scheme for the insuing action or actions; so taking leave, went home, and drew it: which is as followeth.

---

[271] Church was now in the last year of his residence at Fall River (then Tiverton). [Part I. xxxiii.] This is by the present direct route scarcely more than 51 miles from Boston; and the more circuitous roads then existing could hardly bring it up to 70. I think Col. Church, when dictating this paragraph, forgot that he had not, at the date here referred to, removed, as he did so soon after, back to Little Compton; or the Governor might have been absent from Boston fifteen or twenty miles northward, at that time, so as to have lengthened his journey by that much.

[100]

Tiverton, February 5. 1703, 4.

May it please your Excellency,

According to your request when I was last with your Self; and in obedience thereunto, I present you with these following lines, that concern the preparation for next Springs Expedition, to Attack the Enemy. According to my former Direction, for it is good to have a full stroke at them first, before they have opportunity to Run for it; for the first of our action will be our opportunity to destroy them, and to prevent their running away, in way-laying every passage; and make them know we are in good earnest, and so we being in a diligent use of means, we may hope for a blessing from the Almighty, and that He will be pleased to put a dread in their hearts, that they may fall before us and perish: For my advice is,

1st. That Ten or Twelve hundred good able Souldiers, well equip'd be in a readiness fit for action by the first of April *at the furthest*, for then will be time to be upon action.

2ly. That five & forty or fifty good Whale-boats be had ready, well fitted, with five good Oars, and 12 or 15 good Paddles to every Boat: And upon the Wail[272] of each Boat five pieces of strong Leather be fastened on each side to slip five small Ash bars thro', that so when ever they land the Men may step over-board, & slip in said bars a-cross, and take up said Boat, that she may not be hurt against the Rocks. And that two suitable Brass Kittles be provided to

---

[272] The *wale* is the plank that rims the outside of the boat, stiffening it, and giving strength to its curves. — *Totten.*

belong to each Boat, to dreſs the Mens Victuals in, to make their Lives comfortable.

3ly. That 4 or 500 pair of good Indian Shoes be made ready, fit for the Service, for the Engliſh & Indians, that muſt improve the Whale-boats, and Birch Canoo's, for they will be very proper, and ſafe for that Service; and let there be a good Store of Cow Hides, well Tann'd, for a ſupply of ſuch Shoes; and Hemp to make Thread, and Wax, to mend & make more of ſuch Shoes, when wanted, and a good ſtore of Awls.

4ly. That there be a 100 large Hatches[273] or light Axes made pretty broad, & ſteeled with the beſt Steel that can be got, and made by workmen, that may cut very well, and hold, that the Hemlock knots may not brake nor turn them; to widden the landing places up the Falls, for it may happen that we may get up with ſome of our Whale-boats to their Falls or Head-quarters.

5ly. That there be a ſuitable quantity of ſmall Bags, or Wollets provided, that every Man that wants may have one, to put up his Bullets in, of ſuch a ſize as will fit his Gun, (and not ſerved as at Caſco.[274]) That every Mans bag be ſo Marked that he may not change it: for if ſo, it will make a great confuſion in action; that every Mans ſtore of Ball be weighed to him, that ſo he may be accountable, & may not ſquander it away; and alſo his ſtore of Powder, that ſo he

---

[273] Our word "hatchet" comes from the diminutive of the French *hache*, a little axe. Very likely Church uſed the common Canadian name for what he wanted to deſcribe, ſo that this is not a miſprint for "hatchets," but the plural of the French.

[274] See p. 22, *ante*.

[101]

may try his Powder & Gun be [101] fore action. And that every particular Company may have a Barrel of Powder to themselves, and so marked that it by no means may be changed; that men may know before hand, and may not be cheated out of their Lives, by having bad Powder; Or not knowing how to use it: and this will prove a great advantage to the action.

6ly. That Col John Gorham, if he may be prevailed with may be concerned in the management of the Whale-boats, he having been formerly concerned in the Eastern Parts, and experienced in that affair. And Whale-men then will be very serviceable in this Expedition, which having a promise made to them, that they shall be released in good season to go home a Whaling in the Fall; your Excellency will have men enough.

7ly. That there may be raised for this Service 300 Indians at least, & more if they may be had; for I know certainly of my own knowledge, that they exceed most of our English in hunting & sculking in the woods, being always us'd to it; and it must be practised if ever we intend to destroy those Indian Enemies.

8ly. That the Souldiers already out Eastward in the Service; By men of known judgment may take a survey of them and their Arms; and see if their Arms be good, and that they know how to use them, in shootting right at a Mark; and that they be men of good Reason & Sence, to know how to manage themselves in so difficult a piece of Service, as this Indian hunting is; for bad men are but a clogg and hindrance to an Army, being a trouble and vexation to good Commanders, and so many Mouths to devour the Countries Provision, and a hindrance to all good action.

9ly. That special care be had in taking up the whale-boats, that they be good and fit for that Service; that so the Country be not cheated, as formerly, in having rotten-Boats; and as much care that the Owners may have good satisfaction for them.

10ly. That the Tenders or Transports, Vessels to be improved in this action be good Deck'd Vessels, not too big, because of going up several Rivers; having 4 or 6 small Guns a-piece for defence, and the fewer Men will defend them. And there is enough such Vessels to be had.

11ly. To conclude all, *If your Excellency will be pleased to make your Self Great and us a happy People*, as to the destroying of our Enemies, and easing of our Taxes, &c. be pleased to draw forth all those Forces now in Pay in all the Eastward Parts, both at Saco & Casco-Bay; for those two Trading-Houses never did any good, nor never will, and are not worthy the name of Queens Forts; and the first building of them, had no other Effect, but to lay us under Tribute to that wreached Pagan Crew; and I hope will never be wanted, for that they were first built for: but sure it is, they are very serviceable to them, for they get many a good advantage of us to destroy our Men, and laugh at us for our folly, that we should be at so much cost & trouble to do a thing that does us so much harm, and no manner of good: but to the contrary, when they see all our Forces drawn *forth, and in the pursuit of them, They will think that we begin to be rouzed up and to be awake, and will not be satisfied with what they have pleas'd to leave us, but are resolved to Retake from them, that they formerly took from us, and drive them out of their Country also. The which being done, then to build a Fort at a suitable time and in a convenient place; and it* [102] *will be very honourable to your Excellency & of great Service to Her Majesty, & to the enlargement of her Majesty's Government: (The Place meant being at* Port Royal.)

12ly. *That the objection made against drawing off the Forces in the* Eastward *Parts will be no damage to the inhabitants; for former Experience teacheth us, that so soon as drawn into their Country they will presently forsake ours to take care of their own: And that there be no failure in making preparation of these things afore-mentioned, for many times the want of small things, prevent the compleating of great Actions; and that every thing be in a readiness before the Forces be raised, to prevent Charges; and the Enemy having Intelligence: And that the General Court be moved to make suitable Acts, for the incouraging both* English *&* Indians; *that so men of business may freely offer Estates and Concerns to Serve the Publick.*

This hoping what I have taken the pains to Write in the sincerity of my heart and good affection, will be well accepted; I make bold to subscribe, as I am your Excellency's most Devoted and Humble Servant,

Benjamin Church.

Then returning to his Excellency prefented the faid Scheme, which his Excellency approv'd of; and return'd it again to Maj. *Church* and defired him to fee that every thing was provided telling him that he fhould have an Order from the Commiffary General to proceed. Then returned home and made it his whole bufinefs to provide Oars and Paddles and a Veffel to carry them round; and then return'd again to his Excellency, who gave him a Commiffion: which is as followeth.

JOSEPH DUDLEY Efq;[273] *Captain General and Governour in Chief in and over Her Majefty's Provinces of the* Maffachufetts-Bay *&* New-Hampfhire *in* New-England *in* America, *and Vice Admiral of the fame.*

To Benjamin Church *Efqr*; *Greeting.*

'BY Virtue of the Power & Authority in & by her
' M jefty's Royal Commiffion to me granted I do by
' thefe prefents, Repofing fpecial Truft and Confidence in
' your Loyalty, Courage and good Conduct, Conftitute and
' Appoint you to be Colonel of all the Forces raifed and to

---

[273] *Jofeph Dudley* was fon of Gov. Thomas, of Roxbury; freeman, 1672; Deputy, 1673-5; Artillery Company, 1677; Affiftant, 1676-85; went to England in 1682; Prefident of the Colonies of Mafs. and N. Hamp., 1686; was of Andros's Council, and Chief Juftice of the unconftitutional Supreme Court; was imprifoned here; went to England in 1689; was Deputy Governor of the Ifle of Wight eight years; came home 1702, as Governor of Mafs. Col., which place he filled until Nov. 1715; died 2 April, 1720. His wife was Rebecca, dau. of Edward Tyng; they had Thomas, Edward, Jofeph, Paul, Samuel, John, Rebecca, Catharine, Ann, William, Daniel, Catharine, and Mary. [Savage's *Gen. Dict.* ii: 76; *N. E. Hift. and Gen. Reg.* i: 71.]

[103]

'be raised for Her Majesty's Service against the *French* &
'*Indian* Enemy and Rebels, that shall be improved in the
'Service to the *Eastward* of *Casco-Bay;* And to be Cap-
'tain of the first Company of the said Forces. You are
'therefore carefully and diligently to perform the Duty of
'a Colonel and Captain, by Leading, Ordering & Exer-
'cising the said Regiment & Company in Arms, both In-
'feriour Officers & Souldiers; and to keep them in good
'Order and Discipline. Hereby commanding them to
'Obey you as their Colonel and Captain; And with them
'to do and Execute all acts of hostility against the said
'Enemy & Rebels. And you are to observe & follow
'such Orders and Directions as you shall receive from my
'Self or other your Superiour Officer, according to the
'Rules & Discipline of War, pursuant to the Trust reposed
'in you. Given under my Hand & Seal at Arms at *Boston*
'the 18*th* day of *March*. In the Third Year of Her Ma-
'jesty's Reign. *Anno Dom.* 1703, 4.

By his Excellency's Command, Isaac Addington *Secr.*

J. DUDLEY. [103]

Col. *Church* no sooner received his Commission, but
proceeded to the raising of Men Volunteers, by going into
every Town within the three Counties which was formerly
Plymouth Government;[276] advising with the Chief Officer

---

[276] When Plymouth Colony was merged in Massachusetts, in 1692, it comprised *Plymouth* County (including Plymouth, Duxbury, Scituate, Marshfield, Bridgewater, Middleborough, and Accord Pond plantation [Abington]); *Bristol* County (including Taunton, Rehoboth, Dartmouth, Swansea, Bristol, Little Compton, Freetown, and Pocasset [Tiverton]); and *Barnstable* County

of each Company, to call his Company together, that so he might have the better opportunity to discourse & incourage them to Serve their Queen and Country; treating them with Drink convenient; told them he did not doubt but with God's blessing to bring them all home again; all which, with many other arguments animated their hearts to do Service, so that Col. *Church* enlisted out of some Companies near 20 Men, & others 15. He having raised a sufficient number of *English* Souldiers, proceeded to the enlisting of *Indians* in all those parts where they dwelt, which was a great fategue & expence; being a People that need much treating, especially with Drink *&c.* Having enlisted the most of his Souldiers in those parts, who daily lay upon him; was not less than 5 *l. per* day expences, some days, in Victuals & Drink; who doubtless thought (especially the *English*) that the Country would have re-imburst it again, otherways they would hardly accepted it of him. Col. *Church's* Souldiers both *English* and *Indians* in those parts being raised, March'd them all down to *Nantasket*,[277] according to his Excellency's directions; where being came, the following Gentlemen were Commissionated to be Commanders of each particular Company, *viz* Lieut. Col. *Gorham*, Captains *John Brown*,[278]

(including Barnstable, Sandwich, Yarmouth, Eastham, Rochester, Falmouth, Mashpee, and Monamoy or Chatham). [Baylies's *Plym. Col.* Part IV: 97.]

[277] *Nantasket* was what is now Hull, accessible by land over the neck which unites it to Hingham and Cohasset, and favorably situated toward Boston harbor — of whose entrance its Point Allerton is one of the gateposts — for the embarkation of troops.

[278] *John Brown* was "approved as Captain of the town of Swansey, 4 June, 1686." [*Plym. Col. Rec.* vi: 189.]

Conſtant Church,²⁷⁹ *James Cole,*²⁸⁰ *John Dyer,*²⁸¹ *John Cook, Caleb Williamſon* ²⁸² and *Edward Church,*²⁸³ of the Forces raiſed by Col. *Church*, each Company being filled up with *Engliſh* & *Indians* as they agreed among themſelves, and by the Colonel's directions; Capt. *Lamb*,²⁸⁴ and Capt. *Miricks* ²⁸⁵ Company, who were raiſed by his Excellency's direction, were ordered to joyn thoſe aforeſaid under the Command of Col *Church*. Matters being brought thus far on, Col. *Church* waited upon his Excellency at *Boſton* to know his pleaſure, what further meaſures were to be taken; and did humbly move that they might have liberty in their Inſtructions to make an Attack upon *Port Royal*: ²⁸⁶ Being very well ſatisfyed in his opinion, that with the bleſſing of God, with what Forces they had or ſhould have; and Whale-boats ſo well fitted with Oars & Pad-

---

²⁷⁹ See references to his name in the Index of Part I.

²⁸⁰ *James Cole* was admitted freeman of Swanſea, 1682; Enſign, 1686: Lieutenant, 1689; Deputy, 1690. [*Plym. Col. Rec.* vi: 86, 189, 223, 240.]

²⁸¹ I cannot certainly identify this captain; nor *Cook*, next named.

²⁸² *Caleb Williamſon,* of Barnſtable, was perhaps ſon of Timothy of Marſhfield; married Mary Cobb; had Mary, William, Timothy, Sarah, Ebenezer, Mercy, and Martha. He removed to Hartford, Conn., where he died 24 Dec., 1738, æt. 87. [Savage's *Gen. Dict.* iv: 572.]

²⁸³ [See Part I. xliv.]

²⁸⁴ Col. *Joſhua Lamb,* ſon of Thomas of Roxbury, in 1713, one of the firſt proprietors of Leiceſter? [Barry's *Hiſt. Framingham,* 311; Waſhburn's *Hiſt. Leiceſter,* 9, 10.]

²⁸⁵ There was an *Iſaac Mirick,* ſon of James of Newbury, who was now, if alive, near 40 years old; having been born 6 Jan., 1665. [Coffin's *Hiſt. Newbury,* 310.] This captain's name further on is ſeen to have been Iſaac (p. 119, orig. paging.)

²⁸⁶ *Port Royal* was a fort upon the inlet of that name almoſt due ſouth from the outlet of the St. John, acroſs the Bay of Fundy, which is here ſome two leagues wide. It was named by *De Monts,* and was exceedingly difficult of acceſs becauſe of the narrowneſs of the mouth of the bay; only one ſhip being able to enter at a time, and

[104]

dles, as they had with them, might be sufficient to have taken it. His Excellency (looking upon Col *Church*) replyed, He could not admit of that, by reason he had by the advice of Her Majesty's Council writ to Her Majesty about the taking of *Port Royal* Fort, and how it should be disposed of when taken, *&c.* However Col. *Church* proceeding to get every thing ready for the Forces down at *Nantasket*, which was the place of Parade. He happening one day to be at Capt. *Belchers*,[287] where his Excellency happened to come; who was pleased to order Col. *Church* to put on his Sword, and walk with him up the Common; which he readily complyed with: where being come, he saw two Mortar pieces with Shells, and an Ingineer trying with them, to throw a Shell from them to any [104] spot of ground where he said it should fall: Which when Col. *Church* had seen done, gave him great incouragement & hopes that it would promote their going to *Port Royal*, which he had solicited for; and returning from thence after they had seen them try'd by the said Ingineer, and performing what was proposed. Coming near to Capt. *William Clarks*[288] -house over against the

---

that stern foremost, and with great precautions. [Champlain's *Voyages*, 21; Shea's *Charlevoix*, i: 253.]

[287] *Andrew Belcher* (Part I. notes 52 and 138) was son of Andrew, of Sudbury and Cambridge; lived first at Hartford, then at Charlestown, and then at Boston; freeman, 1677; of Com. of Safety in the Andros Insurrection; Counsellor, 1702, to his death, 31 Oct.,

1717. He married Sarah, dau. of Jonathan Gilbert, of Hartford; had Andrew, Deborah, Deborah, Mary, Ann, Martha, Elizabeth, and Jonathan, the Governor. He was a "very rich and leading man in the town." [Savage's *Gen. Dict.* i: 156. Drake's *Hist. Bost.* i: 539.]

[288] *William Clarke* was "of North Boston" in 1699, and one of the peti-

Horse-shoe,[229] his Excellency was invited by Capt. *Clark* to walk over and take a Glass of Wine; which he was pleased to accept of, and took Col. *Church* with him; and in the time they were taking a Glass of Wine, Col. *Church* once more presumed to say to his Excellency; Sir, I hope that now we shall go to *Port Royal* in order to take it; those Mortars being very suitable for such an Enterprize. His Excellency was pleas'd to reply; Col. *Church* you must say no more of that matter, for the Letter I told you of I writ by the advice of her Majesty's Council, now lyes at home on the board before the Lords Commissioners of her Majesty's foraign Plantations, &c. After some days every thing being ready to Embark, Col. *Church* received his Instructions: which are as followeth.

By his Excellency JOSEPH DUDLEY *Esq; Captain General and Governour in Chief in and over Her Majesty's Province of the* Massachusetts-Bay, &c. *in* New-England, *and Vice Admiral of the same.*

Instructions *for Colonel* Benjamin Church *in the present Expedition.*

'IN Pursuance of the Commission given you to take the
' Chief Command of the Land and Sea Forces by me
' raised, equipped and set forth on Her Majesties Service,

---

tioners for a bankrupt law "as in England"; constable, 1700; 1711, a "searcher" for provisions for Hovenden Walker's Canada fleet; 1722, was one of the purchasers of pews in Christ's Church. [Drake's *Hist. Bost.* i: 518, 521, 540, 567; Snow's *Hist. Bost.* 220.]

[229] The "Horse-shoe" was a tavern, believed to have been at the North End.

'against her open declared Enemies the *French*, and *In-
'dian* Rebels. You are to Observe the following Instruc-
'tions.

'First. You are to take care, That the duties of Reli-
'gion be attended on board the several Vessels, and in the
'several Company's under your Command, by daily Pray-
'ers unto God, and Reading his holy word; And that the
'Lords Day be observed & duly Sanctifyed to the utmost
'of your power, as far as the circumstances and the necef-
'sity of the Service can admit; that so you may have the
'presence of God with, and obtain His Blessing on your
'Undertaking.

'You are to take care, That your Souldiers have their
'due allowance of Provisions & other necessaries; That
'their Arms be well fixt, and kept fit for Service, and that
'they be furnished with a suitable Quantity of Powder and
'Ball, and be alwayes in readiness to pass upon duty.

'That good Order & Discipline be maintained; And
'all disorders, drunkenness, prophane Swearing, Cursing,
'Omission or neglect of Duty, disobedience to Officers,
'Mutiny, Desertion, and Sedition be duely punished ac-
'cording to the Rules & Articles of War; The which you
'are, once a Month or oftner, to cause to be published &
'made known to your Officers and Souldiers for their
'Observance & Direction in their duty. Let notorious &
'Capital Offenders be sent away to the next Garisons, there
'to be Imprisoned until they can be proceeded with. [105]

'Let the Sick and wounded be carefully look'd after,

'and accommodated after the beſt manner your circum-
'ſtances will admit of, and be ſent either to *Caſco Fort*, or
'to Mr. *Peperels*[290] at *Kittery*, which may be eaſieſt, ſo
'ſoon as you can.

'You are forthwith to ſend away the Forces & Stores
'by the Tranſports, with the Whale-boats to *Piſcataqua*,
'on *Kittery* ſide, there to attend your coming; whither
'you are to follow them with all Expedition.

'You are to Embark on the Province Galley, Capt.
'*Southack* Commander, And let Lieut Col. *Gorham* go on
'board Capt. *Gallop;*[291] who are both directed to attend your
'Motion on the *French* ſide; after which they are to return.
'Let the Commanders of all the Store Sloops & Tranſports
'know that they Sail, Anchor and Serve at your direction.

'When you Sail from *Piſcataqua*, keep at ſuch diſtance
'off the Shoar, that you be not obſerved by the Enemy to
'Alarm them. Stop at *Montinicus*,[292] and there Embark
'the Forces in the Whale-boats for the Main, to range
'that part of the Country, in ſearch of the Enemy, to
'Mount *Deſart;* ſending the Veſſels to meet you there;
'and after having refreſhed & recruited your Souldiers,

---

[290] *William Pepperell* was a native of Cornwall, Eng.; emigrated to the Iſles of Shoals, 1676; thence removed to Kittery point, Me., where he carried on a large fiſhery; was a diſtinguiſhed merchant and magiſtrate, and died 15 Feb., 1734, *æt.* 85. He married Margaret, dau. of John Bray, of Kittery; had Andrew, Mary, Margery, Joanna, Meriam, Dorothy, Jane, and [Sir] William. [Savage's *Gen. Dict.* iii. 392; Williamſon's *Hiſt. Me.* i: 687.]

[291] *Samuel Gallop*, ſon of Samuel, and grandſon of John, of Boſton?

[292] *Matinicus* is an iſland off the coaſt of Maine, early inhabited; containing 750 acres. It is 17 miles S. E. of Owl's Head (Thomaſton), and 10 E. of *Metinic*. [Williamſon's *Hiſt. Me.* i: 63.]

' proceed to *Machias*, and from thence to *Paſſamequado;*
' And having Effected what ſpoils you poſſibly may upon
' the Enemy in thoſe parts, Embark on your Veſſels for
' *Menis* and *Signecto*, touching at *Grand Manan*, if you
' ſee cauſe, and from *Menis* & *Signecto* to *Port Royal Gut;*
' And uſe all poſſible Methods for the burning and deſtroy-
' ing of the Enemies Houſing, and breaking the Dams of
' their Corn grounds in the ſaid ſeveral places, and make
' what other Spoils you can upon them, and bring away
' the Priſoners. In your return call at *Penobſcot*, and do
' what you can there, and ſo proceed Weſtward.

' This will probably imploy you a Month or Six Weeks;
' when you will draw together again, and by the latter end
' of *June* conſider whither you can march to *Norrigwack*,
' or other parts of their Planting to deſtroy their Corn &
' Settlements: And keep the Expedition on foot until the
' middle of *Auguſt* next.

' Notwithſtanding the particularity of the afore-going
' Inſtruction, I lay you under no reſtraint, becauſe I am
' well aſſured of your Courage, Care, Caution and Induſtry;
' But refer you to your own Reſolves, by the Advice of
' your Commiſſion Officers, not under the degree of Cap-
' tain's, and the Sea-Commiſſion Captains (whom you will,
' as often as you can, Adviſe with) according to the Intel-
' ligence you may receive, or as you may find needful upon
' the Spot.

' You are by every opportunity, and once a Week cer-
' tainly, by ſome means, either by way of *Caſco*, *Piſcata-*

'*qua*, or otherwise to acquaint me of your proceedings
'and all occurrents, and what may be further necessary for
'the Service. And to observe such further & other In-
'structions as you shall receive from my Self. [106]

'As often as you may, Advise with Capt. *Smith*[293] and
Capt. *Rogers*[294] Commanders of Her Majesty's Ships.

'Let your Minister, Commissary & Surgeons be treated
'with just respects.

'I Pray to God to preserve, prosper and succeed you.

'Given under my hand at *Boston*, the Fourth Day of
'*May*, 1704.   J. DUDLEY.

Pursuant to his Instructions he sent away his Transports,
and Forces to *Piscataqua*, but was oblig'd himself to wait
upon his Excellency by Land to *Piscataqua* in order to
raise more Forces, in the way thither; and did raise a
Company under the Command of Capt. *Harridon*;[295] taking
care also to provide a Pilot for them in the *Bay* of *Fundee*:
Col. *Church* being directed to one —— *Fellows*,[296] whom
he met with at *Ipswich*. And going from thence to *Pis-*

---

[293] *Thomas*, commander of the frigate *Jersey*. [Drake's *Church* (ed. 1827), 257.]

[294] *George*, commander of the frigate *Gosport*. [*Ibid.*]

[295] *John Haraden* (*Harradin, Harrendine*) was son of Edward, who went to Gloucester from Ipswich 1657; he led a maritime life; 1709, was master of a sloop fitted out to capture a French privateer; 1711, he was pilot of ship "Montague" in the expedition to Canada, for which service he received an allowance from the General Court, 1714; died 11 Nov., 1724. He married Sarah Giddings, by whom he had several children. [Babson's *Hist. Gloucester*, 98.]

[296] *William Fellows* was one of the first settlers of Ipswich, and left a large family, from which this pilot was probably descended. [Felt's *Hist. Ipswich*, 11.]

cataqua with his Excellency, was there met by that worthy Gentleman Maj. *Winthrop Hilton*,[297] who was very helpful to him in the whole Expedition, whofe Name & Memory ought not to be forgot. Being ready to Embark from *Pifcataqua*; Col. *Church* requefted the Commanders of her Majefty's Ships, Capt. *Smith* & Capt. *Rogers* to tarry at *Pifcataqua* a Fortnight, that fo they might not be difcovered by the Enemy before he had done fome fpoil upon them. Then moving in their Tranfports, as directed, Got fafe into *Montinucus* undifcovered by the Enemy. Next Morning early fitted out two Whale boats with men, Capt. *John Cook* in one, and Capt. *Conftant Church* in the other; and fent them to Green-Ifland[298] upon a difcovery; and coming there they parted, one went to one part, and the other to the other part, that fo they might not mifs of what could be difcovered; where they met with old *Lafaure*[299] with his two Sons *Thomas* & *Timothy*, and a *Canada Indian*. The Enemy feeing that they were difcovered, threw down their Ducks and Eggs, who had got a con-

---

[297] *Winthrop Hilton* was fon of Edward of Exeter, and grandfon of Edward of Dover; born about 1671; was the leading military man of the Province; 1706, was made Judge of Com. Pleas, which office he held to his death; was appointed Counfellor, but was killed by the Indians, 23 June, 1710, in that part of Exeter which is now Epping. He married Ann Wilfon, who afterwards married Col. Jonathan Wadleigh. They had Judith, Ann, Deborah, Elizabeth, Bridget, and Winthrop. [*N. E. Hift. and Gen. Reg.* vii: 51.]

[298] There are two "Green" iflands N. E. of *Matinicus*, and near to it, each of 2 or 3 acres only.

[299] Penhallow calls him "*Monfieur Lafebure*, and his two fons, with a Canada Indian." [*Indian Wars* (ed. 1859). 28.] Church himfelf calls him *Le Faver*, further on (p. 110, old paging).

fiderable quantity of each, and ran to their Canoo's, getting into them, ftood directly for the Maine; looking behind them, perceived the Whale-boats to gain fo faft upon them, clapt fide by fide and all four got into one Canoo, which prov'd of little advantage to them, for the Whale boats gained fo much upon them, and got fo near that Capt. *Cook* firing at the Stores-man [300] which was the *Indian*, & happen'd to graze his skull, and quite fpoil'd his Paddling: upon which old *Lafaure* and Sons feeing their companions condition foon beg'd for quarter, and had it granted: the two Captains with their fuccefs prefently return'd to their Commander, taking care that their Captives fhould not difcourfe together before they were examined; when brought to Col. *Church*, he order'd them to be apart; and firft proceeded to examine old *Lafaure*, who he found to be very furly & crofs, fo that he could gain no manner of intelligence by him; upon which the Commander was refolved to put in practice what he had formerly done at *Segnecto*;[301] ordering his *Indians* to make two large heaps of dry wood at fome diftance one from the other, and to fet a large ftake in the ground clofe to [107] each heap; then ordered the two Sons *Thomas & Timothy* to be brought and bound to the Stakes; alfo ordering his *Indians* to paint themfelves with colours which they had brought for that ufe. Then he Colonel proceeded to examine firft *Timothy*; and told him, He

---

[300] Steerfman; *i.e.*, the paddler in the ftern of the canoe.

[301] Stiles and Southwick reprint this Senecto.

had examin'd his Father already; and that if he told him
the truth he would fave his Life, and take him into his
Service; and that he fhould have good pay & live well.
He anfwer'd, That he would tell him the truth; and gave
him an account of every thing he knew; which was all
Minuted down: He being ask'd whither his Brother
Thomas did not know more than he? His anfwer was,
Yes. For his Brother *Thomas* had a Commiffion fent
him from the Governour of *Canada*, to Command a Company of *Indians* who were gathered together at a Place
where fome French Gentlemen lately arrived from *Canada*, who were Officers to Command the reft that were to
go Weftward to fight the *Englifh*, and that there was fent
to his Father and Brother *Tom*, a confiderable quantity of
Flower, Fruit, Ammunition and Stores, for the fupply of
the faid Army. He being ask'd, Whither he could Pilot
our Forces to them? faid, No: But his Brother *Tom*
could, for he had hid it and that he was not then with
him. The Colonel ask'd him, What Gentlemen thofe
were that came from *Canada*? He anfwered Monfieur
Gordan,[302] and Mr. *Sharkee*.[303] Being ask'd where they
were? Anfwered at *Paffamequado;* building a Fort there.
Being alfo ask'd, What number of *Indians* and *French*

---

[302] Penhallow (ed. 1859, p. 29) makes this *Guorden;* Stiles and Southwick make it *Gourdan;* and Church, when referring (p. 110, old paging) to his capture, does the fame. The name was probably *Gourdon*. [Hutchinfon's *Hift. Mafs.* ii: 133.]

[303] Penhallow fays *Sharkee* (his name feems to have been *Chartiers* [Hutchinfon's *Hift. Mafs.* ii: 133]) was taken prifoner by this expedition; which, it will be feen further on, is an error, Col. Church having "miffed" him on this foray. [*Indian Wars*, 29.]

there were at *Penobscot?* He answered, there were several Families, but they liv'd scattering. Ask'd him further, If he would Pilot our Forces thither? Answered, He would if the Commander would not let the Salvages Rost him. Upon which the Colonel ordered him to be loosed from the Stake, and took him by the hand, told him, He would be as kind to him as his own Father; at which he seemed to be very thankful. And then the Colonel proceeded to examine his Brother *Tom*, and told him that he had examined his Father and Brother, and that his Brother had told him every tittle he knew; and that he knew more than his Brother *Timothy* did; and that if he would be Ingenious & confess all he knew, he should fare as well as his Brother, but if not, the Salvages should Rost him. Whereupon he solemnly promised that he would; and that he would Pilot him to every thing he knew, to the value of a Knife and Sheafe (which without doubt he did.) Then the Colonel immediately gave orders for the Whale-boats to be ready, and went directly over where the said Goods & Stores were, and found them as inform'd, took them on board the Boats, and returned to their Transports; and ordering Provisions to be put into every Mans Snapsack for 6 or 8 days; so in the dusk of the Evening left their Transports, with Orders how they should act; and went directly for the Mainland of *Penobscot*, and Mouth of that River with their Pilots *Tom* & *Timothy*, who carried them directly to every Place & Habitation both of *French* & *Indians* there-abouts, with the assistance of one *De*

[108] *Young*,[304] whom they carried out of *Boston* Goal for the same purpose, who was very serviceable to them: being there we kill'd and took every one both *French* & *Indians*, not knowing that any one did escape in all *Penobscot*; among those that were taken was St. *Casteens* Daughter, who said that her Husband was gone to *France*, to her Father Monsieur *Casteen*:[305] She having her Children with her, the Commander was very kind to her and them. All the Prisoners that were then taken, held to one Story in general, which they had from *Lafaure*'s Sons; that there were no more *Indians* there-abouts, but enough of them at *Passamequado*; upon which they soon return'd to their Transports with their Prisoners & Plunder. The Commander giving order immediately for the Souldiers in the Whale-boats to have a recruit of Provisions for a further pursuit of the Enemy, giving orders to the Transports to stay a few days more there, and then go to Mount *Desart* (and there to stay for her Majesty's Ships, who were directed to come thither) and there to wait his further order. Then Col. *Church* with his Forces immediately imbark'd on board their Whale-boats, & proceeded to scour the Coast, and to try if they could discover any of the Enemy coming from *Passamequado*; making their stops in the day time (at all the Points & Places where they were certain

---

[304] Penhallow (orig. ed. 17) has this name *D'Young;* which in the reprint of the New Hampshire Historical Society (*Collections*, i: 33), and in the Cincinnati reprint of 1859, is made *D. Young*. The man was doubtless a French Canadian prisoner; probably one of *Villeau's* men. [See note 195, *ante*.]

[305] See note 34, *ante*.

[108]

the Enemy would Land, or come by with their Canoo's) and at Night to their Paddles. Then coming near where the Veſſels were ordered to come, having made no diſcovery of the Enemy, went directly to Mount *Deſart*, where the Tranſports were juſt come; and taking ſome Proviſions for his Souldiers, gave direction for the Ships & Tranſports in 6 days to come directly to *Paſſamequado*, where they ſhould find him & his Forces. Then immediately mov'd away in the Whale-boats & made diligent ſearch along ſhore, as formerly, inſpecting all Places where the Enemy was likely to lurk: Particularly at *Machias*; but found neither Fires nor Tracks. Coming afterwards to the Weſt Harbour at *Paſſamequado*, where they entred upon action; an account whereof Col. *Church* did communicate to his Excellency, being as followeth.

May it pleaſe your Excellency,

'I Received Yours of this Inſtant *Octob.* 9*th*. with the 'two incloſed Informations, that concern my actions 'at *Paſſamequado*; which I will give a juſt and true ac- 'count of as near as poſſible I can (*viz*) on the 7*th* of *June* 'laſt 1704. In the evening we entred in at the Weſtward 'Harbour at ſaid *Paſſamequado*;[306] coming up ſaid Har- 'bour to an Iſland,[307] where landing, we came to a French

---

[306] There are three paſſages into Paſfamaquoddy bay, the weſtern, the middle or ſhip channel, and the eaſtern. The weſtern is that firſt reached in coaſting from Machias, and lies between weſt Quoddy head and the iſland of *Campo-bello.*

[307] *Mooſe* iſland, on which Eaſtport now ſtands? The lay of the land ſuggeſts that it might be that.

'houfe, and took a French Woman, and Children, the
'Woman upon her Examination faid, her Husband was
'abroad a Fifhing I ask'd her, whither there were any
'*Indians* thereabouts? She faid, Yes. There were a
'great many, and feveral on that Ifland. I ask'd her,
'whither fhe could Pilot me to them? Said, No. They
'hid in the Woods. I ask'd her, when fhe faw them?
'Anfwered, Juft now, or a little while fince. I ask'd [109]
'her, whether fhe knew where they had laid their Canoo's?
'Anfwered, No. They carried their Canoo's into the
'woods with them. We then haftened away a-long fhore,
'feizing what Prifoners we could, taking old *Lotriel*[303] and
'his Family. This intelligence caus'd me to leave Col.
'*Gorham*, and a confiderable part of my Men (and Boats)
'with him at that Ifland, partly to guard and fecure thofe
'Prifoners, being fenfible it would be a great trouble to
'have them to fecure and guard at our next landing, where
'I did really expect, and hope to have an opportunity, to
'fight our *Indian* Enemies; for all our French Prifoners,
'that we had taken at *Penobfcot*, and a-long fhore had in-
'formed us, That when we came to the Place, where thefe
'*Canada* Gentlemen lived, we fhould certainly meet with
'the Salvages to fight us, thofe being the only Men that
'fet the *Indians* againft us, or upon us, and were newly
'come from *Canada*, to manage the War againft us (plead-
'ing in this account and information their own Innocency)
'and partly in hopes that he the faid Col. *Gorham* would

[303] See note 255, *ante*.

'have a good opportunity in the Morning to deftroy fome
' of thofe our Enemies, (we were informed by the faid
' French Woman as above,) with the ufe of his Boats, as
' I had given direction. Ordering alfo Maj. *Hilton,* to pafs
' over to the next Ifland, that lay Eaft of us [309] (with a fmall
' Party of Men and Boats) to furprize & deftroy any of the
' Enemy, that in their Canoo's might go here or there,
' from any place, to make their flight from us, and as he
' had opportunity to take any *French* Prifoners. We then
' immediately moved up the River in the dark Night thro'
' great difficulty, by reafon of the Eddys and Whirlpools,
' made with the fiercenefs of the current.[310] And here it
' may be hinted that we had information that *Lotriel* had
' loft fome of his Family paffing over to the next Ifland,
' falling into one of thefe Eddys were drowned; which the
' two Pilots told to difcourage me. But I faid nothing of
' that nature fhall do it; for I was refolved to venture up,
' and therefore forthwith Paddling our Boats, as privately
' as we could, and with as much expedition as we could
' make with our Paddles, and the help of a ftrong Tide, we
' came up to Monfieur *Gourdans,* a little before day; where
' taking notice of the Shoar, and finding it fomewhat open
' and clear, I ordered Capt. *Mirick* and Capt. *Cole,* (having
' Englifh Companies) to tarry with feveral of the Boats to
' be ready, that if any of the Enemy fhould come down

[309] Deer ifland?
[310] The tide rifes here from 24 to 28 feet, and, except at favorable hours, the rufh of waters coming down through thefe narrow inlets from the *Schoodic* or *St. Croix* river makes "eddys," "whirlpools," and "a fierce current," as Church defcribes it.

'out of the brush into the Bay, (it being very broad in
'that place) [311] with their Canoo's, they might take and
'destroy them. Ordering the remainder of the Army,
'being landed,[312] (with my self and the other Officers)
'to March up into the Woods, with a wide Front, and
'to keep at a considerable distance; for that if they should
'run in heaps, the Enemy would have the greater advan-
'tage: and further directing them that if possible, they
'should destroy the Enemy with their Hatches, and not
'fire a Gun. This order I alwayes gave at landing, tell-
'ing them the inconveniency of firing, in that it might be
'first dangerous to themselves, they being many of
'them Young Souldiers, (as I had sometimes observed,
'that one or two Guns being fired, many others would
'fire, at they knew not what; as happened presently after)
'and it would alarm the Enemy, and give them the oppor-
'tunity to make their escape; and it might alarm the whole
'Country, and also prevent all further action from taking
'effect Orders being thus passed, we moved directly
'towards the Woods, *Le Faver*'s Son directing us to a
'little Hutt or Wigwam, which we immediately sur-
'rounded with a few Men, the rest Marching directly up
'into the Woods, to see what Wigwams or Hutts they
'could discover; my self made a little stop, Ordering the
'Pilot to tell them in the Hutt, that they were surrounded

[311] They had now emerged from the narrow western entrance into upper Passamaquoddy bay, which is some 8 or 10 miles in width.

[312] They must have landed upon what is now the town of Perry, Me.; or possibly further up, in Robbinston, or the lower part of Calais.

' with an Army, and that if they would come forth, and
' furrender themfelves, they fhould have good quarter, but
' if not, they fhould be all knock'd on the head and die:
' One of them fhewed himfelf, I ask'd, Who he was? He
' faid *Gourdan;* and begg'd for quarter: I told him he
' fhould have good quarter; adding further, That if there
' were any more in the houfe they fhould come out: Then
' came out two men; *Gourdan* faid, They were his Sons,
' and asked quarter for them, which was alfo granted.
' Then came out a Woman, and a little Boy; fhe fell upon
' her knees, begg'd quarter for her felf and Children, and
' that I would not fuffer the *Indians* to kill them. I told
' them they fhould have good quarter and not be hurt.
' After which I ordered a fmall guard over them, and fo
' mov'd prefently up with the reft of my Company, after
' them that were gone before, but looking on my right
' hand over a little run, I faw fomething look black, juft
' by me, ftopped, and heard a talking, ftepped over, and
' faw a little Hutt or Wigwam with a crowd of People
' round about it, which was contrary to my former direc-
' tions: Ask'd them what they were doing? They reply'd
' there was fome of the Enemy in a houfe, and would not
' come out. I ask'd what Houfe? They faid a Bark-
' houfe. I haftily bid them pull it down, and knock them
' on the head, never asking whether they were *French* or
' *Indians*; they being all Enemies alike to me. And paff-
' ing then to them, and feeing them in great diforder, fo
' many of the Army in a crowd together, acting fo con-

'trary to my Command & Direction, expofing themfelves,
' and the whole Army to utter ruine, by their fo diforderly
' crowding thick together; had an Enemy come upon
' them in that interim, and fired a Volley amongft them,
' they could not have mifs'd a fhot; and wholly neglecting
' their duty, in not attending my orders, in fearching dili-
' gently for our lurking Enemies in their Wigwams, or by
' their fires, where I had great hopes, and real expectation
' to meet with them. I moft certainly know that I was in
' an exceeding great Paffion, but not with thofe poor mif-
' erable Enemies; for I took no notice of half a dozen of
' the Enemy, when at the fame time, I expected to be en-
' gaged with fome hundreds of them, of whom we had a
' continued account who [111] were expected from *Port
' Royal* fide. In this heat of action, every word that I then
' fpoke, I cannot give an account of, and I prefume it is
' impoffible.[313] I ftop'd but little here, but went directly

[313] Church pleads for himfelf here as if he had been blamed, which was the fact. Hutchinfon fays, " Church feeing fome of his men hovering over another hut, he called to them to know what they were doing; and upon their reply, that there were people in the houfe who would not come out, he, haftily bid his men knock them in the head; which order they immediately obferved. He was much blamed for this after his return, and excufed himfelf but indifferently. He feared the enemy might fall upon his men, whom he faw were off their guard, which put him in a paffion." [*Hift. Mafs.* ii : 133.] No one can properly eftimate his conduct, without remembering that he had been led, by the ftatements of his prifoners, to believe that he was near to a very large force of the enemy, who might fall upon his little company at any moment in overwhelming force, aided, as they would be, by darknefs, the foreft, and their own fuperior knowledge of the ground; and that he alfo felt, that the moral effect of fome feverity would be good upon his favage and half-favage foes. It will be feen, that, afterward on his arrival at *Baye les Mines*, he made ufe of what happened here to good refults.

'up into the woods, hoping to be better imployed, with
'the reſt of the Army, I liſten'd to hear, and looked earn-
'eſtly to ſee what might be the next action; but meeting
'with many of the Souldiers, They told me, they had diſ-
'covered nothing; we fetching a ſmall compaſs round,
'came down again. It being pretty dark, I took notice,
'I ſaw two men lay dead as I thought, at the end of
'the houſe, where the door was, and immediately the
'Guns went off, and they fired every man as I thought,
'and moſt towards that place where I left the guard with
'Monſieur *Gourdan*. I had much ado to ſtop their firing,
'and told them, I thought they were mad, and I believed
'they had not killed and wounded leſs than 40 or 50 of
'our own Men. And I asked them what they ſhot at?
'They anſwered at a French man that ran away: but to
'admiration no man was kill'd, but he, & one of our own
'men wounded in the Leg; and I turning about, a French
'man ſpoke to me, and I gave him quarter. Day-light
'coming on and no diſcovery made of the Enemy, I went
'to the place where I had left Monſieur *Gourdan*, to ex-
'amine him, and his Sons, who agreed in their examina-
'tions; told me two of their men were abroad: It prov'd a
'damage; and further told me, That Monſieur *Sharkee*
'lived ſeveral Leagues up at the head of the River, at the
'Falls;[314] and all the *Indians* were fiſhing, and tending
'their Corn there; and that Monſieur *Sharkee* had ſent

---

[314] Great Falls, — "where the water deſcends 20 feet in a ſhort diſtance"? [Williamſon's *Hiſt. Me.* i : 86.]

'down to him, to come up to him to advise about the
'*Indian* Army, that was to go Westward; but he had
'returned him answer, his business was urgent, and he
'could not come up: and that *Sharkee*, and the *Indians*,
'would certainly be down that day, or the next at the fur-
'thest, to come to conclude of that matter. This was a
'short Nights action, and all sensible Men do well know,
'that actions done in the dark (being in the Night as
'aforesaid) under so many difficulties, as we then laboured
'under, as before related, was a very hard Task for one
'Man, matters being circumstanc'd as in this action; which
'would not admit of calling a Council; and at that time
'could not be confin'd there-unto; at which time I was
'transported above fear or any sort of dread; yet being
'sensible of the danger in my Armies crowding so thick
'together, and of the great duty incumbent on me to pre-
'serve them from all the danger I possibly could, for fur-
'ther improvement, in the Destruction of our implacable
'Enemies; am ready to conclude, that I was very quick &
'absolute in giving such Commands & Orders, as I then ap-
'prehended most proper and advantagious. And had it not
'been for the Intelligence I had received from the *French*
'we took at *Penobscot*, as before hinted, and the false re-
'port the *French* Woman (first took) gave me, I had not
'been in such haste. I question not but those *French* men
'that were slain, had the same good quarter of other
'Prisoners. But I ever look'd at it a good Providence of
'Almighty God, that some few of our cruel & bloody

' Enemies, were made fenfible of their bloody Cruelties,
' perpetrated on my dear & loving friends and Country-
' men; and that the fame meafure (in part) meeted to
' them, as they had been guilty of in a barbarous manner
' at *Deerfield*, & I hope juftly. I hope God Almighty will
' accept hereof, altho' it may not be eligible to our *French*
' implacable Enemies, and fuch others as are not our
' friends. The fore-going Journal and this fhort annex-
' ment, I thought it my duty to exhibit, for the fatisfaction
' of my Friends & Country-men, whom I very faithfully &
' willingly ferved in the late Expedition; and I hope will
' find acceptance with your Excellency, the Honourable
' Council & Reprefentatives now Affembled, as being done
' from the zeal I had in the faid Service of Her Majefty,
' and her good Subjects here.

I Remain your moft humble & obedient Servant,
Benjamin Church.

This Nights Service being over immediately Col. *Church* leaves a fufficient guard with *Gourdan*, and the other Prifoners, mov'd in fome Whale-boats with the reft; and as they were going fpy'd a fmall thing upon the Water, at a great diftance, which proved to be a birch Canoo, with two *Indians* in her; the Colonel prefently ordered the lighteft boat he had to make the beft of her way and cut them off from the Shore: but the *Indians* perceiving their defign run their Canoo a-fhore & fled. Col. *Church* fearing they would run directly to *Sharkee* made all the expedition imaginable; but it being ebb and the water low, was obliged to land & make the beſt of their way thro' the woods, hoping to intercept the *Indians*, and get to *Sharkee*'s houſe before them; which was two Miles from where our Forces landed. The Colonel being Ancient & Unwildly, deſired Serjeant *Edee*[315] to run with him, and coming to ſeveral Trees fallen, which he could not creep under or readily get over, would lay his breaſt againſt the Tree, the ſaid *Edee* turning him over, generally had Cat luck, falling on his feet, by which means kept in the Front: and coming near to *Sharkee*'s houſe, diſcovered ſome *French* & *Indians* making a Wair[316] in the River, and preſently diſcovered the two *Indians* afore-mentioned, who call'd to them at work in the River; told them there was an Army of *Engliſh* and *Indians* juſt by; who immediately left their work and ran, endeavouring to get to *Sharkee*'s houſe; who hearing the noiſe, took his Lady & Child, and ran into the woods. Our Men running briskly fired & kill'd one of the *Indians*, and took the reſt Priſoners. Then going to *Sharkee*'s houſe found a Woman and Child, to whom they gave good quarter: and finding that Madam *Sharkee* had left her Silk Clothes & fine linen behind her, our Forces was deſirous to have purſued and

---

[315] This was probably a member of one of the families in the Old Colony deſcended from *Samuel Eddy* (*Ede, Edy, Eady, Eadey, Edie, Edee*), who ſettled in Plymouth from Cranbrooke, Kent, 1630, and left a numerous and noble poſterity. [*See N. E. Hiſt. and Gen. Reg.* iii: 336; viii: 201-206; *Congregational Quarterly*, iv: 223-238.]

[316] *Weir*, — a fence of ſtakes and bruſh ſet in a river for the purpoſe of catching fiſh.

taken her: But Col. *Church* forbid them, saying he would have her run and suffer, that she might be made sensible, what hardships our poor People had suffered by them, *&c.* Then proceeded to examine the Prisoners newly taken, who gave [113] him the same account he had before; of the *Indians* being up at the Falls, *&c.* It being just Night prevented our Attacking of them that Night. But next Morning early they mov'd up to the Falls (which was about a Mile higher:) But doubtless the Enemy had some Intelligence by the two afore-said *Indians*, before our Forces came, so that they all got on the other side of the River and left some of their goods by the Water-side, to decoy our Men, that so they might fire upon them; which indeed they effected: But thro' the good Providence of God never a Man of ours was kill'd, and but one slightly wounded. After a short dispute Col. *Church* ordered that every Man might take what they pleased of the Fish which lay bundled up, and to burn the rest, which was a great quantity. The Enemy seeing what our Forces were about; and that their stock of Fish was destroyed, and the season being over for getting any more, set up a hedious Cry, and so ran all away into the woods; who being all on the other side of the River,[317] ours could not follow them. Having done, our Forces March'd down to their Boats at *Sharkee*'s, and took their Prisoners, Bever, and other Plunder which they had got, and put it into their Boats, and

---

[317] The New-Brunswick side; the river being here the dividing line between the States and the British possessions.

went down to *Gourdans* houfe, where they had left Lieut. Col. *Gorham* & Maj *Hilton*, with part of the Forces to guard the Prifoners; (and kept a good look-out for more of the Enemy) who upon the Colonels return, gave him an account that they had made no difcovery of the Enemy fince he left them, *&c.* Juft then Her Majefty's Ships and Tranfports arriving. The Commanders of Her Majefty's Ships told Col. *Church* that they had orders to go directly for *Port Royal Gut*, and wait the coming of fome Store-Ships, which were expected at *Port Royal* from *France*; and Col. *Church* advifing with them, propofed that it was very expedient and ferviceable to the Crown, that Capt. *Southack* in the Province Galley fhould accompany them, which they did readily acquiefce with him in. Upon which the Colonel immediately embark'd his Forces on board the Tranfports, and himfelf on board Capt. *Jarvis*;[318] ordering the Commiffary of the Stores, the Minifter, Surgeons & Pilots all to embark on board the fame Veffel with him; ordering all the Whale-boats to be put on board the Tranfports and then all to come to Sail. The Ships ftanding away for *Port Royal Gut*,[319] and Col. *Church* with the Tranfports for *Menis*:[320] In their way the Colonel inquired of the Pilot —— *Fellows*,[321] What depth of Water there was in the Crick near the Town of *Menis?* He anfwered him that there was Water enough near the

---

[318] Commander of the frigate *Adventure*; as will be feen from the document commencing on the next page.

[319] See note 286, *ante*.

[320] See note 238, *ante*. *Les Mines* was about half-way from *Port Royal* to *Beau-bafin*, or *Chieguecto*.

See note 296, *ante*.

[114]

Town to flote that Veffel they were in at low Water. So when coming near, Col. *Church* obferved a Woody Ifland [322] between them and the Town, that they run up on the back-fide of the faid Ifland, with all their Tranfports undifcovered to the Enemy, and came to Anchor. Then the Colonel and all his Forces embark'd in the Whale-boats, it being late in the day mov'd directly for the Town, and in the way ask'd for the Pilot, whom he expected was in one of the Boats; but he had given him the flip, and tarried behind. The Colonel not know[114]ing the difficulties as might attend their going up to the Town; immediately fent Lieut. *Gyles*,[323] who could fpeak *French*, with a Flag of Truce up to the Town with a Summons, which was writ before they landed, expecting their furrender: which is as followeth.

Aboard Her Majefty's Ship Adventure near the Gut of Menis, *June 20. 1704   An agreement made by the Field Officers commanding Her Majefty's Forces for the prefent Expedition againft the* French *Enemies, and* Indian *Rebels.*

   Agreed.

THat a Declaration or Summons be fent on Shoar at Menis and Port Royal, under a Flag of Truce.

---

[322] From Charlevoix's map, this would feem to be *Groffe Ifle*.

[323] *John Gyles* was fon of Thomas (who lived firft in Merry-meeting bay, was made prifoner, efcaped to England, came back to live on Long Ifland, went thence to Pemaquid, where he was Juftice, and was killed by the Indians, 2 Aug., 1689); was captured at his father's death, when 14 years of age, and carried to Canada; whence, after a fervitude of feveral years, he was purchafed

[114]

Particularly,

We declare to you, the many Cruelties and Barbarities that you and the Indians *have been guilty of towards us, in laying waste our Country here in the East at* Casco, *and the Places Adjacent: Peculiarly, the Horrid action at* Deerfield *this last Winter, in Killing, Massacring, Murdering and Scalping without giving any notice at all, or opportunity to ask quarter at your Hands; and after all carrying the Remainder into Captivity in the heighth of Winter (of which they kill'd many in the Journey,) and expos'd the rest to the hardships of Cold and Famine, worse than death it self. Which Cruelties we are yet every day exposed unto, and exercised withal.*

We do also declare, That we have already made some beginnings of Killing and Scalping some Canada *Men (which we have not been wont to do or allow) and are now come with a great number of* English & Indians, *all Volunteers, with resolutions to subdue you, and make you sensible of your Cruelties to us by treating you after the same manner.*

At this time we expect our Men of War and Transport Ships to be at Port Royal. *(we having but lately parted with them.)*

by a French trader during Col. Hawthorn's Eastern Expedition, and restored to his home and friends; he thereafter for many years served the Government in the army, and as an interpreter; he printed, 1736, a memoir of his father; died 1755. [Savage's *Gen. Dict.* ii: 326; Sewall's *Anc. Dom. Me.* 195-204; Willis's *Law, Courts, and Lawyers, Me.* 32.]

164

In the laſt place, We do declare to you, That inaſmuch as ſome of you have ſhown kindneſs to our Captives, and Expreſs'd a love to and deſire of being under the Engliſh Government, We do therefore notwithſtanding all this, give you timely Notice, and do demand a Surrender immediately, by the laying down your Arms, upon which we promiſe very good Quarter; if not, you muſt expect the utmoſt Severity.

To the Chief Commander of the Town of Menis, *& the Inhabitants thereof, & we expect your anſwer poſitively within an hour.*	Benjamin Church *Colonel.* John Gorcham *Lieut. Col.* Winthrop Hilton *Major.*

Then moving to the Crick expecting to have had Water enough for the Boats, as the Pilot had inform'd them, but found not Water enough for a Canoo; ſo were oblig'd to land,[324] intending to have been up at the Town before the hour was out, that the Summons expreſſed: (For their return was, That if our Forces would not hurt their Eſtates, that then they would Surrender, if otherwiſe intended, they ſhould fight for them, *&c.*) But meeting with ſeveral Cricks near 20 or 30 foot deep, which were very Muddy and Dirty, ſo that the Army could not get over them; was oblig'd to return to [115] their Boats again, and wait till within Night before the Tide ſerved for them to go up to the Town; and then intended to

---

[324] That is, their boats ſoon grounding, they were obliged to get out of them into the mud, and wade toward the ſhore; which they were unable to accompliſh ſucceſſfully on account of the intervention of ſome creeks of deep water, which forced them back to the boats, and compelled them to wait in them for the tide to riſe, — under the circumſtances, a proſaic reſult!

go up pretty near the Town, and not to fall on till Morning, being in hopes that the banks of the Cricks would shelter them from the Enemy: but the Tides rising so high expofed them all to the Enemy; who had the Trees & Woods to be-friend them. And so came down in the Night & fired smartly at our Forces; but Col. *Church* being in a Pinis[325] that had a small Cannon plac'd in the head, ordered it to be charg'd feveral times, with Bullets in small bags, and fired at the Enemy, which made fuch a rattling amongſt the Trees, that caufed the Enemy to draw off; and by the great Providence of Almighty God not one of our Forces was hurt that Night; (but as I have been informed they had one *Indian* kill'd, and fome others wounded, which was fome difcouragement to the Enemy.) Next Morning by break of Day, Col. *Church* ordered all his Forces, (and plac'd Maj. *Hilton* on the right wing,) to run all up driving the Enemy before them, who leaving their Town to our Forces, but had carried away the beſt of their Goods (which were foon found by our Souldiers.) The bulk of the Enemy happening to lye againſt our right Wing caufed the hotteſt difpute there, who lay behind Logs and Trees, till our Forces, and Maj *Hilton* who led them, came on upon them, and forc'd them to run; and notwithſtanding the ſharp firing of the Enemy at our Forces, by the repeated Providence of God there was never a Man of ours kill'd or wounded. Our Souldiers not having been long in Town before they found

[325] Pinnace.

[115]

confiderable quantities of Strong Drink (both Brandy & Clarat) and being very greedy after it, efpecially the *Indians*, were very diforderly, firing at every Pig, Turky or Fowl they faw, of which were very plenty in the Town; which indanger'd our own Men: Col. *Church* perceiving the diforder, and firing of his own Men, ran to put a ftop to it, had feveral fhot come very near him; and finding what had occafion'd this diforder, commanded his Officers to knock out the heads of every Cask of Strong Liquor they could find in the Town,[326] to prevent any further difturbance amongft his Army; knowing it was impoffible to have kept it from them, efpecially the *Indians*, if it was faved, *&c.* Then fome of the Army who were defirous to purfue the Enemy, having heard them driving away their Cattel, Requefted the Colonel to let them go; who did: and gave them their orders. Capt. *Cooke*, and Capt. *Church* to lead the two Wings, and Lieut. *Barker*[327] who led the Colonels Company in the Center: and the faid Capt. *Cooke* and Capt. *Church* defired Lieut. *Barker*

---

[326] A practical "temperance" movement, deferving extended imitation!

[327] There may have been three "Lieut." Barkers then living, who might have been connected with Church's company: Lt. Robert, and Lt. Francis, both of Duxbury, and both fons of Robert; and Lt. John, of Andover, fon of Richard. The latter died 1722; Robert had a dau. born 18 April, 1704; Francis, I do not trace later than 1689. As Church's company would be likelieft to be officered from Plymouth Colony, it feems probable that one of the Duxbury brothers is the one referred to; and, of thefe, I incline to the opinion that it was Robert. [Savage's *Gen. Dict.* i: 115; Winfor's *Hift. Duxbury*, 223; Abbot's *Hift. Andover*, 200; *Plym. Col. Rec.* vi: 218] Charlevoix fays that the "Lieutenant-General of the Englifh forces" was killed — a miftake of Barker's rank. [*Hift. Nouv. France.*]

not to move too faft; fo that he might have the benefit of their affiftance, if he had occafion; but the faid Lieutenant not being fo careful as he fhould have been, or at leaft was too eager, was fhot down, and another Man; which were all the Men that were kill'd in the whole Expedition. Towards Night Col. *Church* ordered fome of his Forces to pull down fome of the Houfes, and others to get Logs [116] and make a Fortification for his whole Army to lodge in that Night, that fo they might be together: and juft before Night ordered fome of his Men to go fee if there were any Men in any of the Houfes in the Town; if not, to fet them all a fire: which was done, and the whole Town feemed to be of a fire all at once, *&c.* The next Morning the Colonel gave orders to his Men to dig down their Dams,[328] and let the Tide in to deftroy all their Corn, and every thing that was good, according to his Inftructions; and to burn the Fortification which they had built the Day before: And when the Tide ferv'd to put all their Plunder which they had got into the Boats. Then ordering his Souldiers to March at a good diftance one from another; which caus'd the Enemy to think that there was

---

[328] Haliburton fays that there are vaft marfhes fkirting this *Baye les Mines* (Bafon of Mines), which, "when enclofed with dikes, and well drained, are exceedingly fertile, yielding, for feveral years in fucceffion, abundant crops of wheat, and alternate rotations of hay and grain, without the aid of manure." He adds: "the marfhes, formed by the rivers emptying into the Bafon of Mines, are very fuperior to thofe in other parts of the Province — the water of that extraordinary refervoir being not only difcolored, but actually turbid, with the great quantity of matter held in folution by it." [*Hift. Nov. Scot.* ii: 363.] The Acadians had probably already begun this form of tillage, and thefe dikes to which Church here refers are thus exp'ained.

not lefs than a thoufand Men (as they faid afterwards:) and that their burning of the Fortification, and doing as they did, caufed the Enemy to think that they were gone clear off and not to return again. But it proved to the contrary, for Col. *Church* and his Forces only went aboard their Tranfports, and there ftaid till the Tide ferv'd; in the Night embarked on board their Whale-boats, landed fome of his Men, expecting they might meet with fome of the Enemy mending their Dams; which they did, and with the Boats went up another branch of the River, to another Town or Village;[329] upon fuch a furprize took as many Prifoners as they could defire. And it happened that Col. *Church* was at the French Captains Houfe when two Gentlemen that came Poft from the Governour of *Port Royal* to him, who was the Chief Commander at *Menis*, with an Exprefs to fend away two Companies of Men to Defend the Kings Fort there; and to give him an account, That there was three *Englifh* Men of War come into *Port Royal Gut* or Harbour; and that the Men fent for muft be Pofted away with all fpeed. Col. *Church*, as was faid before, being there, treated the two Gentlemen very hanfomely, and told them, He would fend them back again Poft to their Mafter upon his bufinefs; and bid them give him his hearty thanks for fending him fuch good News, that part of his Fleet was in fo good a Harbour. Then reading the Summons to them that he had fent to *Menis*. Further added, That their Mafter the Governour of *Port Royal* muft im-

[329] *Pigiguit*, on the river of the fame name, now the Avon?

[117]

mediately send away a Post to the Governour of *Canada* at *Quebeck*, to prevent his further sending any of his cruel & bloudy *French* and Salvages, as he had done lately upon *Deerfield*, where they had committed such horrible and bloudy outrages upon those poor People, that never did them any harm, as is intollerable to think of; and that for the future, if any such Hostilities were made upon our Frontier Towns, or any of them, He would come out with a thousand Salvages, and Whale-boats convenient, and turn his back upon them, and let his Salvages Scalp & Rost the *French*; or at least treat them as their Salvages had treated ours: Also gave them an account of part of that action at *Passamequado*, and how that his Souldiers had Kill'd & Scalp'd some *Canada* Men [117] there, and would be glad to Serve them so too, if he would permit them. Which terrifyed them very much,[330] *&c.* The two French Gentlemen that came Post made solemn Promises that they would punctually do the Colonel's Message to their Governour. So with the desire of the French People there that the Governour might have this Intelligence, Col. *Church* dismiss'd them, and sent them away; telling the same Story to several of the Prisoners, and what they must expect if some speedy course was not taken to prevent further outrages upon the *English*. The number of Prisoners then Present (which were considerable) did unanimously intreat of Col. *Church*, that he would take them under the Protection of the Crown of *England*;

---
[330] See note 313. *ante.*

[117]

making great Promises of their fidelity to the same, begging with great Agony of Spirit to Save their Lives, and to protect them from his Salvages, whom they extreamly dreaded: As to the matter of the Salvages, He told them, It would be just Retaliation for him to permit his Salvages to treat the *French* in the same manner, as the *French* with their Salvages treated our friends in our Frontier Towns: But as to his taking them under the Protection of the Crown of *England*, he utterly refused it, urging to them their former Perfidiousness; they also urging to him, that it would be impossible for any *French* to live any where in the Bay of *Fundy*, if they were not taken under the *English* Government; for with the benefit of those Whaleboats,[331] (as the *English* called them) they could take and destroy all their People in the Town of *Menis* in one Night: But he reply'd to them, It should never be; alledging to them that when they were so before, when *Port Royal* was taken last by the *English* that it prov'd of very ill consequence to the Crown of *England*, & the Subjects thereof in our Frontiers; for that our *English* Traders supplying them; enabled them (which opportunity they im-

---

[331] The stress laid upon "whaleboats," both by Church in his report of his last expedition (p. 147) and his letter to Gov. Dudley (p. 131), and by the enemy, is explained by the fact that the enormous rise and fall of the tides in and near the Bay of Fundy made landing from, and coasting in, ordinary vessels — in that day when wharf conveniences were of the most primitive description — exceedingly difficult; a difficulty which the boats removed, since they could act as tenders, and leave the ship in deep water; and by the fact, that their swiftness made them more formidable in the pursuit of canoes than any other craft then in use, and their light draft enabled them to go in shallow water, and their lightweight made them especially available at the *portages*.

prov'd) to supply the *Indians* our bloudy Enemies; and therefore he could make no other Terms of Peace with them than that; if they the *French* at *Menis, Signecto* and *Canada,* would keep at home with their bloudy Salvages, and not commit any Hostilities upon any of our Frontiers, we would return home & leave them; for that we lived a great distance off, and had not come near them to hurt them now had not the blood of our poor Friends and Brethren in all the Frontiers of our Province cryed for Vengeance; especially that late unheard of Barbarity committed upon the Town of *Deerfield;* which wrought so generally on the hearts of our People, that our Forces came out with that Unanimity of Spirit, both among the *English* and our Salvages, that we had not, nor needed a Press'd Man among them. The Colonel also telling them, That if ever hereafter any of our Frontiers East or West were Molested by them, as formerly, that he would (if God spared his Life,) and they might depend upon it, Return upon them with a thousand of his Salvages, if he wanted them, all Volunteers, with our Whale-boats, and would pursue them to the last Extremity. The Colonels warm discourse with them [118] wrought such a consternation in them, which they discovered by their Panick fears and trembling, their hearts sensibly beating, and rising up as it were ready to choke them; confessed they were all his Prisoners, and beg'd of him, for JESUS sake, to Save their Lives, and the Lives of their poor Families; with such melting Terms as wrought relentings in the Colonels

[118]

Breaſt towards them; but however, he told them, That his intent was to carry as many Priſoners home as he could, but that he had taken ſo many, they were more than he had occaſion for, nor deſired any more; and therefore he would leave them.³³² The Colonel reſolving the next day to compleat all his action at *Menis*, and ſo draw off. Accordingly, ſent his orders to Col. *Gorcham* and Maj *Hilton*, with all the *Engliſh* Companies both Officers and Souldiers, except ſome few, which he thought he might have occaſion for to go with the *Indians* in the Whale-boats up the Eaſtward River,³³³ where a third part of the Inhabitants Lived; that ſo he might prevent any reflection made on them, in leaving any part of the Service undone. And therefore in the evening ordered all the Whale-boats to be laid ready for the Nights Service; and accordingly when the Tide Served, he went with his *Indians* up the River, where they did ſome ſpoil upon the Enemy going up. In the Morning ſeveral of their Tranſports came to meet them, to their great rejoycing, on whom they went on Board, and ſoon came up with the whole Fleet, with whom they joyned, bending their courſe directly towards *Port Royal*, where they were ordered. Coming to *Port Royal Gut* where their Ships were, and calling a Council

---

³³² Penhallow ſays the expedition "took a hundred priſoners." [*Ind. Wars*, 30.]

³³³ The *Cobeguit*, or *Cobequid* bay, terminating in Salmon river; from which was a *portage* over to *Tatamagouche* on Northumberland Strait, perhaps 7 miles in length.

according to his Instructions, drew up their result: Which is as followeth.

Aboard the Province Galley, 4th. July 1704.
In Port Royal Harbour.

Present all the Field Officers and
Captains of the Land Forces.

WE whose Names are hereunto Subscribed, having deliberately consider'd the cause in hand, whether it be proper to Land all our Forces to offend & destroy as much as we can at Port Royal, all or any part of the Inhabitants thereof, and their Estates, We are of Opinion, that 'tis not for our Interest & Honour, and the Countrys whom we Serve, to Land or expose our Selves; but quit it wholly, and go on about our other business we have to do, for this Reason, That we Judge our Selves Inferiour to the Strength of the Enemy; and therefore the Danger & Risque we run, is greater than the advantage we can, or are likely to obtain, seeing the Enemy hath such timely Notice, and long opportunity to Provide themselves against us, by our Ships lying here in the Road about Twelve Days, before we could joyn them from Menis, where we were during that time, and being so very meanly provided with necessaries convenient for such an Undertaking with so small a Number of Men, not being above Four hundred capable and fit for Service to Land; and understanding by all the Intelligence we can get

[119]

from both Englifh & French *Prifoners, that the Fort is exceeding Strong.*

John Gorcham Lieut. Col.	*Winthrop Hilton* Major. [119]	
Having, Purfuant to my Inftruc-	*Jof.*[334] *Brown*	*Conftant Church*
tions taken the advice of the Gen-	*James Cole*	*John Dyer*
tlemen above Subfcribed, and	*John Cook*	*Jofhua Lamb*
confidering the weight of their	*Ifaac Myrick*	*Caleb Williamfon*
Reafons, I do Concur therewith.	*John Harradon*	*Edward Church*
Benj. Church.		

WHereas Col. Church *hath defired our Opinions, as to the Landing the Forces at* Port Royal, *they being but* 400 *Effective Men to Land, and by all the Information both of* French & Englifh *Prifoners, the Enemy having a greater number of Men, and much better provided to Receive, than they are to Attack them, We do believe 'tis for the Service of the Crown, and Prefervation of Her Majefty's Subjects to act as above mentioned.*

Thomas Smith.   Geo. Rogers.   Cypryan Southack.

After this, they concluded what fhould be next done; which was, that the Ships fhould ftay fome Days longer at *Port Royall Gut,* and then go over to Mount *Defart* Harbour, and there ftay till Col. *Church* with his Tranfports came to them. Being all ready, the Colonel with his Tranfports & Forces went up the Bay to *Signecto,* where they needed not a Pilot, being feveral of them well acquainted there: (and had not met with fo many difficul-

---

[334] Mifprint for *John.* This captain's name is diftinctly ftated to be *John* (p. 138). See note 278, *ante.*

ties at *Menis*, had it not been that their Pilot deceiv'd them;[335] who knew nothing of the matter, kept out of the way and Landed not with them, &c.) And coming to *Signecto*,[336] the Enemy were all in Arms ready to receive them, Col. *Church* Landing his Men; the Commander of the Enemy waving his Sword over his head, bid a Challange to them: The Colonel ordering his two Wings to March up a-pace, and come upon the backs of the Enemy, himself being in the Center, and the Enemy knowing him, (having been there before) Shot chiefly at him; (but thro' Gods goodness received no harm, neither had he one Man kill'd, nor but two slightly wounded) and then ran all away into the Woods, and left their Town with nothing in it; having had timely Notice of our Forces, had carryed all away out of the reach of our Army; for Col. *Church* while there with part of his Forces Ranged the Woods, but to no purpose: Then returning to the Town, did them what spoil he could; according to his Instructions, and so drew off, and made the best of their way for *Paſſamequado*, (and going in) in a great Fog, one of their Transports ran upon a Rock, but was soon got off again. Then Col. *Church* with some of his Forces embark'd in their Whaleboats, and went amongst the Islands, with an intent to go to *Sharkee*'s where they had destroyed the Fish;[337] but observing a Springgy place in a Cove, went on Shore to get some Water to drink, it being a Sandy beach, they

---

[335] That is "they would not have met with so many difficulties, &c."

[336] *Beau-baſin.* See note 229, *ante*.

[337] See p. 161.

espy'd Tracks, the Colonel presently ordered his Men to scatter, and make a search; soon found *De Boisses*[338] Wife, who had formerly been Col. *Church*'s Prisoner, and carried to *Boston*; but returned, who seemed to be very glad to see him: She had with her two Sons that were near Men grown; the Colonel ordering them a part, Examined the Woman first, who gave him this account following, That she had lived there-abouts ever since the Fleet went by, and that she had never seen but two *Indians* since, who came in a Canoo from *Norrigiwock*; who ask'd her, what made her to be there alone? She told them, She had not seen a *French* Man nor an *Indian* except those two since the *English* Ships went by. Then the *Indians* told her there was not one *Indian* left except those two, who belong to the Gut of *Cancer*, on this side of *Canada*: for the Fryers coming down with the *Indians* to Monsieur *Gordans*, and finding the French-men slain, and their Hair spoiled, being Scalp'd, put them into a great Consternation; and the Fryers told them it was impossible for them to live there-abouts, for the *English* with their Whale-boats would serve them all so; upon which they all went up to *Norrigiwock*: Also told her that when the *English* came along thro' *Penobscot*, they had swept it of the Inhabitants, as if it had been swept with a Broom, neither *French* nor *Indians* escaping them. Further told her, That when their Fathers the Fryers, and the *Indians*

---

[338] *Du Bois?* probably taken prisoner when Church was here before, in a previous expedition.

met together at *Norrigiwock* they call'd a Council, and the Fryers told the *Indians*, That they muſt look out for ſome other Country, for that it was impoſſible for them to live there; alſo told them there was a River call'd *Moſſippee*[339] where they might live quietly and no *Engliſh* come near them: It being as far beyond *Canada* as it was to it, *&c.* and if they would go and live there, they would live & dye with them, but if not they would leave them, and never come near them again. Whereupon they all agreed to go away; which they did, and left their Ruff houſhold-ſtuff, and Corn behind them, and went all, except thoſe two for *Canada*. Alſo her Sons giving the ſame Intelligence, ſo we had no reaſon to think but that it was true. Col. *Church* having done what he could there, Embark'd on board the Tranſports and went to Mount *Deſart*, where he expected to have met with the Ships from *Port Royal Gut*; and going into the Harbour at Mount *Deſart*, found

---

[339] The *Miſſiſſippi* (Ind. *Miche Sepe;* called by the early Jeſuits *Meſſ-Sipi*). As early as 1669, Father *Marquette* reſolved upon viſiting this wonderful river, of which rumors came to him from the ſavages. It is firſt mentioned in the "*Relations des Jeſuites,*" in 1670, as "*une grande Riviere large d'une lieuë et davantage, qui venant des quartiers du Nord, coule vers le Sud, et ſi loin que les ſauvages qui ont navigé ſur cette Riviere, allant chercher des enemis à combattre, aprés quantité de journées de navigation, n'en ont point trouvé l'embouchere, quie ne peut eſtre que vers la Mer de la Floride, ou celle de Californie.*" [*Relation*, 1670: 80.] In 1673, *Marquette*, with *Louis Jolliet*, reached the river, and deſcended it probably as far as the mouth of the Arkanſas. (His narrative of this journey may be found in Shea's *Diſcovery and Exploration of the Miſſiſſippi Valley;* having been firſt publiſhed, in 1681, in Thévenot's *Recueil de Voyages.*) Of courſe, his information had added certainty to all vague floating rumors before exiſting; and the Jeſuits in Canada, before the date of this expedition of Col. Church, were able to ſpeak with ſome confidence of this wonderful ſtream. [See *Relations des Jeſuites*, 1670: 91, 100; 1671: 24, 47.]

no Ships there, but a Runlet[340] rid off by a line in the Harbour, which he ordered to be taken up, and opening of it found a Letter, which gave him an account that the Ships were gone home for *Boston*. Then he proceeded & went to *Penobscot*; where being come, made diligent search in those Parts for the Enemy, but could not find or make any discovery of them, or that any had been there since he left those Parts, which caus'd him to believe what *De Boisses* Wife had told him was true. (I will only by the way just give a hint of what we heard since of the Effects of this Expedition, & then proceed.) [First, That the *English* Forces that went next to *Norrigiwock* found that the Enemy was gone, & had left their Ruff houshold-stuff and Corn behind them; also not long after this Expedition, there were several Gentlemen sent down from *Canada* to concert with our Governour about the settling of a Cartile[341] for the Exchange of Prisoners; and that the Governour of *Canada* has never since sent down any Army upon our Frontiers (as I know of) except some times a Scout of *Indians* to take some Prisoners, that he might be informed of our State, and what we were acting *&c.* and always took care that the Prisoners so taken should be Civily Treated, and safely Returned, as I have been informed; that some of the Prisoners that were taken gave an account; so that we have great cause to be-

---

[340] "*Rundlet* (probably *q. d. Roundlet*),—a close cask for Liquors, containing from three to twenty Gallons."—*Bailey*.

[341] *Cartel* (from *cartellus*, from *chartula*, diminutive of *charta, i.e.*, a "little writing"),—a writing, or agreement, between States at war, as for the exchange of prisoners. [*Webster*.]

lieve that the Message Col. *Church* sent by the two *French* Gentlemen from *Menis* to the Governour of *Port Royal* took Effect, and was a means to bring Peace in our borders, &c.] Then Col. *Church* with his Forces embark'd on board the Transports, and went to *Casco Bay*, where they met with Capt. *Gallop* in a Vessel from *Boston*, who had brought Col *Church* further Orders; which was to send some of his Forces up to *Norrigiwock* in pursuit of the Enemy; but he being sensible that the Enemy were gone from thence, and that his Souldiers were much wore-out & fategu'd in the hard Service they had already done, & wanted to get home, call'd a Council, and agreed all to go home, which accordingly they did. To Conclude this Expedition, I will just give a hint of some treatment Col. *Church* had before & after he came home: for all his great Expences, Fategues & Hardships in and about this Expedition. (*viz*) He received of his Excellency *Fifteen* Pounds as an earnest Peny towards Raising of Volunteers; and when he came to receive his Debenture [342] for his Colonels Pay, there was 2 s. 4 d. due to him; and as for his Captains Pay,[343] & Man *Jack* he has never received any thing as yet. Also after he came home some ill minded Persons did their endeavour to have taken away his Life, for that there was some of the *French* Enemy Kill'd this Expedi-

---

[342] *Debenture*, — a writing or certificate signed by a public officer in evidence of a debt due: so called because, in Latin, such documents used to begin *Debentur mihi*, &c.

[343] His commission was twofold (see p. 136, appointing him Captain of the first company of his command, as well as Colonel of all the forces embarked upon the expedition.

tion:[344] but his Excellency the Governour, the Honourable Council and Houſe of Repreſentatives ſaw cauſe to Clear him, and gave him Thanks for his good Service done.[345]

[344] Church's language here might almoſt ſuggeſt that ſome attempt had been made to bring him to a capital trial for alleged malfeaſance in the matter at *Paſſamaquoddy* (p. 157). But I find no evidence of any thing of the ſort.

[345] The original edition of 1716 gives evidence of that "cutting the coat according to the cloth," which was not unuſual in books of that time, and which is not wholly unknown now. In the endeavor to come out even at the end of a page and of a ſignature, the laſt two pages are ſet in type of ſmaller ſize than the reſt of the volume, the "ſpaces" are made thinner, and 51 lines are crowded into a page whoſe meaſure has been 42. In this proceſs of compreſſion, the *MSS*. doubtleſs ſuffered ſomewhat; and, could we recover the laſt page from which Green's compoſitors worked, we ſhould be quite likely to find one or two cloſing remarks from the blunt yet courtly old warrior, which the inexorable demands of the "form" excluded.

FINIS.

CHRONOLOGICAL TABLE OF EVENTS.

Chronological Table of Events.

(☞ It will be noticed that the dates are comparatively few which can be exactly identified.)

Day of Week.	Day of Month.	Year.	EVENT.	Page.
—	Last of Oct.	1688	Church received Andros's express at Little Compton	1
—	,, ,,	,,	Church went to Boston	2
—	,, ,,	,,	,, Returned home	3
Th.	18 April	1689	The Revolution which deposed Andros	3
—	– July	,,	Church waited on Governor Bradstreet, by request	4
—	– ,,	,,	Church went to Rhode Island to ask assistance	5
—	– Aug.	,,	Church returned to Boston, reporting progress, and goes to raising volunteers	5
F.	6 Sept.	,,	Church commissioned by Governor Hinkley for the First Expedition	6
M.	16 ,,	,,	Church received his instructions from Danforth	8
T.	17 ,,	,,	Church received his commission from Massachusetts, as Major	9
W.	18 ,,	,,	Church received his instructions from Massachusetts, as Major	11
—	– ,,	,,	Church sailed for Falmouth, Me.	16
—	——	,,	,, Had a fight with the Indians	20
—	——	,,	,, Ranged the country	28
M.	11 Nov.	,,	,, Held a council of war at Scarborough	29

CHRONOLOGICAL TABLE OF EVENTS.

Day of Week.	Day of Month.	Year.	EVENT.	Page.
W.	13 Nov.	1689	Church held a council of war at Falmouth	29
—	– Jan.	16$\frac{89}{90}$	Church returned home	32
W.	16 ,, ?	,,	,, Went back to Boston, to plead for the down-easters . .	32
Th.	6 Feb.	,,	Church left his plea for them on the Council Board, and went home in disgust	33
—	– April	1690	Church goes to Charlestown, when the Canada Expedition is about to sail, to see his friends off . .	37
—	——	,,	Church has an interview with the Governor and Council	39
	——	,,	Church goes to Barnstable, to see Governor Hinkley	40
—	——	,,	Church raises forces, and marches them to Plymouth	41
T.	2 Sept.	,,	Church is commissioned for the Second Expedition, by Governor Hinkley.	42
W.	3 ,, ?	,,	Church reaches Portsmouth . . .	47
T.	9 ,,	,,	,, Receives Major Pike's Instructions	48
—	——	,,	Church sailed for Pejepscot, and marched to Androscoggin . .	50
S.	14 Sept.	,,	Church took the fort	51
—	——	,,	,, Went to *Maquait* . . .	56
W.	17 Sept.	,,	,, Reached Saco	56
—	——	,,	,, Chased the Indians . . .	57
S.	20 Sept.	,,	,, Bivouacked at *Purpooduck*	60
M.	22 ,,	,,	,, Came to "Cape Neddicke"	64
T.	23 ,,	,,	,, Sent scout to Saco . . .	64
F.	26 ,,	,,	,, Got back to Portsmouth .	65
S.	——	,,	,, Sailed for Boston in the sloop Mary	66
—	– Oct.	,,	,, Lodged at Captain Alden's	67
T.	– ,,	,,	,, Borrowed 40s. of Brayton .	68
—	——	,,	,, Rode home on a borrowed horse	68

CHRONOLOGICAL TABLE OF EVENTS.

Day of Week.	Day of Month.	Year.	EVENT.	Page.
Th.	27 Nov.	1690	Church wrote to some Eastern gentlemen	69
M.	29 June	1691	The Eastern gentlemen replied	79
—	—	1692	Church, on request of Major Walley, from Governor Phips, goes to Boston to consult about the Third Eastern Expedition	83
M.	25 July	—	Church receives Phips's commission	83
—	—	—	,, Raises volunteers.	84
—	- Aug.	—	,, Embarks for *Pemaquid*	85
—	—	—	,, Works on the fort there	86
Th.	11 Aug.	—	,, Is commissioned for Penobscot, &c.	87
—	—	—	,, Ranged those regions, destroying corn, &c.	89–90
—	—	—	,, Returned to *Pemaquid*.	90
—	—	—	,, Has more orders for the *Kennebec*	90
—	—	—	,, Had a fight, and burned *Teconnet* Fort.	91
—	—	—	,, Returned to *Pemaquid*.	92
—	—	—	,, Came back to Boston and Bristol	92
—	—	1696	,, Is at Boston as Deputy from Bristol	93
—	—	,,	,, Is persuaded to go East on a Third Expedition	93
—	—	,,	,, Raises volunteers	93
M.	3 Aug.	,,	,, Is commissioned by Lieutenant Governor Stoughton	94
W.	12 ,,	,,	Church receives his instructions	96
S.	15 ,,	,,	,, Sailed for Portsmouth	99
S.	22 ,,	,,	,, ,, York	100
—	,,	,,	,, ,, Monhegan	101
—	- Sept.	,,	,, (in boats) went up the Penobscot Bay	101
—	—	,,	,, Had a skirmish, and took captives	103–7
—	—	,,	,, Back to the ships	108

CHRONOLOGICAL TABLE OF EVENTS.

Day of Week.	Day of Month.	Year.	EVENT.	Page.
—	——	1696	Church sailed for *Beau Basin*	109
—	——	,,	,, Thence to St. John	116
—	——	,,	,, On their way home from thence interrupted and superseded by Colonel Hathorne	123
—	——	,,	Church home again	127
—	1 Feb.	170¾	,, Waited on Governor Dudley to offer his services against the Indians and French, being moved thereto by late shocking outrages	130
S.	5 ,,	,,	Church writes Governor Dudley his ideas on the best way of carrying on another expedition	131-135
—	——	,,	Church goes to work to fit out the Fifth Expedition	136
S.	18 March	,,	Church receives Dudley's commission	136
—	- ,,	,,	Church raises volunteers in all the towns of the three counties of the Old Colony	137
—	——	1704	Church marches his troops to Nantasket	138
Th.	4 May	,,	,, Receives his instructions	141
—	——	,,	,, Went by land to Portsmouth	145
—	——	,,	,, Raises another company there	145
—	——	,,	,, Moves to *Matinicus*	146
W.	7 June	,,	,, Takes prisoners who give him information	146
—	- ,,	,,	,, Went up the river, had a fight, and took prisoners, some of whom were knocked on the head	150-157
—	- ,,	,,	Church failed to take *Chartier*	160
—	- ,,	,,	,, Burned the Indians' fish	161
—	- ,,	,,	,, Returned, went on board the transports, and sailed for *Port Royal* and *Les Mines*	162

CHRONOLOGICAL TABLE OF EVENTS.

Day of Week.	Day of Month.	Year.	EVENT.	Page.
T.	20 June	1704	Church reached *Les Mines*, and summoned its surrender . . .	163–5
W.	21 ,,	,,	Church burned the town, and took many prisoners	166–8
Th.	22 ,,	,,	Church dug down their dams, and spoiled their crops; and at night captured *Pigiguit*	168–169
F.	23 ,,	,,	Church took *Cobeguit*, &c. . . .	173
—	— ,,	,,	,, Sailed for *Port Royal* . .	173
T.	4 July	,,	,, Had a council of war at *Port Royal*	174–175
—	— ,,	,,	,, Went up to *Beau Basin*, which they spoiled again	175
—	——	,,	,, Sailed for *Passamaquoddy*	176
—	——	,,	,, Took Du Bois's wife prisoner	177
—	——	,,	,, Sailed for *Mount Desert*, and so to Casco, and home . .	178–180
—	——	,,	The Governor, Council, and House of Representatives clear Colonel Church of all imputations of misconduct, and give him thanks for his good service done	181

INDEX.

INDEX.

The Roman numerals refer to pages in the Introduction. The Arabic figures refer to pages in the "History," the numbering in all cases being found at the bottom of each successive page. The names of Indians are in *italics*.

A.

Adams, Rev. William, of Dedham, xiv.; Nathaniel, 77 *note*.
Addington, Isaac, notice of, 11 *note*.
Alden, Capt. John, a naval commander, 66 *note*, 67 *note*, 74; mention of him, 110, 120; William, 107.
Alexander, or *Wamsutta*, son of *Massasoit*, succeeds his father, xx.; brought to Plymouth, xxi.; not ill treated there, xxii.; the facts stated, *ibid.*; dies, *ibid.*
Alger, Andrew, killed, 27 *note*.
Allen, Rev. James, of Boston, xiii.
Allyn, Samuel, of Barnstable, 42.
Amos, Capt., commands an Indian company, 7 *note*.
Andrews, Elisha, 29 *note*, 64 *note*, 74; James, 64 *note*; Samuel, *ibid.*
Andros, Sir Edmund, his history, 1 *note*; sends for Capt. Church, 1; sent prisoner to England, 32; date of this event, *ibid. note*.
Androscoggin, or Amerascogen, described, 49 *note*.

Arnold, Rev. Samuel, of Marshfield, xiii.
Atherton, Rev. Hope, of Hatfield, xv.
Austin, Matthew, 73 *note*.

B.

Baker, Rev. Nicholas, of Scituate, xiv.; Thomas, a prisoner to the Indians, escapes, 58; notice of him, *ibid. note*.
Barbarities of the Indians, 129.
Barker, Lieut., killed at Les Mines, 168.
Barnard, Benjamin, 54 *note*.
Bassett, William, 29 *note*.
Belcher, Andrew, 140 *note*.
Berry, Thomas, 27 *note*.
Billingsgate Point, described, 42 *note*.
Bit, a silver coin, its value, 85 *note*.
Black Point, where, 28 *note*; a fort there, *ibid.*
Blue Point, where, 29 *note*.
Boad, Henry, 107 *note*.
Bourne, Rev. Richard, missionary, xvii.
Bowers, Rev. John, of Branford, xiv.
Brackett, Anthony, 17 *note*; account of, 21 *note*; shot by the Indians, *ibid.*,

INDEX.

27 *note;* his children, 21 *note;* Anthony, his fon, efcapes, 60; again mentioned, 104, 120.

Bradford, William, deputy-governor, xxi. xxii. 40 *note.*

Bradftreet, Rev. Simon, of New London, xiv.; Simon, governor of Maffachufetts, 3; his hiftory, *ibid. note;* fends for Church, 4.

Bramhall, Mr., of Cafco, mortally wounded, 27 *note.*

Brayton, Stephen, of Portfmouth, R.I., a drover, 68; lends money to Church, *ibid.;* Francis, *ibid.*

Bridgway, or Bourgeois, Jarman, 111, 112, 113.

Brimfmead, Rev. William, of Marlborough, xv.

Brock, Rev. John, of South Reading, xiv.

Brown, John, captain in Church's Fifth Expedition, 138, 175; notice of him, 138 *note.*

Browne, Rev. Edmund, of Sudbury, xiv.; Thomas, of Cafco, wounded, 27 *note.*

Buckingham, Rev. Thomas, of Saybrook, xiv.

Bulkley, Rev. Edward, of Concord, xiii.; Rev. Gerfhom, of Wethersfield, xiv.

Burton, Thomas, 27 *note.*

Buttolph, Prifcilla, 10 *note.*

Byfield, Nathaniel, of Briftol, 40 *note,* 69 *note.*

C.

Carter, Rev. Thomas, of Woburn, xiv.

Cafco, in danger from Indians, 17; fight with Indians there, 23–26; arrangements made by Church for their fafety, 30; he returns home, 31; Cafco taken by the Indians, and the inhabitants killed or carried away, 36; the dead remain unburied two years, 85 *note;* buried by Phips's foldiers, *ibid.*

Caftin, Vincent de St., account of, 19 *note;* his lucrative trade with the Indians, *ibid.;* violates the capitulation of Cafco, and deftroys the inhabitants, 36; commands an Indian force at the taking of Fort William Henry, Pemaquid, 98 *note;* his daughter and her children taken prifoners by Church, 150.

Cawley, or Caule, Robert, of Pemaquid, 107; notice of him, *ibid. note.*

Chartier. See *Sharkee.*

Chauncey, Rev. Nathaniel, of Windfor, xiii.

Chubb, Pafco, furrenders Fort William Henry to the Indians, 98 *note;* is murdered at Andover, with his wife, *ibid.*

CHURCH, Capt. BENJAMIN, at Saconet, Little Compton, 1; is fent for by Gov. Andros, *ibid.;* arrives in Bofton, 2; the Governor propofes an Eaftern expedition, 3: Church declines the undertaking, *ibid.;* is fent for by Gov. Bradftreet after the overthrow of Andros, 4; comes to Bofton, *ibid.;* undertakes an expedition againft the Indians " in the Eaftern Parts," *ibid.;* goes to Rhode Ifland to obtain affiftance, and returns to Bofton, 5; his commiffion from the Council of War, 6; commiffion from the Prefident of Maine, 8; commiffioned as Major by the Governor and Council of Maffachufetts Bay, 9; inftructions from the Commiffioners of the United Colonies, 11; his FIRST EASTERN EXPEDITION, 16; arrives at Cafco, *ibid.;* hears of Indians in the

INDEX.

neighborhood, 17; orders given by him, 19; embarraffed by the bullets furnifhed being too large, 22; his force attacked by a body of Indians, *ibid.*; their repulfe, 26; he vifits the garrifons at Black Point, &c., 28; holds a council of war at Scarborough, 29 *note*; makes arrangements for the fecurity of the Eaftern fettlements, 30; returns home at the approach of winter, 31; fpends three weeks in Bofton, 33; reprefents to the Governor and Council the expofed condition of the Eaftern fettlements, 33-35; this reprefentation not attended to, 36; flender compenfation of Church, *ibid.*; his SECOND EASTERN EXPEDITION, 37; he comes again to Bofton, 38; the Council confult him in refpect to the war, 39; his anfwer, 40; goes to Barnftable to fee Gov. Hinckley, *ibid.*; raifes a force, and marches with it to Plymouth, 41; finds no preparation there, *ibid.*; commiffioned by the Council of War of Plymouth Colony for a fecond expedition to Maine, 42; their inftructions to him, 44-47; arrives at Pifcataqua [Portfmouth], 47; receives inftructions there from Major Pike, 48; fails for Pejepfcot, 50 *note*; lands at Maquoit in Freeport, *ibid.*; releafes two Englifh captives, 51; takes the fort at Pejepfcot [Brunfwick], *ibid.*; fpares an Indian captive, 55; kills others, *ibid.*; returns to Maquoit, 56; fails to Winter Harbor [Saco], *ibid.*; puts the Indians to flight, 57; difagreement between him and his captains, 59; arrives at Purpooduck, 60; encounters Indians there, 62; comes to Wells, 64; and to Portfmouth, 65; fends home his foldiers, 66; fails for Bofton in floop Mary, *ibid.*; deftitute of money, and gets none from the government, 67, 68; tries to borrow a fmall fum, and is refufed, 67; borrows forty fhillings of a drover, 68; returns home, *ibid.*; a lofer by his patriotic fervices, *ibid.*; his letter to Wheelwright and others, refpecting the mifreprefentations which had been made of his conduct, and his confequent lofs of favor from the government. 69-76; ftate of things in Maine after Church's departure, 74; application to him from gentlemen at the eaftward for help againft the Indians, 79, 80; his anfwer, 81; his THIRD EASTERN EXPEDITION, 82; invited by Gov. Phips to accompany him in his expedition into Maine, 83; Church confents, and receives a commiffion, *ibid.*; is forced to borrow money in order to go, 84; arrives at Pemaquid, 85; is difinclined to have a fort built there, 86; is fent to fight the Indians on the Penobfcot, *ibid.*; his inftructions from Phips, 87; ranges thofe parts, and deftroys the enemy's corn, 90; returns to Pemaquid, *ibid.*; is ordered to the Kennebec, *ibid.*; has a brufh there with the Indians, *ibid.*; returns once more to Pemaquid, 92; returns to Bofton, and again deprived by the government of his juft dues, *ibid.*; is a deputy in the General Court from Briftol, 93; his FOURTH EASTERN EXPEDITION, *ibid.*; raifes a volunteer force, *ibid.*; receives a commiffion from Lieut. Gov. Stoughton, 94; his inftructions to Church, 96, 97; fails for Pifcataqua, 99; lands at York, 100; proceeds to Saco, *ibid.*; arrives at Monhegan, 101; afcends

INDEX.

Penobscot Bay and River as far as Old Town, 102, 103; returns to his vessels at the mouth of the river, 106; visits Mount Desert and other places, but finds no enemy, 108; sails up the Bay of Fundy and lands at Beau Basin, 110; the enemy take to flight, 111; Church takes several prisoners, 112, 113; penetrates into the country, and returns to Beau Basin, 114; his discourse with the Acadians, 114, 115; restrains his Indian followers from hurting them, 115; enters the river St. John, 116; skirmish with the French, 117; is superseded by Col. Hathorne, 123; returns to Boston, 127; his FIFTH EASTERN EXPEDITION, 128; he offers his services again to the government, 130; his plan for a campaign against the Indians, 131-135; his commission from Gov. Dudley, 136; raises volunteers, 137; in this incurs heavy expense, not re-imbursed, 138; requests permission to attack Port Royal in Acadia, 139; is denied, 140, 141; his instructions from Gov. Dudley, 141-145; proceeds on the expedition, 146; takes prisoners and obtains information from them, 147-149; takes Castin's daughter at Penobscot, 150; scours the coast as far as Passamaquoddy, 150, 151; writes to Dudley a history of his proceedings, 151-159; his actions at Passamaquoddy, 152; is greatly displeased with a party of his own soldiers, and why, 156; a busy night, 157; embarks for Les Mines, 162; demands the surrender of that town, 163; the document inserted, 163-165; takes possession of the town, 166; makes a "temperance movement," 167; burns the town, 168; takes many prisoners, 169; sends a threatening message to Port Royal and Quebec, with good results, 170; his conference with the prisoners taken at Mines, 171; tells them of Deerfield, and threatens retaliation, 172; the prisoners greatly frightened, *ibid.*; he sails for Port Royal, 173; a council of war dissuade from an attack on that place, 175; the document given, *ibid.*; takes possession of Chignecto, or Beau Basin, after a skirmish, 176; returns to Passamaquoddy, *ibid.*; receives information that the Indians had gone to Norridgewock, 177; sails to Mount Desert, 178; to Casco, and returns to Boston, 180; receives thanks, but no pay, 180, 181. See Chronological Table, at the close of the volume.

Church, Caleb, of Watertown, brother of Benjamin, 68; notice of him, *ibid. note;* his children, *ibid.*; Constant, captain in the Fifth Eastern Expedition, 139, 146, 175; Edward, captain in the same expedition, 139, 167, 175.

Clark, Thaddeus, of Falmouth, 25 *note*, 29 *note;* killed by Indians, *ibid.*; his family, *ibid.*; Walter, governor of Rhode Island, notices of him, 5 *note;* his family, *ibid.*; Isaac, *ibid.*; William, captain, notice of him, 140 *note.*

Cobbet, Rev. Thomas, of Ipswich, xiii.

Cole, James, captain in the Fifth Eastern Expedition, 139, 153, 175.

Collins, Rev. Nathaniel, of Middletown, xv.

Connecticut, towns settled therein, in 1675, x.

Converse, Capt. James, of Woburn, with Church, 60; notices of him, *ibid. note;* comes to Boston with Church, 66; destitute of money, 67.

INDEX.

Cook, John, captain in Church's Fifth Eastern Expedition, 139, 146, 167, 175.
Cooke, Dr. Elisha, 15 *note*.
Cotton, Rev. John, of Plymouth, xiii.; Rev. Seaborn, of Hampton, xiii.
Cushing, John, of Scituate, 40 *note*.
Cutt, Richard, 76 *note*; John, 80 *note*.

D.

Dane, Rev. Francis, of Andover, xiv.
Danforth, Rev. Samuel, of Roxbury, xiii.; Thomas, president of Maine, his commission to Church, 8; notices of him, 9 *note*.
Daniel, Capt., leader of an Indian company, 7 *note*.
Davis, Ambrose, 29 *note*; Silvanus, notices of, 14 *note*; his residence, 18 *note*; present at a council of war, 29 *note*.
Deerfield destroyed by the Indians, 128, 129; this moves Church to undertake his Fifth Eastern Expedition, 130; he threatens the French with similar treatment, 164, 170.
Deering, James, 21 *note*.
Doney, half Frenchman, half Indian, 51 *note*, 57 *note*.
Drake, Abraham, 21 *note*.
Dudley, Joseph, governor of Massachusetts, his commission to Church, 136; notices of him, *ibid. note*; his family, *ibid.*; his instructions to Church, 141-145.
Dummer, Rev. Shubael, of York, xv.
Dyer, John, captain in Church's Fifth Expedition, 139, 175.

E.

Easton, John, his account of a conference between Philip and the English, xxviii.

Eaton, Daniel, 37 *note*.
Ebens [Evans], Edward, 27 *note*.
Eddy, Edee, sergeant, 160.
Eliot, Rev. John, of Roxbury, xiii. xvii.; Rev. Joseph, of Guilford, xiv.
Elliot, Robert, of Scarborough, 80 *note*.
Elkins, Henry, 17 *note*.
Emerson, Rev. John, of Gloucester, xiv.; Rev. Joseph, of Mendon, xv.
Estabrook, Rev. Joseph, of Concord, xiii.
EXPEDITION, First, 16.
    Second, 37.
    Third, 82.
    Fourth, 93.
    Fifth, 128.

F.

Fellows, William, 145.
Fernald, William, of Kittery, surgeon, 80 *note*.
Finney, Jeremiah, of Bristol, R.I., 70 *note*; Josiah, *ibid*.
Fiske, Rev. John, of Chelmsford, xv. Rev. Moses, of Quincy, xiv.
Fitch, Rev. James, of Norwich, xv.
Flint, Rev. Josiah, of Dorchester, xiii.
Fobes, William, 85.
Foxwell, Philip, 29 *note*; Richard, *ibid*.
Freeman, John, of Eastham, 40 *note*.
Freeze, James, mortally wounded, 27 *note*.
Frontenac, Count, his expedition against the Maquas or Iroquois, 104 *note*.
Frost, Charles, Major, notice of, 77 *note*.
Fryer, Nathaniel, of Portsmouth, N.H., 76 *note*.

G.

Gallison, Elisha, 29 *note*.
Gedney, Col. Bartholemew, commands a force at York, 99; notices of him, *ibid. note*; John, *ibid*.

INDEX.

Gendall, Walter, 17 *note*.

Glover, Rev. Pelatiah, of Springfield, xiii.

Goodwin, Ozias, 16 *note*.

Gorham, Capt. John, second in command under Church in his Fourth Expedition, 97; notice of him, *ibid. note;* is sent by Church to Winter Harbor [Saco], 100; second in command under Church in his Fifth Expedition, 138, 152, 162, 165, 173, 175.

Gourdon, or Gourdan, a Frenchman, 148, 153, 155.

Green, Samuel, dies of small-pox, 32 *note*.

Gyles, John, sent with a flag of truce to demand the surrender of Les Mines in Nova Scotia, 163, 203.

H.

Hale, Rev. John, of Beverly, xv.

Hall, Nathaniel, 10 *note*, 12, 27, 29 *note*, 30 *note*.

Hanford, Rev. Thomas, of Norwalk, xv.

Haraden, John, of Gloucester, 145 *note*, 175; Edward, *ibid*.

Hathorne, Col. John, supersedes Church in the command of the Fourth Eastern Expedition, 123, 124.

Hawkins, John, an Indian. See *Kankamagus.*

Haynes, Rev. Joseph, of Hartford, xiii. xv.

Heard, Ann, of Cochecho [Dover], 54 *note*.

Higginson, Rev. John, of Salem, xiii.

Hill, John, 30 *note*.

Hilton, Edward, 146; Winthrop, major in Church's Fifth Eastern Expedition, 146, 153, 162, 165, 173, 175.

Hinckley, Thomas, governor of Plymouth Colony, 6; notices of, *ibid. note*, 40 *note*.

Hobart, Rev. Jeremiah, of Topsfield, xiv.; Rev. Nehemiah, of Newton, xv.; Rev. Peter, of Hingham, xiii.

Holmes, Rev. John, of Duxbury, xlii.

Homes, David, killed, 27 *note*.

Hooke, Francis, of Kittery, 80; notices of, *ibid.*, *note*.

Hooker, Rev. Samuel, of Farmington, xv.

Huckins, James, of Oyster River [now Durham, N.H.], 54 *note;* Robert, *ibid.;* his wife intercedes for an Indian captive, 54.

Hunniwell, Richard, 30 *note*, 58 *note;* notices of, 77 *note;* "the Indian killer," *ibid.;* with Church at St. John, 120.

I.

Iberville, Lemoine d', a skilful naval commander, his name strangely metamorphosed by Church, 105; founds a colony on the Mississippi, *ibid. note.*

Indians, their numbers in 1675, x. Indians, Praying, their numbers in 1675, xvi.; improved condition of the Indians, xix.; causes of the Indian war, xxxi.; Indians accompany Church in his expedition, 20; Indians attack Church at Casco, 22; are repulsed, 26; take the fort at Pejepscot Falls [Brunswick], 39; evacuate it, 50; are put to flight at Saco, 57; and at Purpooduck, 63; kill several prisoners, 64; ask for peace, 74; their treacherous conduct, 79; attacked by Church, and their fort at Taconick [Winslow] burned, 91, 106; some are slain by

INDEX.

Church's soldiers on the Penobscot, 103; Indian barbarities at Deerfield, 128, 129.
Ingersoll, George, 29 *note*.
Inventory and equipments of a French fort, 117 *note*.

J.

Jacob, Richard, 10 *note*.
Jacobs, Nicholas, of Hingham, 72 *note*.
Jones, Rev. Eliphalet, of Stamford, xiv.
Jordan, Dominicus, 28 *note*, 57 *note*; Rev. Robert, 28 *note*.
Jose, Richard, 17 *note*.

K.

Kankamagus, or *John Hawkins*, a sachem of Pennacook, 53 *note*, 64.
Keith, Rev. James, of Bridgewater, xv.

L.

Lafaure. See *Lefevre*.
Lamb, Joshua, captain in Church's Fifth Expedition, 139, 175.
Lane, Edward, son of Edward, of Boston, 2 *note*; his name changed to Paige, *ibid*.
Larkin, captain with Church at St. John, 120.
Lathrop, or Lothrop, John, of Barnstable, 41; his family, *ibid. note*; Joseph, of Barnstable, notice of, 73 *note*; his family, *ibid*.
Lawrence, Robert, 29 *note*, 30 *note*.
Lee, Abram, 17 *note*; Esther, his wife, gives information concerning Indians, 19; Samuel, minister of Bristol, R.-I., his history, 70 *note*.

Lefevre, Lafebure, or Lafaure, a prisoner to Church in his Fifth Expedition, 147.
Lightfoot, a friendly Indian captain, 22.
Little, Isaac, of Marshfield, 40 *note*.
Littlefield, John, son of Edmund of Wells, 73 *note*.
Losses sustained by the colonies in Philip's War, xxxi.
Loyall, Fort, in Falmouth, 17 *note*.

M.

Maine, progress of colonization in, in 1675, ix.
Mashpee Indians furnished soldiers in Church's expeditions, and in the Revolutionary War, 20 *note*.
Martin, or Martyn, Richard, notice of, 80 *note*.
Mason, Samuel, notice of, 15 *note*; John, killed, 27 *note*.
Massachusetts, progress of colonization therein, in 1675, ix.
Massachusetts Indians, number in 1675, x.
Mather, Rev. Increase, of Boston, xiv.
Maxwell, James, notice of, 39 *note*.
Mayflower company, survivors in 1675, xi.
Mayhew, Rev. John, of Tisbury, xv; Experience, 7 *note*.
Mitton, Michael, 21 *note*, 25 *note*, 64 *note*.
Moody, Rev. Joshua, of Portsmouth, xv.
Myrick, or Mirick, Isaac, captain in Church's Fifth Eastern Expedition, 139, 153, 175.

N.

Narragansetts, their number in 1675, x.
New England, its condition in 1675, ix. xvii.; losses by Philip's War, xxxi.

INDEX.

New Hampshire, progress of colonization in, in 1675, ix.
Newman, Rev. Noah, of Rehoboth, xiv.
Newton, Rev. Roger, of Milford, xiv.
Nipmuk Indians, number in 1675, x.
Numpas, a friendly Indian in Church's First Expedition, 7 *note*, 20 *note*, 27, 37 *note*.

O.

Oakes, Rev. Urian, of Cambridge, xiii.

P.

Paige, Nicholas, of Boston, meets Col. Church in Braintree, 2; his history, *ibid. note*.
Paine, John, 110.
Palmer, Mr., of Casco, wounded, 27 *note*; John, 29 *note*.
Palfgrave, John, 81 *note*.
Parker, Rev. Thomas, of Newbury, xiii.
Pautucket Indians, number in 1675, x.
Pemaquid, extent of application of the word, 85 *note*; Church, as second in command to Gov. Phips, arrives there, 85; description of the fort built there by Phips [Fort William Henry], 86 *note*; the fort taken by the enemy four years after, 98.
Pepperell, William, notice of, 143 *note*.
Pequots, their numbers in 1675, x.
Perkins, Rev. William, of Topsfield, xiv.
Philip, or *Pometacom*, the Indian chief, accused of plotting against the English, xxiii.; goes to Plymouth, xxiv.; misconceptions of his character and plans, xxv.; had not been ill-treated by the English, *ibid.*; extravagantly overrated, xxvi.; Dr. Palfrey's account of him more just, *ibid.*; no proof of any extensive plot of his, *ibid.*; reported conference between him and the English, xxviii.
Phillips, Rev. Samuel, of Rowley, xiv.
Phips, Sir William, his eventful history, 82 *note*; invites Church to accompany him on his Eastern Expedition. 83; gives him a commission, *ibid.*; constructs a strong fort at Pemaquid [Fort William Henry], 86 *note*; returns to Boston, 91; his wife signs a discharge for a lady accused of witchcraft, *ibid. note*.
Pike, Robert, Major, of Salisbury, raises soldiers for Church, 48; his instructions to Church, 48-50; notice of him, 48 *note*; letter of Church to him, respecting reports circulated to Church's disadvantage, 77.
Pitkin, William, account of, 15 *note*, 49 *note*.
Plaisted, Ichabod, 66.
Plymouth Colony, its slow progress in wealth and population, xviii.; pays the debt incurred in Philip's War, xxxi.; engages in the war with the Eastern Indians, 6; its commission to Church, 6, 42; schedule of the number of soldiers required of each town in 1689, 6 *note*; a similar schedule in 1690, 43 *note*; debt incurred by the Colony for the Eastern war, *ibid.*
Pokanokets, number in 1675, x.
Pollard, William, an inn-keeper in Boston, 38 *note*.
Portsmouth, Church arrives there, 47; small-pox there, 65; Church there again, *ibid.*; its name changed from Strawberry Bank, 66 *note*.
Prince, Samuel, 7 *note*.
Prout, Timothy, 31 *note*.

INDEX.

R.

Ramsdell, Joseph, of Lynn, slain by Indians, 63 *note*.
Reyner, Rev. John, of Dover, xiii.
Rhode Island, progress of colonization in 1675, x.; its condition at that time, xvii.
Rogers, George, 145, 146, 175.
Row, Giles, killed, 27 *note*.
Rowlandson, Rev. Joseph, of Lancaster, xv.
Russell, Rev. John, of Hadley, xv.

S.

Saffin, John, 15 *note*.
Saffamon, discloses Philip's plot against the English, xxiii.; murdered, xxiv.
Scammon, Richard, 17 *note;* Anne, *ibid.;* Humphrey, of Saco, 57 *note*.
Scottow, Joshua, 28 *note;* Thomas, *ibid.;* notices of him, 31 *note*, 36.
Sewall, Samuel, notices of him, 38 *note*.
Sharkee, or Chartier, 148, 157, 158, 159, 160, 161.
Shepard, Rev. Thomas, of Charlestown, xiii.
Sherman, Rev. John, of Watertown, xiii.
Shove, Rev. George, of Taunton, xiii.
Small-pox in Boston, 32, 37; in Portsmouth, 65; on board of some of Church's transports, *ibid.;* some of his men seek to deceive him in regard to it, *ibid*.
Smith, Rev. John, of Sandwich, xiii.; Thomas, commander of the frigate Jersey, 145, 146, 175.
Southack, Cyprian, commander of the Province galley, 123 *note*, 143, 162, 175.

Southworth, William, a lieutenant in Church's First Expedition, 27; account of him, *ibid. note;* chosen by the Indians their captain, 37 *note*.
Sparrow, Jonathan, of Eastham, 40 *note*.
Sprague, William, of Hingham, 68 *note*.
Spurwink, where, 28 *note*.
Stoddard, Rev. Solomon, of Northampton, xv.
Story, Joseph, 73, 76.
Stoughton, William, Lieut. Gov., his commission to Church, 94; notice of him, *ibid. note;* his letter to Church, transferring the command to Col. Hathorne, 123, 124.
Street, Rev. Nicholas, of New Haven, xiv.
Swain, Jeremiah, notice of, 13 *note*.
Swarton, John, from the island of Jersey, 23; killed by Indians at Casco, *ibid. note;* Hannah, taken by Indians, *ibid.;* Joshua and Joanna, *ibid.;* Mary, *ibid*.

T.

Thacher, Rev. Thomas, of Boston, xv.; John, of Yarmouth, 40 *note*.
Thaxter, Thomas, 27 *note*.
Thomas, Nathaniel, notices of, 72 *note;* his family, *ibid*.
Thorpe, Robert, of York, 107 *note*.
Tolman, Peter, of Newport, 68 *note*.
Torrey, Rev. Samuel, of Weymouth, xiii.
Trading-houses, or truck-houses, Church's opinion of them, 134.
Treat, Rev. Samuel, of Eastham, xiv.
Tyng, Edward, 25 *note*, 136 *note*.

V.

Vaughan, William, of Portsmouth, N. H., 76 *note;* his family, *ibid.;* he and

INDEX.

others apply to Church for help against the Indians, 79; George, 81 *note*.

Villebon, Chevalier, 114 *note*.

W.

Wakeman, Rev. Samuel, of Fairfield, xiv.

Waldron, or Walderne, Major Richard, 17 *note*; his children, *ibid.*; Esther, his daughter, a captive to the Indians, *ibid.*

Walker, Rev. Zechariah, of Woodbury, xv.

Walley, Major John, 10 *note*, 15 *note*, 37, 40 *note*; is desired by Gov. Phips to speak to Church about going again to Maine, 83; Rev. Thomas, of Barnstable, xiv. 42 *note*.

Walton, Shadrach, colonel and judge, 51 *note*; his family, *ibid.*; George, *ibid.*; Benjamin, *ibid.*

Ward, Rev. John, of Haverhill, xiv.

Waterhouse, Richard, 81 *note*.

Wells, Rev. Thomas, of Amesbury, xv.

Whale-boats, much used in Church's Fifth Expedition, 131, 139, 147, 150, 151, 159, 169, 171, 177; explanation of their special value in such an affair, 171 *note*.

Wheelwright, Rev. John, of Salisbury, xiv.; John, Esquire, of Wells, 73 *note*, 75; letter addressed to him by Church, 69-76.

Whiting, Rev. Samuel, of Lynn, xiii.; Rev. Samuel, of Billerica, xv.

Whitman, Rev. Zechariah, of Hull, xiv.

Wigglesworth, Rev. Michael, of Malden, *ibid.*

Willard, Rev. Samuel, xv.; Simon, notices of, 10 *note*, 29 *note*.

William Henry, fort at Pemaquid, described, 86 *note*; taken by the French and Indians, 98 *note*.

Williams, Eunice, wife of Rev. John, of Deerfield, slain by Indians, 128.

Williamson, Capt. Caleb, 139, 175; notice of, 139.

Wilson, Rev. John, of Medfield, xiv.

Wincol, John, of Kittery, 80 *note*.

Winslow, Josiah, brings Alexander, the Indian sachem, to Plymouth, xxi.

Winter, John, notice of, 56 *note*.

Winter Harbor, 56 *note*.

Witchcraft delusion, 91 *note*.

Witherell, Rev. William, of Scituate, xiv.

Withington, Mary, 9 *note*.

Woodbridge, Rev. Benjamin, of Windsor, xv.; Dorothy, 76 *note*; Rev. John, of Killingworth, xv.

Woodman, John, of Little Compton, 84.

Worombos, an Indian sachem, 53, 64.

Y.

York, Joseph, pilots Church up the Penobscot, 102, 105, 106.

NOTE.

My attention has been kindly called, by the Rev. J. A. Vinton, — who has prepared the foregoing Index, — to sundry statements in note 323 (p. 163), concerning the Gyleses, father and son, which he conceives to be inaccurate. Those statements were made upon the testimony of Sewall, who expressly refers, in regard to some of them, to an incomplete MSS. narrative of the Rev. Mr. Vinton, of the date of 1853, and who was therefore supposed to have, in this case, special authority. In order to place the reader in possession of all the facts, however, I gladly append here the following, prepared by Mr. Vinton, — containing facts subsequently brought to light, — which note, if it had not been too late, would have been substituted for the note referred to.

H. M. D.

John Gyles (p. 163 *ante*), born in what is now the town of Topsham, Me., about the year 1678, was son of Thomas Gyles (who, after a residence of some years on Merrymeeting Bay, where the Androscoggin joins the Kennebec, went to England to attend to some family matters, then returned to New England, and purchased a large farm at Pemaquid, where he was Chief-Justice, under the ducal government, of the County of Cornwall, and was killed by the Indians, Aug. 2, 1689); was carried off by the Indians, after his father's death, to their savage haunts on the upper waters of the river St. John, in the present province of New Brunswick. After severe sufferings among them during six years, he was purchased by a French gentleman residing on that river, who treated him kindly, and who, three years afterward, permitted him to return to his friends at Boston. He served the Government of Massachusetts thirty-eight years, with some interruptions, as interpreter in their transactions with the Indians, and as commander of several military posts on the frontiers; was a man of great courage, and of stern, unbending integrity; retired from the military service in 1737, and took up his residence in Roxbury, near Boston, where he died in 1755, aged 77. In 1736, he printed a narrative of his adventures, which is still extant. [Vinton's *Giles Memorial*, pp. 103-111, 122-129.]